THE JEWS AMONG PAGANS AND CHRISTIANS

Religious life within and around the Roman Empire – the context into which Christianity emerged and where it spread – is a topic of the widest interest. Yet this context was not that of a completely pagan world, for Judaism was already firmly established and continued as a vigorous contender in the field throughout the first four centuries after the death of Christ – a fact not always well-recognized.

Historically, Christianity's relationship with Judaism continued to be intimate but ambivalent long after their separation. This has distorted scholarly perceptions right down to our own day, when the religious history of the period still tends to be written from a Christianizing perspective. The suggestion of this book is that we can and should reassess, from a more neutral position, how the competition between these three religions influenced the development of each of them.

The Jews Among Pagans and Christians offers a new model of this complex area by drawing on a variety of types of material and method. The essays, by some of the leading scholars in the field, explore facets of the main theme in a challenging and unorthodox way. They are written without excessive technicality but concentrate on specific historical problems rather than offering a generalized overview. Together with the overall assessment offered by the Introduction they show that to understand the significance of Judaism is also to transform our ideas of how the other religions developed and how the societies worked.

The book will be of interest to all those working in the areas of Ancient History, Jewish Studies, and the study of the New Testament and early church, and to all concerned with the nature and history of religious groups and their relationship to one another.

Dura Europos Synagogue: the defeat of the pagan gods (the ark in the land of the Philistines).
Photo reproduced by kind permission of Yale University Art Gallery, the Dura Europos Collection.

THE JEWS AMONG PAGANS AND CHRISTIANS

In the Roman Empire

Edited by

Judith Lieu, John North and Tessa Rajak

London and New York

First published 1992
by Routledge
11 New Fetter Lane, London ECP 4EE

First published in paperback 1994 by Routledge

Simultaneously published in the USA and Canada
by Routledge
29 West 35th Street, New York, NY 10001

Phototypeset in 10/12 Garamond by Intype, London
Printed and bound in Great Britain by
TJ Press (Padstow) Ltd, Padstow, Cornwall

British Library Cataloguing in Publication Data
The Jews among pagans and Christians in the Roman Empire.
1. Roman Empire. Judaism. History
I. Lieu, Judith   II. North, John   III. Rajak, Tessa
296.2872

Library of Congress Cataloging in Publication Data
The Jews among pagans and Christians: in the Roman Empire/edited by
Judith Lieu, John North, Tessa Rajak.
p. cm.
Includes bibliographical references and index.
1. Judaism–History–Talmudic period. 10–425.   2. Christianity–
Early church. ca. 30–600. 3. Rome–Religion. 4. Judaism–
Relations–Christianity. 5. Christianity and other religions–
Judaism.   I. Lieu, Judith   II. North, John A.   III. Rajak, Tessa
BM177.J49 1992
296'.09'015–dc20 91–16866

ISBN 0–415–11448–9

CONTENTS

CONTENTS

LIST OF CONTRIBUTORS

Han Drijvers is Professor in the Institute of Semitic Languages and Literatures in the University of Groningen.

Martin Goodman is Reader in Jewish Studies in the University of Oxford.

Martin Hengel is Professor of New Testament and Early Judaism in the University of Tübingen.

Judith Lieu is Lecturer in Christian Origins and Early Judaism in King's College London.

Fergus Millar is Camden Professor of Ancient History in the University of Oxford.

John North is Professor of History in University College London.

Tessa Rajak is Reader in Classics in the University of Reading and Head of the Department of Classics.

Michael Weitzman is Lecturer in Hebrew and Jewish Studies in University College London.

PREFACE

The conception of this book, and most of its chapters, derive from a series of Ancient History seminars organized by the editors, at the Institute of Classical Studies in London. The plan was to work towards correcting the prevailing distorted picture of the religious history of the Roman Empire, a picture which springs essentially from privileging the rise of Christianity as the only truly significant event in that history. The distortion had concealed the Jewish role in a number of important respects, so the task was to restore the Jews to view. The roots of the distortion were theological as much as historical; we therefore felt from the beginning that, in order to tackle the 'triumphalist' view of Christian history, it was essential to call on scholars from at least three different disciplines, Ancient History, Jewish Studies and Theology (while Semitic Philology also had a part to play). The published version also reflects this wide variety of approaches. We have tried to make all the chapters as generally accessible as possible. All, in our view, make fundamental contributions to the task of reinterpretation. And, apart from the more general benefits of cross-fertilization between normally separate spheres of study, the justification for publishing the papers together is, precisely, that it is enlightening to read them together. The editors' shared concern with understanding the role of religion in society has, it is hoped, shaped the identity of the volume.

We are grateful to all who contributed to the seminars, not least to those who gave papers which could not be included in the present volume – Professor Stuart Hall, Professor E. P. Sanders and Dr Joan Taylor – and to those who took part in the very lively discussion. We owe thanks to Dr Loveday Alexander for her advice and to Saul Rajak for his draftsmanship. The seminar series was generously assisted by grants from the British Academy, the Institute of Jewish Studies of University College London and the Institute of Classical Studies, London.

Minor changes and bibliographical additions have been made in the paperback edition, 1994.

ABBREVIATIONS

ANRW	*Aufstieg und Niedergang der römischen Welt*, edited by H. Temporini and W. Haase
CCL	Corpus Christianorum, Series Latina
CIJ	*Corpus Inscriptionum Iudaicarum*, ed. J. B. Frey (Vol. 1, rev. edn B. Lifshitz)
Cod.Theod.	*Codex Theodosianus* = Theodosian Code
Const.Sirmond.	*Constitutiones Sirmondianae*
CPJ	*Corpus Papyrorum Iudaicorum*, ed. V. Tcherikover, A. Fuks, M. Stern
CSCO	Corpus Scriptorum Christianorum Orientalium
EPRO	*Etudes préliminaires aux religions orientales dans l'empire romaine*
ILS	*Inscriptiones Latinae Selectae*, ed. H. Dessau
JIWE I	*Jewish Inscriptions of Western Europe* I, ed. D. Noy
PL	*Patrologia Latina*, ed. J.-P. Migne
SEG	*Supplementum Epigraphicum Graecum*

NOTE ON TRANSLITERATION

Transliteration of Greek, Hebrew and Syriac follows a simple phonetic system except where holding to an established custom or where the argument demands philological precision.

GLOSSARY OF JEWISH SOURCES AND TERMS

Apocrypha	Books largely surviving in the LXX which are not part of the Hebrew canon
b	The Babylonian Talmud (sixth century AD), used in naming the different tractates, as bShabbat, bPes, etc.; English translation I. Epstein, London 1935–52
halakhah	Religious law or custom covering ritual and practical behaviour
j	The Palestinian Talmud (fifth century AD), used in naming the different tractates, as jSotah, jAbodah Zarah, etc.; no complete English translation; French translation: M. Schwab (1871–89) *Le Talmud de Jérusalem*, Vols 1–11, Paris; reprinted (1969), Paris
Kaddish	A central prayer in the liturgy, sanctifying God
LXX = Septuagint	The major surviving Greek translation of the Hebrew Bible (started in the third century BC)
m	The Mishnah (*c.* AD 200), used in naming the different tractates, as mBerakoth, mAboth, etc.; English translation H. Danby, London 1933
Midrash	A method of scriptural interpretation; also used of rabbinic Biblical commentaries using this method
mitzvah	A Biblical or rabbinic commandment
MT (Massoretic text)	The received Hebrew text of the Hebrew Bible
Pentateuch	The first five books (= the first division) of the Hebrew Bible
talmid hakham	A sage: the self-designation of members of the rabbinic class and their pupils
Targum	Biblical versions in Aramaic for use in the synagogue
Torah	The Pentateuch: the body of Law and doctrine revealed to Moses
Tosefta	Additional material to the Mishnah (*c.* AD 230)
Writings	The third division of the Hebrew Bible (after the Prophets and Pentateuch)

CHRONOLOGICAL GUIDE TO THE JEWISH DIASPORA UNDER ROMAN RULE

BC

139   Jews expelled from Rome

63   Pompey takes Jerusalem and Judaea becomes subject to Rome

49–43   Roman decrees securing Jewish rights issued to various cities by Julius Caesar and Mark Antony (with mediation of the Jewish ethnarch Hyrcanus II)

37–4   Herod rules as 'client king' in Judaea

31–12   Octavian/Augustus or his governors issue decrees favourable to Jews in several provinces

14   Nicolaus of Damascus, Herod's minister, defends the rights of Jews in Ionia in front of Marcus Agrippa

AD

19   Expulsion of Jews from Rome by Emperor Tiberius

30–40   Conversion to Judaism of royal house of Adiabene

? 31–4   Conversion of Paul

38–41   Violence between Jews and Greeks in Alexandria

41   Emperor Claudius' edict retaining status quo on the Jews in Alexandria

? 45   Death of Philo

66–73   Attacks on Jews in Diaspora Greek cities sparked by Jewish resistance to Rome in Palestine

70   Fall of Jerusalem; destruction of the Temple

70   Vespasian institutes *fiscus Iudaicus*, levying tax on Jews

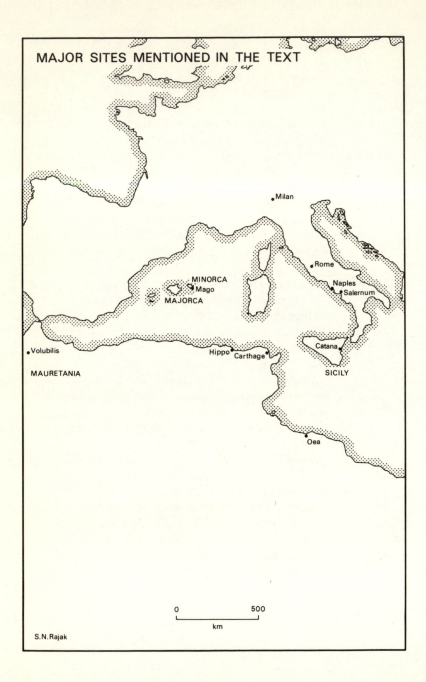

MAJOR SITES MENTIONED IN THE TEXT

Milan

Rome

Naples
Salernum

MINORCA
Mago
MAJORCA

Volubilis

Hippo Carthage

Catana

MAURETANIA

SICILY

Oea

0   500
km

S.N.Rajak

xvi

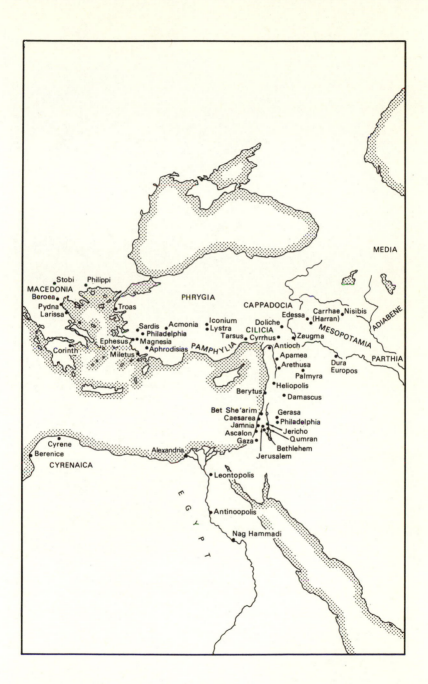

MACEDONIA
Stobi
Philippi
Beroea
Pydna
Larissa
Troas
Corinth
Ephesus
Magnesia
Miletus
Sardis
Philadelphia
Aphrodisias

PHRYGIA

Acmonia
Iconium
Lystra
Tarsus
PAMPHYLIA

CAPPADOCIA

Doliche
CILICIA
Cyrrhus
Antioch
Apamea
Arethusa
Palmyra
Heliopolis
Berytus
Damascus

Edessa
Carrhae Nisibis
(Harran)
Zeugma
MESOPOTAMIA
Dura
Europos

MEDIA

ADIABENE

PARTHIA

Bet She'arim
Caesarea
Jamnia
Ascalon
Gaza
Jerusalem
Gerasa
Philadelphia
Jericho
Qumran
Bethlehem

Cyrene
Berenice
CYRENAICA
Alexandria

Leontopolis

E G Y P T

Antinoopolis

Nag Hammadi

xvii

INTRODUCTION

Judith Lieu, John North and Tessa Rajak

Any account of the religious history of the Roman Empire has to incorporate the victory of Christianity and the defeat of paganism, or – to put it in another way, which is perhaps only a little less one-sided – the conversion of the pagans. For the course of history, as for the contemporary victims of the conflict, it may well have been the outcome of the confrontation that mattered more than the details of its development. Meanwhile, scholars, both those writing from a theological perspective and those concerned with the study of ancient history, have tended to be satisfied, for their own different reasons, with this 'triumphalist' interpretation. As for the Jews, who were, of course, central to the beginning of the story and scarcely less so (as we shall show) later on, their viewpoint has tended to drop out of sight. A major purpose of this book is to look at the same story without the familiar preconceptions and with the Jewish role in mind, and to discover how different a pattern of development then emerges.

The first step is simply to recognize that there were patterns of religious activity not included within the pagan or the Christian but inescapably engaging with both. Our particular purpose is to highlight the groups of Jews who lived their lives in the cities of the Roman Empire or to the east of it and who must in one way or another have influenced the ideas and behaviour of their pagan and Christian neighbours. Even if it is not as much as we would like, we know enough about them to explore from a number of angles both their own experience and their place in the general religious situation of their time. To do this is to expose the weakness of the notion that the period was dominated by an all-important collision between pagans and Christians.

A new reconstruction of the religious and social context within

1

which Jews, pagans and Christians alike were living their lives is then required. Over the centuries of Roman rule in the Mediterranean world, radical changes were taking place in the relationship between society and religion. What we find in the later Empire (from perhaps the third century) is a plurality of religious groups in some or perhaps all of the cities, each propounding its own distinctive mix of ideas, philosophies, tales and ritual practice. In other words, it was a situation not unlike those familiar to us from more recent societies. Familiar it may be; but in relation to the traditional religious practices of the Graeco-Roman world of earlier centuries, all this represents nothing less than a revolution in the nature of the individual's religious existence.

This revolution could be defined in terms of movement away from a monopolistic situation, in which citizens shared a common, generally accepted religious adherence, and towards what has been called a 'market-place' in religions, in which religious adherence became a matter of debate, anxiety and doubt (see the chapter by John North). The simplest model on which these changes might in theory be organized is to describe Christianity as an intrusion from the outside which by its very arrival caused the disturbance of traditional patterns and expectations. Once again, such an approach has the effect of reducing the problem to one about the relations between pagans and Christians – pagans inert, Christians aggressive. And, once again, this fails to explain much of what was happening. There are, first of all, solid reasons for believing that the religious revolution was already beginning in the Hellenistic period, two or three centuries before the spread of Christianity. Second, far from being in a passive or negative state, pagan cults in the Roman imperial period display both vigour and the capacity to innovate.

Above all, however, the simple conflict model excludes too many of the participants in the story and offers too rigid a framework for explaining how all of them interacted. In particular, to ignore the presence of Jews in much of the Empire is to ignore a major element in the picture. And to focus on them provides a unique opportunity for an overall reinterpretation.

The militaristic conflict model has had a dominant influence both in imposing its language of victory or triumph on the debate and also in denying the historical role of Judaism. Deep ideological roots have nourished this attitude. Histories of the early Church have often been the work of authors with theological interests,

2

not least those histories written at the turn of the century which did so much to determine scholarly and wider opinion. They commonly located the 'preparation for the Gospel' in the political and religious circumstances of the Roman Empire; their aim was to identify, on the one hand, such insights of paganism as Christianity assimilated, and, on the other, the weaknesses that Christianity remedied, that is to say, the inability of paganism to satisfy the deepest human needs. Despite a saga of obstacles overcome, threats avoided and wholesale attacks repulsed, the final (!) triumph was never in doubt – in this perspective.

It is an important part of this essentially Christian conception of the final triumph that the spread has been seen as 'universal', despite the fact that a substantial majority of the population remained pagan until well after the time of Constantine; becoming universal means, in essence, that Christianity was leaving behind its roots in Judaism, for Judaism is negatively defined as the antithesis of the universal. Such presentations as these never tried to deny the deeply Jewish character of early Christian institutions or theology, since Christianity was obviously born from Judaism. In accordance with Luke's picture in the Acts of the Apostles, they have conceded that the early expansion of the Church started in the synagogues of the dispersion and have identified the dispersion itself as part of the 'preparation of the Gospel'. Yet they have gone on to characterize Christianity as stripping Judaism of its assets and in doing so they have incorporated into 'history' what the early church writers had presented as primarily 'a theological necessity'. The contention was that, in rejecting Jesus, the Jews had denied their character as the people of God and hence effectively cut themselves off from any source of life or from any serious contribution to history.

A number of factors were involved in support of this picture. One of these was a particular view of the Old Testament, highly influential within Christian scholarship, that the prophets of the pre-exilic and exilic periods (Amos, Hosea, Isaiah, Jeremiah) had achieved a peak in the understanding of God. From this peak, the post-exilic period brought a decline marked by the disappearance of prophecy and, most of all, by a growing tendency to focus on the Law. It was this alleged characteristic, often disparagingly described as 'legalism' or 'exclusivism', that led to the labelling of the Judaism of this period as 'late Judaism'. It seemed only natural that no further exercise of life or influence could follow.

This picture seemed to gain support from the dominant idea that the surviving literature of Judaism was oblivious to the outside world, concerned only with the regulation of its own life and the interpretation of its own sacred texts, in particular the Law. The sheer volume of Talmudic literature seemed to discourage access, yet it also helped to promote the idea that the Talmud, as interpreted in the light of the Christian concept of 'orthodoxy', represented the whole of Jewish life. The consequence was that any other Jewish beliefs or types of life, as in the case of those implied by the archaeological and epigraphic remains, were seen as peripheral or corrupted and accordingly called by many 'syncretistic'. The main concerns of Jewish study of this literature and of the history of the Jews of this period were not such as to produce any contradiction of this view. Therefore, on this interpretation, an almost exclusive reliance on the literary remains of Judaism reinforced the extraordinary claim that triumphant Christianity had left behind it a Judaism theologically and historically moribund, at least as regards external influence.

Another factor behind this earlier model was that the Christians too were viewed as a self-contained group – in the words of the early Christian writers a 'new people' or 'race'. The history of the early Church was often seen as a matter of internal development or of 'the Church' against society, rather than as something rooted in the realities of day-to-day life in the city. This whole approach, with its implicit assumption of confident boundaries and tight Jewish identity, is brought into question by the market-place model that is in different fashions explored in this book. Many new insights have stimulated this questioning, but the catalyst has been reassessing the position of the Jews.

One new insight is the dissolution of the formerly favoured distinction between a supposedly uncontaminated Palestinian Judaism and the Hellenizing Judaism of the Diaspora communities. It has become increasingly clear from recent work that the distinction between Palestine and the Diaspora cannot be expressed within this framework. The Judaism from which Christianity was born was far from monolithic and was already part of the cultural interchange of the Graeco-Roman world; this is well demonstrated here by Martin Hengel in his exploration of Paul's Jerusalem background. As Hengel then goes on to suggest, the identification of what was 'new' in Christianity and in its structures and thought must consequently be reassessed. Moreover, if

4

Christianity shared with and even learned from Judaism some of its responses to the world around it, the reasons for which the two groups separated and came into conflict also need more sensitive description.

For the post-70 period, the need for a new interpretation is even greater. There has long been something paradoxical in the way that scholars have accepted a picture of post-70 Judaism dominated by the Palestinian rabbis and by their Babylonian successors while also accepting high (if not inflated) estimates of the Jewish population of the Diaspora. Archaeological remains, such as the magnificent third- or fourth-century synagogue at Sardis discovered in the late 1960s or the more recently published inscription erected by Jews in the city of Aphrodisias, testify, if testimony were needed, that Jews did not retreat into a ghetto nor did Judaism gracefully die after the birth of Christianity. Rather the Jews maintained a self-confident life in the busy thoroughfares of the city. Tessa Rajak and, for the later period, Fergus Millar assess the possibilities of reconstructing this life. The Judaism we glimpse from this evidence cannot be confined within the straitjacket of (Palestinian) Judaism as traditionally defined or be interpreted as somehow 'less genuine'. Michael Weitzman proposes a similar picture for the Jewish communities in Edessa as the best explanation of the characteristics of the Syriac version of the Hebrew Bible known as the Peshitta. How much contact there was between the rabbinic centres and the Diaspora communities remains an important area of debate; but whatever the degree of contact or of recognition of the rabbis' authority, Diaspora Judaism cannot be labelled marginal, let alone unauthentic or syncretistic. Rather we must explore how these Jewish communities sustained their sense of identity on their own terms, despite still forming part of the cities to which they had long committed themselves.

An important element in the traditional model which stands in need of examination is the assumption that, in Palestine and also throughout the Diaspora, Judaism compelled isolation and self-seclusion, at the very least from its full adherents. Christian interpretation, as we have said, assumed this to be part of the acceptance of the 'burden' of the Law, while ancient historians seem simply to have taken it on trust. Reinforcement for the view has been supplied by the lurid picture of Jewish xenophobia painted by those familiar caricatures of Judaism which appear in

Latin literature, especially in the fifth book of Tacitus' *Histories* (with its Greek antecedents) and in the incidental jibes of the poets. On this point, it has been rather too easy to take the writers at face value.

Time and again, confrontation tends to be seen as the dominant mode of relations between Jews and others, acted out in different ways between the different parties and sometimes erupting in physical conflict. Such conflict was, of course, by no means absent from the scene; nor, however, was it omnipresent. Fergus Millar's survey of the evidence for the Diaspora in the later Roman Empire reveals, indeed, a pattern of increasing religious hostility and destructive violence in the years between AD 312 and the 430s. But it also reveals the high profile still adopted by the Jewry of a number of cities in those years; and it shows how coexistence and confrontation could be two sides of the same coin.

The market-place model preferred by us gives primacy to the overall pattern of coexistence, within which both interaction and breakdown can find their place. This model acknowledges, as we have said, what was in effect a society developing towards pluralism: varied options, each carrying its own attractions, its own advantages and liabilities, became available. This is clearly the situation in the Edessa discussed by Han Drijvers, even though he also shows how erratic the swing between detachment and mutual influence can be.

The model of the market-place also seems to imply not only a variety of wares but that at least a part of what was on offer would be on public display and that vendors would copy one another, competing over what they stocked and how they presented it. However, in this particular market-place, not all the shopkeepers saw fit to pressurize their potential customers. Martin Goodman's contribution argues that the Jews do not seem to have done so until at least the third century, and that it may in fact have been under Christian influence that Jewish behaviour altered. Yet, if there was no Jewish mission, there still existed among Jews a sophisticated mechanism for receiving outsiders with a greater or lesser degree of completeness. The Jewish inscriptions in Greek, and above all the major new evidence in the inscription from Aphrodisias (see Tessa Rajak's chapter), bring the demand that we give this remarkable social phenomenon its due weight.

The very same evidence also indicates that not everybody in this religious world regarded the choices as mutually exclusive:

6

thus, Jewish 'sympathizers' could be in some sense pagans and in some sense Jews; while Christian Judaizers in fourth-century Edessa and Antioch went both to church and synagogue, as we see in Han Drijvers's chapter, and the vitriol of preachers who purported to find the latter practice unacceptable only goes to show how embedded the habit was.

Yet the possibility of choice does not mean that we can explore the inner motives of individuals, still less their supposed 'spiritual needs'. Although this approach may seem attractive and has often been attempted in the past, it is necessarily subjective; for the most part, the evidence is not of the kind necessary for such analysis, but points in other directions.

The question of the nature of the evidence and of its interpretation is a central one in any discussion of ancient religion. For Judaism after the end of the first century AD, it has been seen as particularly problematic. Fergus Millar's chapter, on the later Roman Empire, shows the difficulties of reconstructing the story of a period of the history of Diaspora Jewry that has left no literature. Yet he also shows how much can be done by pulling together the scattered evidence from different milieux, in different languages. The special contribution of Christian references to the doings of the Jews emerges clearly: from a Christian literature that is often polemical and may sometimes, as Judith Lieu indicates, have been more concerned with theology than with real situations, fragments of history can still be disentangled by subtle analysis. Evidence may also be drawn from sources not usually studied by historians and that is the value of Michael Weitzman's painstaking study of the Peshitta; he shows how historical implications may be drawn from a comparison of its translations and interpretations with those of other versions. Han Drijvers, it will be noted, adheres to a different position, which leaves the Syriac Bible still firmly in the Christian domain, rather than in that of an 'unorthodox' Diaspora Judaism. Here further detailed study may well make a decision possible.

Together the contributions to this volume thus both illustrate and provide test cases for the new view point which has been explored. They also suggest areas where further questions need to be asked. Whereas what we have termed the militaristic conflict model tended to work with a monochrome picture of the warring parties, here, as appropriate in a market-place, we become aware of considerable variety in different settings. This is a variety both in the inner self-identity and in the pattern of relationships with others. It is a variety which must allow for change and development through the course of the Roman Empire. In particular there is room for more detailed studies of local situations, drawing on all the evidence available even where it does not fit in with the expected pattern.

These are but possibilities for the further exploration and testing of the model suggested by this book. Like all models, it may often prove inadequate or misleading, but if it promotes a fresh understanding of the religious interaction of the Roman Empire and a fresh base for the co-operation of the different disciplines involved in its study, then it will have served its purpose.

1

THE JEWISH COMMUNITY
AND ITS BOUNDARIES

Tessa Rajak

THE JEWISH DIASPORA

After rejecting the theological animus, as well as the historical
absurdity, in claims that Judaism effectively vanished when Christianity arose, we may still wonder whether the followers of a faith
apparently organized around self-separation could really play a
full part in any plural society. And yet we see the Jews doing just
that in the post–70 era, as already before it. This discussion exam-
ines that seeming contradiction, suggesting reasons why it may in
fact be inappropriate to speak of Diaspora Jews as separated from
their neighbours by metaphorical high walls and, on the other
hand, enquiring about the meaning and the limits of the types of
interaction known to us.

In Acts, Peter offers the centurion Cornelius a grossly unfair
representation of the Jews as forbidden by their religion 'to visit
or associate with a man of another race' (Acts 10:28). Discounting
the exaggeration, we may still be inclined to feel that there is an
element of truth here. We may recall that pagan outsiders even
more than Christian, saw Jews as misanthropic, self-sufficient,
unwilling to share a table with any but their own kind or even
to render basic human assistance (Stern 1974: 1980). This is indeed
the regular, virtually automatic response of Roman writers to
Jews, or to the thought of them, and before that of certain
Hellenistic Greek writers. Take away the hostility, and here too
there may remain a degree of verisimilitude. After all, Balaam had
long ago prophesied for Israel a future as 'a people that dwells
alone, that has not made itself one with the nations' (Numbers
23:9). And Philo's comment (*Life of Moses* I. 278) had explained
this in terms of the distinctiveness of Jewish customs. Modern

9

experience readily leads us to believe that the life-arrangements required by completely orthodox Judaism, as we today know it, presuppose an intensely communal existence and scarcely leave room for more than superficial mixing.

It is undeniable that the crystallization and the increasing influence of rabbinic Judaism constituted by far the most prominent development in Jewish life and thought over the first five centuries of the Christian era. From the inside, this is usually viewed as a supreme achievement (which it undoubtedly was, by any intellectual standards); from the outside, often with wilful ignorance, as a regrettable, even a culpable, narrowing. The fact, either way, cannot be forgotten; yet what it means for the communities under consideration is by no means self-evident.

The communities of Jews who lived in the cities of the Roman Empire were in no sense a marginal phenomenon. The first-century authors Philo and Josephus tell us that in their day there existed already a large and ubiquitous Jewish Diaspora. In some places its origins went back to long before Alexander the Great. We may perhaps distrust their exaggerations, as also the supposed citation from Strabo about the Jewish people (Josephus, *Antiquities* XIV 115) that 'it has already made its way into every city, and it is not easy to find any place in the habitable world which has not taken this race in and which it does not dominate'. Josephus appears to have picked up a nasty remark in Strabo (or else quoted from Strabo) and then attempted to turn it to his own purpose.[1] Josephus' statement in the *Jewish War* (II 462–3) that, at the war's outbreak in AD 66, every city in Syria had in it both Jews and Judaizers, has a somewhat greater claim on our attention. However, we do not have to rest on these subjective utterances to be confident that Jews were to be found in number in many of the cities of the eastern empire, and of course in Rome, and tentatively to suggest that they are likely to have spread around the west as well by the mid-first century AD. Inscriptions attest urban settlement; while we cannot say much about rural settlement, it has been suspected for Cyrenaica, where an inscription refers to the Jews of the region (Applebaum 1979), and is clearly demonstrated by papyri for Egyptian villages. There is no need to enter into discussion here about highly speculative figures.

Diaspora communities were grouped around the institution of the *synagōgē*, also called *proseuchē*, of which there would be more than one in a large city – eleven are attested for Rome in the

catacomb epitaphs (Leon 1960). Inscriptions reveal synagogue officials to have been prominent figures. But the word *synagōgē*, which means assembly, unlike *proseuchē*, meaning prayer, carries an important ambiguity, and we cannot always tell whether a building is intended, or merely the particular community, viewed as an association, *conventus*, or *synodos* in Greek (Applebaum 1974: 490). Nor is it impossible for both implications to be carried at the same time. Thus, while we can readily say that the synagogue was central to Diaspora Judaism, we are in no position to say how far the religious life of individuals expressed itself through the synagogue. Furthermore, we have clear knowledge from inscriptions that synagogues might consist of more than just halls for the reading of the Law and the recital of prayers, and might, as at Macedonian Stobi (*CIJ* 694; Lifshitz 1967, no. 10; Hengel 1966) or in the Theodotus synagogue of pre-70 Jerusalem (*CIJ* 1404; Lifshitz 1967: 79; Levine 1987: 17), contain also dining-halls (Stobi had a *triclinium*) or hostelries or other communal facilities. Therefore, the labelling of an individual as belonging to a particular synagogue becomes even less easy to interpret.

If the role of synagogue affiliation and the demarcation there between the religious and the social are opaque to us, the practices and observances of Diaspora Jews in their daily lives are also hard to penetrate. But we can make an attempt to discern something of the implications of rabbinic Judaism for their world, and then to conclude whether it is indeed likely that the demands of that system will have cut them off from the life of the city around them.

RABBINIC JUDAISM

A rough and uncontroversial description of rabbinic Judaism must be the starting-point. Rabbinic Judaism is that form of religion which took shape after the failure of the first revolt against Rome and the destruction of the Temple in AD 70, and in some measure in response to those events; its foundations, however, had been earlier laid by the Pharisees. In Palestine, this replaced the sectarianism which had marked the period between the Maccabees and the destruction, even if the ideal unity that rabbinic literature likes sometimes to depict was not achieved. The emphasis of the rabbis was on study of the Torah (the Pentateuch) and its interpretation, in an ever-increasing body of oral doctrine, whose

main thrust was towards norms of behaviour (*halakhah*), though its range was in fact much wider. The production of written texts began with the Mishnah, a summary of practice in commentary form which was composed in about AD 200, and was supplemented by the longer Tosefta, perhaps a generation later; the process reached its climax, though in no sense its conclusion, with the massive and heterogeneous compilation of the sixth century, known to us as the Babylonian Talmud. It is noteworthy that this was produced not in Palestine but in the Aramaic-speaking Diaspora. The institution of the synagogue, with its regular Torah readings, and (in Palestine) its Aramaic translation, had emerged already before 70; but it assumed a new importance in the absence of the Temple cult (which had drawn many pilgrims) and ensured that the sacred text was widely familiar. It is probably right to see the development of rabbinic Judaism, and perhaps also its beginnings, as in some way a response to the Christian challenge, a sharpening of self-definition (a fashionable term in this field); yet it is highly significant that no such purpose is made explicit: everything in the system is explained in its own terms, with ultimate recourse to divine requirements. Some see the concern of the rabbis with purity and with establishing correct action in every particular as the construction of a fortification against fatal erosion or undermining through compromise of essentials. 'The Rabbis', wrote Momigliano (1987: 401), 'humane and alert as they were, chose or were driven to create a new Jewish culture, which touched only the fringes of Greek culture.'

No less significant than the content of rabbinic Judaism, was the centralized authority structure, based first at Yavneh (or Jamnia), on the coast of Judaea, but later elsewhere; this may be described as a strengthened replacement of the focal point that Jerusalem had been. The rabbinic academy (*beth midrash*), the court of law associated with it,[2] the ordination of one another by the rabbis, who might also be spoken of as *hakhamim* or sages (Levine 1989: 141–2), and the prestige of these scholar-teachers as individuals and as a collective elite, were the components of rabbinic Judaism. The Patriarch (*Nasi*) was the leader of Palestinian Jewry (and perhaps of other Jews too) and in the eyes of the Roman government; he had supreme status by the beginning of the third century if not before, and he was always the upholder of rabbinic authority. Rabbis who were especially esteemed issued ordinances (*takkanot*) and prohibitions, but those were few at

first. The evolution, elucidation and transmission of a much larger and more complex (even sometimes contradictory) network of *halakhot* (which we might call accepted rulings) was the main part of the rabbis' business. Practical rulings about the calendar (which determined the observance of the festivals and many other aspects of Jewish life) were among both the earliest and the most fundamental of the powers assumed by the central institutions. Jewish piety, as understood by the rabbis, rested on the fulfilment of a very large number of approved acts, *mitzvot*, of either a ritual or an ethical character; it was indispensable that these be performed in a spirit of love. They could account, in their totality, for all areas of an individual's life. All activities were seen as sanctified, but study was strongly promoted as a value in itself; one may detect an element of professional interest in the latter. This ever-growing system was generated by way of the spoken word. Large-scale literary formulation of principles was not undertaken until the Mishnah was completed (Strack 1931; Strack-Stemberger 1982; Safrai 1987).

We can discern that the authority of the rabbis did not establish itself immediately; naturally, however, the setbacks suffered by the earlier leaders were not preserved for the record by their successors. For all periods, it is a matter of uncertainty how much of the *halakhah* which the rabbis debated so enthusiastically was seen as theoretical. There were other limitations too. Those *mitzvot* which were to do with land-use (tithing, sabbatical year, etc.) were applicable only to the area regarded as being within the notional confines of the land of Israel. But even there, throughout the Mishnaic period and probably beyond, a whole section of the population, known as *amei ha-aretz* (literally, peoples of the land) appear to have ignored them, with no worse consequences than incurring the snobbish contempt or the abusive comments of the rabbinic class (Oppenheimer 1977; Levine 1989: 112–17). For the Galilee, it has been argued (Goodman 1983: 93–118) that, before the third century, the rabbis attempted to control the population only in matters of specifically *religious* observance, and not at all in practical matters, and that even in the first sphere they were largely unsuccessful. Although there was, on this view, universal observance of the basic requirements of Judaism – the sabbath, circumcision, the festivals, the regulations about sexual cleanness and uncleanness, and widespread practice of the basic dietary laws, that was something which occurred independently of the rabbis.

And even that may be too strong a statement: it relies largely on the negative evidence of absence of complaint by Tannaitic (i.e. pre-Talmudic) rabbis on those cardinal issues. During the third and fourth centuries the situation must have changed somewhat, since Galilee became the heartland of Jewish settlement in Palestine, but it is unclear how this happened.

In the literature, attributions of doctrine or utterance to particular rabbis are often highly dubious (Neusner 1984); none the less, there has been enough investigation to reveal that, far from a unified view, there existed a spectrum of opinion among prominent rabbis on major questions, and this is visible in the case of approaches to the outside world, to association with Gentiles and to levels of permitted contact (Levine 1989: 83–97). The Mishnaic tractate on idolatry, *Avodah Zarah*, exposes a number of such divergences. Palestine, of course, contained its own Greek cities where such problems could be pressing, and the rabbis seem often to have regarded places like Caesarea, Scythopolis and Sepphoris as within their purview.[3] However, while it would be wrong to treat the rabbis as a monolithic group, the possibility which opens before us, in questioning their connection with Diaspora Jewry, is a radical one which makes the matter of their diversity of stance less significant. If the Jewries of the Graeco-Roman Diaspora were far removed from the refined debates taking place in Palestine (or Babylon), they need not have accepted the combination of premisses from which those debates started and, therefore, would have had as little interest in tolerant rabbinic positions as in hard-line ones. In their lives, self-separation for the achievement of purity may not have been perceived as an issue in the same terms.

THE DIASPORA AND THE RABBIS

What, then, can we say about how the rabbis viewed the Diaspora and the Diaspora the rabbis? Those rabbinic sources which contain some kind of answer to the first question, have to be read with the greatest caution, as they have a marked tendency to prefer imaginary constructs of the past to real descriptions. But what at any rate emerges from those texts is that rabbinic interest, at least at times, extended to the dispersed communities. The institution of *shelikhim* (*apostoloi*, emissaries) is attested also in Christian writers and in the Theodosian code (Safrai 1974; cf. Millar, p. 98 of this volume). Talmudic reports ascribe especially hectic travels

14

to the sages of Jamnia, and quite credibly, since they will have been seeking to establish themselves. Journeys like these, or the ones attributed to Rabbi Akiba (who died under Hadrian), took rabbis to Rome, Gaul, Africa, Arabia, Antioch (in Syria), Cilicia, Cappadocia, Babylonia and Media, and could clearly involve visiting Jewish communities and also preaching in synagogues (Safrai 1974: 208–10; Feldman 1989: 301–2). But the journeys also had a political dimension, where negotiations with local or imperial authorities might be required; and we should not forget fundraising; at a certain stage the patriarchate may have been strong enough to exact taxes from Jews abroad; and if the visitors were acceptably received, and, indeed, contributions paid without any compulsion being applied, we may conclude that the rabbis were accorded some respect. This form of contact, if indeed we should take it as historical, would demonstrate that the rabbis of Palestine meant something in the Diaspora; but not, of course, that the system for Jewish living promoted by the rabbis was meaningful there in its entirety or their learning grasped (Kraabel 1982: 454).

The prime rabbinic values of study and teaching are not absent from Diaspora Jewry. Josephus maintained that detailed knowledge of the Torah (which he rendered as *nomos*, law) was derived from regular reading (*Against Apion* II 175), and was a determining characteristic of all Jews, at any rate by the time he wrote the *Against Apion* (towards AD 100). Epitaphs commemorate, from Rome, a *mathētēs sophōn* (the exact Greek equivalent of the Hebrew, *talmid hakham*), a *didaskalos* and a *nomodidaskalos*; from near Rome, a God-fearer (Rufinus) who was *agiōn te nomōn sophiēs te sunistor* (Reynolds and Tannenbaum 1987: 31), from Athens, a *proscholos* (*CIJ* 333; 1158; 201; 715b), and, from Larissa, a *scholastikos*, perhaps of the first century AD (*SEG* XXIX, 197: 537).[4] But here it is only fair to point out that in Greek culture the latter term could mean a 'professor' of rhetoric or even an advocate (Loewe 1974). The inscription from Aphrodisias has now revealed a group (*dekania*) of *philomathōn*, lovers of learning. No literature survives to expose the preoccupations of any of those scholars. Their total number in known inscriptions cannot be said to be high, in proportion to our evidence; and geographically they are also rather confined. Their appearance does seem to reveal, once again, a link with the distant rabbis. At the same time, it is quite possible that the positions and activities they represent were but pale imitations of their counterparts in Palestine. I ignore here any appearances of the term 'rabbi'; this should not be taken as indicative since the term can also serve as a form of respectful address, with no technical meaning (Levine 1989). I do not know whether one should add to the collection Juvenal's begging Jewess who was an 'interpreter of the laws of Jerusalem', as well as being a 'high priestess of the tree' and a decoder of dreams (*Satire* 6, 524–7; Stern 1980, no. 299). The joke there was perhaps meant to be compounded by ascribing legal expertise to a woman.

For the period between about AD 200 and AD 350, there is archaeological evidence of an association in death between Palestinian rabbis and members of Diaspora communities. It became desirable to be interred in the Holy Land. The rock-cut necropolis at Beth She'arim (near modern Haifa) already housed the sarcophagus of the Patriarch R. Judah I, author of the Mishnah, and a number of rabbis after him (Schwabe and Lifschitz 1974). Here were brought the bodies of many wealthy lay individuals, especially from Phoenicia and from Syria, but also from places further afield, such as Pamphylia. All were buried in the same manner, and the use of the Greek language (some 80 per cent of the inscriptions are in Greek) and of figurative designs, including the occasional one from Greek mythology, seems equally acceptable to all groups. It is hard to say how far this indicates shared practices among the living. The existence, to our knowledge, of one single synagogue within reach of the site, constructed towards the end of the third century, may perhaps be taken as a pointer in this direction, if it is right to take it as a place of worship for all who had occasion to stay there. On the other hand, we should remember that the synagogue should, according to Jewish Law, have had nothing to do with the cemetery, and the requisite prayers for the deposition of the sarcophagi would have been pronounced not in any synagogue but in the necropolis itself.

To observe the presence or absence of rabbinic influence or authority anywhere in the Diaspora, we should need to know more than we do about the texture of life, since that is where the principles found their full expression. The sources are inadequate for this; descriptions of practice in them are limited, yet it would be wrong to draw conclusions from this negative evidence. Had Josephus written his promised work 'on Customs and Causes' (*Antiquities* IV 198), we might have been better off. The second book of the *Against Apion* contains an interesting summary of Judaism's salient features, written in the 90s AD, just at the time when rabbinic Judaism was beginning to take shape in Palestine; but the thrust of this account is ethical, serving the work's apologetic argument (Vermes 1982). For the rest, what we find in such Diaspora Jewish writing as we have, are brief remarks, with that in Philo's *On the Creation of the World* (170–2) being the most notable (Mendelson 1988: 29–49).

By far the best-documented practice, which also caught the attention of Roman writers, is the keeping of the sabbath, with its lighting of lamps; and from what is said we can infer that enough Jews treated it seriously as a day of withdrawal from public life, of rest and prayer, to make it stand out as a distinguishing feature (Goldenberg 1979; Rabello 1984). It is, interestingly enough, in a speech ascribed to the hostile Roman prefect of Egypt, Avilius Flaccus, that Philo gives a memorable vignette of how a Jewish sabbath might have looked: the Jews should abandon the observance, says Flaccus; if invasion or disaster were to strike on that day, would they really continue to walk around the streets with their hands in their pockets as usual, or stay in their synagogues, and not budge an inch (*On Dreams* 123–9)? We also learn from Philo that there were problems for Jewish recipients if the Roman grain distribution was made on a Saturday (*Embassy to Gaius* 23, 158). Exemptions from military service because of its incompatibility with sabbath observance are sought in letters cited by Josephus, from Roman officials of the triumviral period to the city authorities of Ephesus and Miletus. The Jews of Ionia regard it as a form of harassment that they are asked to appear before tribunals on the sabbath and (interestingly) on festivals, and this is one of the principal complaints that they lay before Marcus Agrippa as arbiter in 14 BC (Josephus, *Antiquities* XVI 27). The consequent exemption granted by Augustus appeared still in the Theodosian Code (II 8,6 = VIII 8, 8; XVI 8, 2). There is no reason to envisage much change over time in this area, and the impression given in the fourth century by John Chrysostom and in the Laodicea Council canons, of the Jewish sabbath as a happy day, set apart for Bible-reading and repose, has the ring of truth about it.

The sabbath was central to the identity of Jews living among Gentiles. It is possible in similar fashion to track down other basic practices from a combination of sources, with the additional help of Christian literature (Meeks and Wilken 1978: 64–5). Circumcision, ritual immersion and the wearing of *tephillin* (phylacteries) are well attested. Among the festivals, Passover and Tabernacles appear to have been prominent, and an assembly held during the latter is mentioned explicitly in a first-century AD decree in Greek where the Jewish community of Cyrene honours a Roman official (Lüderitz 1983, no. 71).

For the question of boundaries, the dietary laws might be of special significance, since in their very nature they would appear to encourage, even if not necessitating, separate eating: consuming food and drink together with others is an important way of breaking down barriers; and a community's eating habits are a major social distinguishing mark. We need look no further than Josephus to be assured that Diaspora Jews observed at least some of the Levitical regulations, and, indeed, he claims that 'many of our prohibitions in the matter of food' have become widespread (*Against Apion* II 123). Equally, however, this very remark, with its implication that the dietary laws were accessible, suggests that a limited form of observance may have been in question. Certainly, the complicated regulations about preparing and mixing food and about contamination of vessels and utensils, which play so large a part in Talmudic discussions, need not be read into the world of the Graeco-Roman city. In any case it is not inevitable that special dietary laws compel people to eat away from others, even if they may encourage such habits, as well as being best preserved by them. All sorts of arrangements are feasible, where there is a social reason to make them. And again, where we do suspect a high level of punctiliousness in eating habits, it would be wrong on this basis simply to assume a high degree of self-segregation from outsiders in every sphere. There is no necessary connection, and practices at any particular moment in history do not always form a harmonious unity.

What we know of Diaspora observance need not point beyond what might be called a minimal Judaism, comparable, perhaps, with that ascribed by Goodman (1983) to the Galileans in the Mishnaic age. For the Diaspora, such an interpretation is not entirely new (Sanders 1990: 255–83). Feldman (1989: 300–5) has suggested that in the third century the Jews of non-coastal Asia Minor were particularly cut-off from rabbinic influence. Kraabel (1981; 1982) has argued primarily on the basis of architecture and iconography for a non-halakhic Diaspora Judaism.[5] It is the implications of such a view that are interesting: a Judaism of the kind proposed does not in itself need to induce a tightly enclosed community. The most that can be said is that the system may tend that way in certain circumstances. Any group needs some boundary, or its identity will vanish. Special practices make a group distinct and also provide a way of making entry meaningful and the membership somewhat select. Equally, any group needs some contact with the world in which it is located, in order to secure its existence, its livelihood and some new blood. Jewish communities will undoubtedly have occupied different places along that continuum which runs from having boundaries that are almost closed to manifesting a high degree of openness (Cohen 1989). They must also have reacted to circumstances and adapted.

Here, the aim is not to illuminate the diversity of possibilities but rather to look at shared characteristics, to determine some leading features. The notion of the typical community has its uses. I shall focus on two aspects which emerge from recent publications. One has been much discussed on a technical level, but its implications perhaps shirked; the other now demands an explanation.

ACTIVITY ON THE BOUNDARIES

The first feature to be highlighted is the intensity of activity on the boundaries: the ease with which it was possible to enter Judaism and the availability of forms of partial membership which were often taken up, it would appear, by both pagans and Christians. Indeed, Marcel Simon (1964; 1986), who, in a work perhaps more noticed by theologians than by historians, was the first systematically to demonstrate the vitality of Judaism between the second and the fifth centuries, spoke of Jewish involvement in a universal syncretism. That concept is in fact best confined to real religious fusions, such as the cult of Zeus the Most High (Zeus Hypsistos) led by an *archisynagōgos* (a term occasionally used for the leader of a pagan club) at Pydna in Macedonia (Cormack 1974: 51–5). But the manifestations which led Simon to invoke the concept widely are very real. He was preoccupied principally with Jewish–Christian relations, and so he made a special study of Christian Judaizers, those individuals who incurred the wrath of their bishops by maintaining Jewish habits and rituals alongside their Christianity; these extended to the use of phylacteries and the celebration of Jewish festivals together with their Jewish neighbours.

Pagan Judaizers are, however, equally important, though perhaps more obscure to us. We have already seen references in Philo and Josephus to the attractions of Judaism. We also meet in Josephus individuals described as 'worshippers of God' (*theosebeis*), normally translated as 'God-fearers' or 'sympathizers'. They appear to correspond with those who are similarly described, though with a slightly different verbal formation, in Acts; and they figure in some inscriptions. Greek and Latin authors have various ways of alluding to sympathizers with Judaism. Rabbinic literature appears to echo the same formulae (see now Feldman 1989: 274–82). Clearly, those partial adherents were distinguished from proselytes and yet they were publicly associated with Judaism, in benefaction, possibly in burial and also, we may suppose, in at least some forms of worship (Kant 1987: 688). Apparently, they were not generally deemed impure. Josephus evidentiy approves them (Rajak 1985: 257–9).

The major inscription recently discovered in the excavation of Aphrodisias in Caria (Reynolds and Tannenbaum 1987) makes it evident, after years of inconclusive debate, that the God-fearers were indeed a category of half-way proselytes, even if the terms have a range of uses beyond that quasi-technical one. It is unnecessary to recall the debate here. The inscription of a dedication for some sort of memorial created by an association (*dekania*) of Jews, perhaps in the early third century. On its second face (which may be later than the first), there appears a list giving the names of fifty-two people described at the top as *theosebis* (*sic*); these include nine Aphrodisian town-councillors (*bouleutai*), members of the city's elite. The *dekania*, which is described in a perplexing introduction on the first side, is that of the *philomathōn* and (apparently) *panteulogētōn* ('lovers of wisdom' and 'all-blessed' or 'all-blessing') of which we have already spoken.[6] The names listed on the first side are presumably those of its full members. There is no necessity to take the God-fearers as also belonging to the club, though it is possible that they did do so and they are linked with it here. At the very least we find them closely associated in a common philanthropic activity with the full Jews, and subscribing, presumably, to the same semi-private memorial.

There emerges the picture of a category of adherent that was kept distinct for formal purposes, but scarcely one that was held at arm's length. The opposite, indeed, would seem to be true, since the picture is complicated by the appearance of two *theoseb-eis*, Antonios and Emmonios, on the first face, among the Jews. Perhaps they were allowed entry because they were closer to Judaism than the *theosebeis* on the second face, and this then would raise the interesting possibility that varying degrees of adherence had different standing (cf. Cohen 1989); or perhaps this happened for quite other reasons. Josephus' formulation, when he tells us of the throngs of Greeks at Antioch in Syria who were in his day attracted to Jewish worship and goes on to say that the Jews had 'in a fashion made them a part of themselves' (*Jewish War* VII 45), seems aptly to describe the situation visible at Aphrodisias.

Also among the eighteen names on the first face of the inscription, there are three proselytes, so designated; these bear Jewish names, Samuel, Joses and Joseph. Presumably, they were circumcised[7] and were deemed to have abandoned pagan practices, having 'made the journey to a better home' (Philo, *On the Virtues* 102). This does not mean that all their fellow Jews will have accepted them as entire equals: both in Qumran texts and in the Mishnah some distinctions are drawn between proselytes and Jews (Cohen 1989: 27–9; cf. Goodman 1983: 71). To cross the boundary wholly no doubt required a decisive and not altogether easy act; though we notice that, even then, not everyone choosing to label himself or herself in an inscription as *Ioudaios* or *Ioudaia* or the like seems fully to have achieved the transition. A pagan-style Latin dedication to an interesting collectivity of deities entitled Iunones was erected by Annia, an Italian freedwoman, who is able to describe herself quite simply as 'Iuda', 'Jewess' (*CIJ* 77; Kraemer 1989: 42).[8] In any case, we can safely say, on the basis of the Aphrodisian categories, that a clear distinction between proselytes and God-fearers was quite operable, whether or not there was some spectrum of degrees of affiliation to be found among proselytes. And we may add that, when it comes to God-fearers, there need be no uncertainty on the latter point: for them it was possible to sit astride the boundary in comfort, temporarily and probably even permanently.

WOMEN BENEFACTORS AND COMMUNITY PRACTICES

The second issue to be discussed concerns the principles by which Diaspora Jews characteristically conducted their affairs. A prime reason for maintaining closed boundaries is to preserve a particular value system intact, allowing the values and practices of outsiders only limited access. Can the surviving inscriptions, in their fragmentary state, tell us anything of the community life of Greek-speaking (or Latin-speaking) Jews? Again, our purpose is to look for patterns within the local and chronological diversity.

A challenging proposal which has aroused considerable interest is the subject of a book by Bernadette Brooten on woman synagogue leaders (1982). On her view, some very peculiar and certainly unrabbinic practices were to be found in Diaspora communities. Even if the thesis has flaws, the observed phenomenon requires an explanation and leads us to consider the ideology of the Jews in relation to their environment. On the basis of a detailed study of nineteen Greek and Latin inscriptions of varying or sometimes unknown date (together with some supporting material), all of which name a woman as some type of community or synagogue leader, Brooten argues for the existence in the Diaspora of a form of Judaism which allowed women an active role in the religious life of the synagogue. They appear as *archisynagōgoi* as 'elders', as 'mothers' of the synagogue, and, in all these capacities, they can be benefactresses; they might even, it would appear, be categorized as priests. She therefore argues that responsibility for every major facet of synagogue life, including instruction and the ritual itself, might, in principle, have been assigned to a woman. She vigorously contests the traditional explanation of these inscriptions, that the stated offices were honorific in nature, claiming that such explanations can either be shown or suspected to originate in an a priori assumption: the view has been that women simply could not have played the roles ascribed to them by the names of their offices.

That such prejudices were constantly and illegitimately entertained by male scholars need hardly be doubted. The belief seems to have been that women held purely honorific offices while men held proper ones, and for this there is no justification. The problem, however, is that there are also independent, strong arguments for taking the posts named in the inscriptions as essentially honorific for *all* types of holder. First, it should be observed that Brooten discusses, but fails to account for, the presence of children among the office-holders. Kallistos, an *archisynagōgos* at Venosa, was aged 3 years and 3 months, while at Rome there was a youthful (*nēpios*) *archōn* (*CIJ* 120; 587). These children can hardly be regarded as having been functional in their posts. Second, and more fundamentally, she does not take serious account of the parallelism between the honorands of the synagogue inscriptions, and the larger world, where holders of municipal office were regularly honoured with inscriptions. There too, at any rate in Asia Minor, women and children were to be found, among a vast preponderance of men (van Bremen 1983). Both in the larger and in the smaller world, the individuals in question may or may not have been functional in the capacities ascribed to them. This was of secondary importance, and the significant thing about them, whether they were men, women or children, was evidently that they had benefited, or were connected with those who had ben-efited, the honouring institution by their munificence or their patronage. They may have been owners of property in their own right. They are linked into a wider pattern of exchange of benefits between powerful individuals and communities which has come to be known as euergetism. Payment, obligatory or voluntary, by the office-holder for the privilege of office-holding is a crucial part of this system. In the case of the synagogue, these features of office-holding explain well why there are sometimes in the same institution a surprising number of seemingly overlapping offices, and why the post of *archisynagōgos* may have multiple holders. Brooten vastly overestimates the amount of administrative activity that would have surrounded an ancient institution, and her picture of dedicated female rabbis of progressive persuasion, concerned with everything from liturgy to repairs, introduces an anachronistic note.

None the less, Brooten's questioning exposes an important phenomenon: the mirroring of the city's social framework, with its implicit values, within a Jewish context. Those values, by which status and power were tied to demonstrative wealth, obviously ran counter to certain Jewish principles.[9] This mirroring is striking in relation to the post of *archisynagōgos*, rightly described by Brooten as the most widely known Jewish title in the ancient world. What deserves comment is the distance this name has travelled. It would seem to have originated in Hebrew, for it is a literal Greek translation of the Hebrew *rosh kneset*, assembly head: hence the rather odd Greek formation, where the second part of the word does not designate a position, as in *archiereus* and other such titles, but an institution (Brooten 1982: 5). But *archisynagōgos* eventually embedded itself comfortably in the context where we find it when we read the Greek and Latin inscriptions.[10] That context was, in essence, the honour-based system of administration which characterized the cities of the Roman Empire. It may be added that such a change in meaning had surely been facilitated by the fact that Jews, like the nine councillors at Aphrodisias, themselves took a part in that administration: that is attested already for the first century AD and occurred widely after Septimius Severus early in the third century (Rajak 1985; Linder 1987, no. 2). To some extent, they must have internalized its values.

The appearance of women and children as synagogue leaders is the clue which leads us to a plausible and fruitful interpretation of the titulature and the pattern of office-holding in the Jewish community. It will require further testing. If it is correct, then we observe also the hint of an important social mechanism. For the connection of the Jewish world with the patronal system of the city will have provided an easy way in for those who wished to transfer (or partly to transfer) from one side of the boundary to the other. And the interconnection also suggests an obvious source of pressure on some pagan citizens to do just that: if the Jews were prominent in a city, the claims of patronage or of the exchange of benefits could have dictated the move. This, then, would be a powerful force for keeping boundaries open.

There is another observation to be made. If the social pattern surrounding the synagogue not only was intelligible to outsiders, but also rested on the same base of patronage and munificence as their own institutions, then it will have been of use to outsiders to be benefactors of synagogues. And some undoubtedly were, the most notable being the distinguished Julia Severa, a pagan priestess in Acmonia, Phrygia, recorded in an inscription from the time of the Emperor Nero. This priestess used sometimes to be taken by scholars as a syncretizing Jewess, but she has now been firmly put in her place as a great pagan lady; she may, but need not, have been a sympathizer with Judaism (*CIJ* 766; Schürer 1986: 30; Sheppard 1979: 170). It was Julia Severa who built the synagogue in Acmonia. Exactly why she might have done so, must remain a subject for speculation.

EPILOGUE

The institutional and social familiarity of the synagogue world will also have made it easier for those whose motivation was more private to enter this world, whether wholly or partly. The *archisynagōgoi* will surely have made entrants welcome, whatever the degree of their involvement or the irreproachability of their lives. And the rabbis in remote Palestine will not have been consulted.

Closeness, of course, produced tension too, and the major explosions of violence that occurred intermittently over the period are all too well known. But eventually, neither pagan nor Jewish but Christian anxieties were to be responsible for constructing new barriers. And soon, Jewry itself was virtually to forget a remarkable phase of its existence, to an extent where it has become hard to believe that the rabbinic age was for many Jews not a period of looking inward, but rather a time when the world opened out.

NOTES

1 In annotation in the Loeb edn of Josephus (Vol. 7: 509), Marcus suggests that *epikrateitai hup' autou* means 'makes its power felt' in quite a neutral sense, rather than 'is dominated by', but this does not accurately render the Greek.

2 Levine (1989: 76–83) argues that the sources do not attest the existence of a 'Great Sanhedrin' after 70, contrary to common opinion, and he allows only local courts associated with specific rabbis.

3 See Elmsley's edn (1911). Sheppard (1979: 170) comments on the absence in Mishnah *Avodah Zarah* of any discussion about the permissibility of Jews being town councillors (which would involve at the very least being present at pagan rituals; see Rajak 1985: 256–7). Perhaps the matter was simply out of the question in Palestine, and this then would constitute further evidence that the rabbis did not look any further.

4 On these terms, see also Fergus Millar's discussion, pp. 110–11.

5 Goodenough's *magnum opus* (1953-) provides the inspiration for such interpretations of the iconography, though its ascription of a special form of mystical Judaism to the Diaspora is now no longer tenable.

6 The exact nature of the *dekania* is uncertain, the name being unparalleled for a Jewish association. The reading, however, ought to stand, though see Feldman (1989: 280). There is even more doubt about the nature of the so-called *patella*, perhaps some kind of charitable foundation, with which the *dekania* is linked. The exact formation *philomathōn* appears only here in Jewish epigraphy but is common

in Philo and LXX; *panteulogētōn* (the word is damaged in the text) is more contentious: see Reynolds and Tannenbaum (1987): 30–6.
7 There is no evidence that a ban on Gentile circumcision operated in practice, following Antoninus Pius' modification of Hadrian's total prohibition of the act (Reynolds and Tannenbaum 1987: 43–5; Linder 1987: 100). A reiteration by Septimius Severus is not securely attested.
8 See possible examples of similar 'Jewish paganism' in Feldman (1989: 304).
9 See T. Rajak, 'Jews as Benefactors' in *The Jewish Diaspora in the Hellenistic and Roman Periods* (Tel-Aviv University, forthcoming).
10 This argument is reconsidered in Rajak and Noy (1993: 83–4).

BIBLIOGRAPHY

Applebaum, S. (1974) 'The Organization of the Jewish Communities in the Diaspora' in S. Safrai, and M. Stern (eds) *The Jewish People in the First Century* (Compendia Rerum Iudaicarum ad Novum Testamentum 1, 1), Assen, 464–503.
Applebaum, S. (1979) *Jews and Greeks in Ancient Cyrene*, Leiden.
Bremen, R. van (1983) 'Women and Wealth' in A. Cameron and A. Kuhrt (eds) *Images of Women in Antiquity*, London and Sydney, 223–42.
Brooten, B. (1982) *Women Leaders in the Ancient Synagogue* (Brown Judaic Studies 36), Chico, Calif.
Cohen, S. J. D. (1981) 'Patriarchs and Scholarchs', *Proceedings of the American Academy for Jewish Research* 48: 57–85.
Cohen, S. J. D. (1989) 'Crossing the Boundary and Becoming a Jew', *Harvard Theological Review* 82, 1: 13–33.
Cormack. J. (1974) 'Zeus Hypsistos at Pydna', in *Mélanges Helléniques offerts à Georges Daux*, Paris, 51–5.
Elmsley, W. A. L. (1911) *The Mishnah on Idolatry: 'Aboda Zara* (Texts and Studies 8, 2), Cambridge.
Feldman, L. H. (1989) 'Proselytes and "Sympathizers" in the Light of the New Inscription from Aphrodisias', *Revue des Etudes juives* 148, 3–4: 265–305.
Feldman, L. H. (1993) *Jew and Gentile in the Ancient World: Attitudes and Interactions from Alexander to Justinian*, Princeton, NJ.
Forkman, G. (1972) *The Limits of the Religious Community*, London.
Goldenberg, R. (1979) 'The Jewish Sabbath in the Roman World up to the Time of Constantine the Great', *Aufstieg und Niedergang der römischen Welt* [hereafter cited as ANRW] II, 19, 1: Berlin and New York, 414–47.
Goodenough, E. R. (1953-) *Jewish Symbols in the Greco-Roman Period*, Vols 1–11 (Bollingen Series 37), New York.
Goodman, M. (1983) *State and Society in Roman Galilee, A. D. 132–212*, Totowa, N.J.
Hengel, M. (1966) 'Die Synagogeninschrift von Stobi', *Zeitschrift für die Neutestamentliche Wissenschaft* 57: 145–83.

Kant, L. H. (1987) 'Jewish Inscriptions in Greek and Latin' *ANRW* II, 20, 2: Berlin and New York, 671–713.

Kraabel, A. T. (1979) 'The Diaspora Synagogue', *ANRW* II, 19, 2: Berlin and New York, 477–510.

Kraabel, A. T. (1981) 'Social Systems of Six Diaspora Synagogues', in J. Gutmann (ed.) *Ancient Synagogues: The State of Research*, Chico, Calif.

Kraabel, A. T. (1982) 'The Roman Diaspora: Six Questionable Assumptions', *Journal of Jewish Studies* 33: 445–64.

Kraemer, R. S. (1989) 'On the Meaning of the Term "Jew" in Greco-Roman Inscriptions' *Harvard Theological Review* 82: 35–53.

Leon, H. J. (1960) *The Jews of Ancient Rome*, Philadelphia, Pa.

Levine, L. I. (1979) 'The Jewish Patriarch (Nasi) in Third Century Palestine' *ANRW* II, 19, 2: Berlin and New York, 650–88.

Levine, L. I. (ed.) (1987) *The Synagogue in Late Antiquity*, Philadelphia, Pa.

Levine, L. I. (1989) *The Rabbinic Class of Roman Palestine in Late Antiquity*, Jerusalem and New York.

Lifshitz, B. (1967) *Donateurs et fondateurs dans les synagogues juives*, Paris.

Linder, A. (1987) *The Jews in Roman Imperial Legislation* Detroit, Mich. and Jerusalem.

Loewe, R. (1974) 'Rabi Joshua ben Hananiah: Ll.D. or D.Litt?', *Journal of Jewish Studies* 25, 1: 137–54.

Lüderitz, G. (1983) *Corpus jüdischer Zeugnisse aus der Cyrenaika. Mit einem Anhang von J. M. Reynolds*, Tübingen.

Meeks, W. A. and Wilken, R. I. (1978) *Jews and Christians in Antioch in the First Four Centuries of the Common Era* (SBL Sources for Biblical Study 13), Missoula, Mont.

Mendelson, A. (1988) *Philo's Jewish Identity* (Brown Judaic Studies 161), Atlanta, Georgia.

Momigliano, A. D. (1987) review of Meeks, *The First Urban Christians*, in *Ottavo Contributo alla Storia degli Studi Classici e del Mondo Antico*, Rome: 399–402.

Neusner, J. (1973) *The Idea of Purity in Ancient Judaism* (the Haskell Lectures), Leiden.

Neusner, J. (1981) *Judaism: the Evidence of the Mishnah*, Chicago and London.

Neusner, J. (1984) *In Search of Talmudic Biography: the Problem of the Attributed Saying* (Brown Judaic Studies 70), Chico, Calif.

Oppenheimer, A. (1977) *The 'Am Ha-aretz*, Leiden.

Rabello, A. M. (1984) 'L'Observance des fêtes juives dans l'empire romain', *ANRW* II, 21, 2: 1288–1312.

Rajak. T. (1984) 'Was there a Roman Charter for the Jews?', *Journal of Roman Studies* 74: 107–23.

Rajak, T. (1985) 'Jews and Christians as Groups in a Pagan World', in J. Neusner and E. S. Frerichs (eds) *'To See Ourselves as Others See Us': Christians, Jews, 'Others' in Late Antiquity*, Chico, Calif., 247–62.

Rajak, T. and Noy, D. (1993) '*Archisynagogoi*: Office, Title and Social

Status in the Greco-Jewish Synagogue', *Journal of Roman Studies* 83: 75–93.

Reynolds, J. and Tannenbaum, R. (1987) *Jews and Godfearers at Aphrodisias* (Cambridge Philological Society, Supplementary Volume 12), Cambridge.

Safrai, S. (1974) 'Relations between the Diaspora and the Land of Israel', in S. Safrai and M. Stern (eds) *The Jewish People in the First Century* (Compendia Rerum Iudaicarum ad Novum Testamentum 1, 1) Assen, 184–215.

Safrai, S. (ed) (1987) *The Literature of the Sages* (Compendia Rerum Iudaicarum ad Novum Testamentum 2, 3, 1), Assen and Philadelphia, Pa.

Sanders, E. P. (1990) *Jewish Law from Jesus to the Mishnah. Five Studies*, London and Philadelphia.

Sanders, E. P., Baumgarten, A. and Mendelson, A. (eds) (1981) *Jewish and Christian Self-Definition* Vol. 2, London.

Schürer, E. (1986, 1987) *History of the Jewish People in the Age of Jesus Christ*, ed. G. Vermes, F. Millar and M. D. Goodman, Edinburgh.

Schwabe, M. and Lifschitz, B. (1974), *Beth Shearim*, Vol, II, Jerusalem.

Sheppard, A. R. R. (1979) 'Jews, Christians and Heretics in Acmonia and Eumeneia', *Anatolian Studies* 29: 169–80.

Simon, M. (1964) *Verus Israel: études sur les relations entre Chrétiens et Juifs dans l'empire romain (135–425)*, Paris; English translation (1986), Oxford.

Stern, M. (1974, 1980, 1984) *Greek and Latin Authors on Jews and Judaism*, Vols 1, 2 and 3, Jerusalem.

Strack, H. L. (5th edn. 1931) *Introduction to the Talmud and Midrash*, Philadelphia, Pa. reprinted (1970), New York.

Strack, H. L. (7th Edn, 1982) *Einleitung in Talmud und Midrasch*, ed G. Stemberger, Munich.

Vermes, G. (1982) 'A Summary of the Law by Flavius Josephus', *Novum Testamentum* 24: 289–303.

2

THE PRE-CHRISTIAN PAUL

Martin Hengel[1]

As the first Christian theologian, Paul has uniquely attracted the attention of exegetes. In the process they have almost forgotten Saul *the Jew*. Whereas there is an enormous literature about the Christian apostle, far too little attention has been paid to the former Pharisee. Granted, his verdict on his own pre-Christian past (as on the past of any Christian) is that 'the old has passed away' (2 Corinthians 5:17), but at the same time he tells his readers more about that past than any Christian author before Justin.

In addition to the well-known autobiographical testimonies (Galatians 1: 13–17; 1 Corinthians 15:9; 2 Corinthians 11:22; Romans 11:1; Philippians 3:4–6), there are the indirect conclusions that can be drawn from his theological argumentation, which is incomprehensible apart from its *Jewish* roots. Knowledge of Saul the Jew is a precondition of understanding Paul the Christian.

In addition we have information from Luke, which many scholars nowadays dismiss as unreliable. But we should never forget how difficult it would be to give Paul a historical setting if we did not have Acts.

ORIGIN AND CITIZENSHIP

Let us begin with Paul's origin. At the forefront of his own testimonies is the Pharisee connected with Jewish Palestine; only from Luke do we learn that he came from Tarsus and that he was a citizen of both Tarsus and Rome (Acts 21:39; 16:37f.; 22:25; 23:27).

In other words, only Luke describes Paul as a Diaspora Jew with privileged origins. It is remarkable that despite the tendency to question everything that Luke says, this information is rarely doubted, although the apostle never speaks of his home city and on the basis of his letters we should have, rather, to assume that he came from Palestine (Acts 22:3; cf. 9:11, 30; 11:25; 21:39). Here, however, people have been ready to believe Luke because if Paul came from Tarsus it was possible to connect him with Hellenistic culture and syncretism from his earliest youth.

However, it is questionable whether the young Paul in Tarsus acquired any of the Greek education that flourished there. Granted, we have commonplaces of popular philosophy in his letters, but these come from synagogue preaching; we do not find in him any of the knowledge of classical Greek literature which formed part of the general canon of education. I doubt whether he was trained in one of the usual schools of rhetoric. Even the question where he received his elementary education must remain open. Both Jerusalem and Tarsus are possibilities, since in Paul it is impossible to separate Greek education from Jewish. Although to outward appearance he is a 'wanderer between two worlds', his theological thinking displays an astonishing unity. That will already have been the case with the Jew Saul.

According to Luke, Paul was born in Tarsus and was a citizen of Tarsus as well as of Rome. Both these assertions have been disputed recently (Stegemann 1987). The question of the origin and social status of Paul's family is closely connected with this.

There are problems in supposing that Paul was a citizen of the city in which he was born. He describes himself as a Jew and 'from Tarsus in Cilicia, the citizen of no mean city' (Acts 21:37–9). The question is how we are to understand the words *Tarseus* and *politēs*. Since the citizenship of a Greek polis was only very rarely bestowed on aliens, it seems to me more probable that from his birth Paul was a member of the Jewish community in Tarsus, which as in other places had certain privileges, but not full citizenship, and that here as in the Septuagint, *politēs* and *Tarseus* denote only his place of origin, but – of course – we cannot gain real certainty in this question.

However, there is no reason for doubting Luke's information that the apostle had Roman citizenship. The reasons brought forward against this are not convincing. Thus Paul may have been flogged three times (2 Corinthians 11:25) because he deliberately kept quiet about his citizenship in order to follow Christ in his suffering. We must also take into account the possibility that the city magistrates may not have felt themselves constrained by his claim to privilege. That Paul never mentions it does not mean anything, since he keeps quiet about almost all private matters. Had he been a mere *peregrinus* Paul would have been condemned in Judaea without much fuss and would not have been sent to the imperial court in Rome.

Nor does the objection that Paul never mentions his complete three-part Roman name mean anything, since this usage was not always customary in Greek-speaking circles and went against the custom of Judaism and of early Christianity. The important thing for Christians was not the privilege of an earthly citizenship but the fact that they were brothers and sisters. So we can only say that Paul did not attach any special value to his citizenship. However, that does not mean that he was not a Roman citizen, who made use of the fact in threatening situations.

The name 'Paul' itself is very rare among non-Romans in the Greek east and does not occur at all among contemporary Jews.[2] It continues to be unclear why the young Jew with the proud biblical name Sha'ul, which emphasized the derivation of his family from the tribe of Benjamin, was given this Latin cognomen. The most plausible reason is that it derived from the personal associations of Paul's father, perhaps with his patron. It is also worth mentioning that with one late exception Saul(os) does not appear among Diaspora Jews but does so quite often in Palestine.

Luke is also our sole source of information about the Hebrew name. The transition to the new name does not take place at the time of the apostle's call – Saulus does not become Paulus then – but at the point where for the first time Paul enters a pagan environment as a missionary; and his eminent 'namesake', the governor Sergius Paulus, appears as the first 'missionary success' (Acts 13:9). That the missionary to the Gentiles uses only his non-Jewish name in the letters may be an indication that the ancient royal name had now become unimportant to him, as was his descent from the tribe of Benjamin (Romans 11:1; Philippians 3:5).

The reality of Paul's Roman citizenship is finally supported by the fact that, so far as geography is concerned, he thinks in Roman categories, and that in his world-wide plans for mission he has only the Empire in view. At an early stage his gaze focuses on the capital, and then extends further as far as Spain (Romans 15:28): his strategy is orientated on the Roman provinces. In these he concentrates on the main cities, and it is no coincidence that Roman colonies like Antioch in Pisidia, Iconium, Lystra, Troas and Philippi also play an important role. Philippians 3:20f. becomes particularly significant in that it comes in a letter from a Roman citizen to the Christian community of a Roman city: it is about the binding nature of 'our citizenship' (*politeuma*), which is quite different from that of Rome.

We can only guess how Paul's ancestors acquired this citizenship. The most important way in which the privilege spread among Jews was through the emancipation of Jewish slaves by Roman citizens.

According to Philo the majority of Jews living in Rome were Roman citizens. Having been brought to Italy as prisoners of war, they were freed by their owners who 'did not compel them to corrupt their ancestral laws'. Augustus 'did not expel them from Rome nor deprive them of Roman citizenship on the grounds of their Jewish faith' (*Embassy to Gaius* 155, 157).

In addition we have information about the return of Jewish freedmen to Judaea. The nucleus of the synagogue 'of the Libertines' mentioned in Acts 6:9 certainly consisted of Roman *libertini*. The Theodotus son of Vettenus who founded a synagogue was also a descendant of such a person; his patronym indicates that he was of Roman origin and the title 'priest' that he was one of the Jewish nobility by birth (*CIJ* 1404; see Hengel 1975). How respectable a freedman could be in Judaea is evident from the tomb of the 'Goliath' family in Jericho, where an ossuary bears the inscription: 'Theodotus, freedman of the Empress Agrippina' (Hachlili 1979). This Theodotus belonged to the 'house of Caesar'; the 'Empress Agrippina' was the wife of Claudius and mother of Nero. Even in Jewish Palestine people were proud of the high rank of this member of the family.

So it seems most likely that Paul's forebears were given Roman citizenship unasked for when they were freed by a Roman citizen. Jerome reports that Paul's parents came from Gischala in Upper Galilee and that they had been carried off to Tarsus in the upheavals of war (*Commentary on Philemon* 23). The young Paul had gone with them. This contradicts Acts 22:28, where Luke makes Paul say that he was *born* a Roman citizen. If Jerome were right, Paul would only be a *libertinus* and not a full citizen. On the other hand, it does seem likely that Paul's forebears became slaves as the result of war. How and why they came to Tarsus remains an open question. The reason might be connected with their Roman master, and they could have come by a roundabout route, even via Rome. Tarsus was a metropolis in which numerous Roman citizens lived.

There is also considerable uncertainty about the apostle's social origins. Ramsay's assumption was that Paul 'belonged to a family of wealth and position' (1908: 34). Eduard Meyer even assumed that 'his father had a factory in which tents were made' (1923: 308). If Paul came from a family of freedmen, these suppositions will have to be toned down somewhat, but it is even less valid to infer from the apostle's remarks about his craft that he had proletarian origins (Stegemann 1987: 226–8). To work as a tent-maker (*skēnopoios*: Acts 18:3) is no indication of poverty. Moreover, Paul need not necessarily have learned the craft in Tarsus; he could have taken it up in connection with his scribal studies or even after he became a Christian, in order to be independent as a missionary.

That despite this craft Paul was not just a member of the proletariat is evident both from the old traditions of his family which had been carefully preserved and from his Graeco-Jewish education. Education in antiquity – above all Greek education – was not to be had for nothing; it presupposed material support. That was true just as much of Jerusalem as of Tarsus.

UPBRINGING AND SCHOOLING

This brings us to a further point of dispute. Where was Paul brought up and where did he go to school – in Tarsus or in Jerusalem? Here we come to a point where, in addition to the texts in Luke, Paul's own evidence becomes significant, and so we are brought up against the central problem of his spiritual home.

Our starting-point must be the information about Paul's education. Here we have a hotly disputed tradition in Luke and some remarks by Paul which supplement it.

The passage in question comes at the beginning of Paul's speech at his arrest in Jerusalem:

I am a Jew, born at Tarsus in Cilicia, but brought up in this city, at the feet of Gamaliel, educated according to the strict manner of the law of our fathers, being zealous for God as you all are this day. (Acts 22:3).

In the introduction to the speech before Agrippa II, Luke makes Paul say:

> My manner of life from my youth, spent from the beginning among my own nation and in Jerusalem, is known by all the Jews. They have known for a long time, if they are willing to testify, that according to the strictest party of our religion I have lived as a Pharisee. (Acts 26:4)

To the Sanhedrin in Jerusalem he confesses:

> Brethren, I am a Pharisee, a son of Pharisees. (Acts 23:6)

These statements by Luke's Paul are intended to present him as a true Jew, obedient to God.

Paul's own testimony has the opposite purpose. It is written in acute controversy with his Judaizing opponents. In it he stresses his distance from the past with which he has broken. He tells the Galatians in 1:13–14:

> For you have heard of my former life in Judaism, how I persecuted the church of God violently and tried to destroy it; and I advanced in Judaism beyond many of my own age among my people, so extremely zealous was I for the traditions of my fathers.

Philippians 3:4–6 is addressed to Jewish-Christian opponents:

> If any other man thinks he has reason for confidence in the flesh, I have more; circumcised on the eighth day, of the people of Israel, of the tribe of Benjamin, a Hebrew born of Hebrews, as to the law a Pharisee, as to zeal a persecutor of the church, as to righteousness under the law blameless.

Despite their diametrically opposed intentions, the content of the information given by Luke, who does not know Paul's letters, and that in Paul's own testimony is very similar.

Now where did Paul get the Jewish (and Greek) education that moulded him: in Tarsus or in Jerusalem? Van Unnik used this alternative as the title of a well-known study (1973a, cf. 1973b). On the basis of a painstaking investigation of Acts 22:3 he came down clearly for Jerusalem. With the three participles 'born' 'brought up', 'educated', Luke uses a biographical scheme which says:

34

Paul was born in Tarsus, it was in Jerusalem that he received his upbringing in the parental home, just as it was in Jerusalem that he received his later schooling for the rabbinate.

In other words, van Unnik assumes that Paul's parents returned to Jerusalem with him when he was still a small child:

This removal took place quite early in Paul's life, apparently before he could peep round the corner of the door and certainly before he went roaming on the street. (1973a: 301)

Thus the pagan Hellenistic milieu could not have 'corrupted' him. A further conclusion of van Unnik is that Paul's mother tongue was Aramaic, and that this was the language in which he thought.

To begin with, we must take the arguments of van Unnik's investigation seriously. Since Mommsen's article on 'The Legal Proceedings over the Apostle Paul' (1901) scholars have indeed argued against any stay of the pre-Christian Paul in Jerusalem by appealing to Galatians 1:22, where Paul claims the Christians did not know him by face (see pp. 46–7), but this is hardly correct. How and why Paul the Pharisee – and here I quote Georg Strecker – 'in whose case according to Galatians 1 it is *very* uncertain whether he lived in Jerusalem before his experience at Damascus' (1979: 232, n.10), came from Tarsus to Damascus (Galatians 1), but is said to have avoided Jerusalem remains completely puzzling – just look at the map! Strecker tried to substantiate his reference to Galatians 1:22 etc. by referring to the smallness of the population of Jerusalem, which Jeremias estimated at 25,000. But here he is on uncertain ground. Most recent investigations work on the assumption that the number of inhabitants grew between the Hasmonaeans and AD 66 from around 32,000 to around 80,000 (Wilkinson 1974; Broshi 1975). Jerusalem was certainly not a village in which everyone knew everyone else.

Acts 22:3 was formulated by Luke, but it is based on older information. This finds support in Paul himself. One might refer first to Romans 15:19, where Paul outlines the span of his missionary work: 'So that from Jerusalem and as far round as Illyricum I have fully preached the gospel of Christ.' This is the apostle's primary missionary work, and the stress on Jerusalem as a starting-point shows how closely he is connected with the holy city, to which he wants to return again before he goes westwards, despite the danger a visit poses to him.

In Paul's own testimony the sequence 'Hebrews', 'Israelites', 'descendants of Abraham' (2 Corinthians 11:22; cf. Romans 11:1) and 'people of Israel', 'tribe of Benjamin', 'Hebrew of Hebrews', 'Pharisee' (Philippians 3:5) is striking. In both cases *Hebraios* (Hebrew) means an Aramaic-speaking Palestinian Jew. In the context it certainly does not mean 'Jew' as opposed to Gentile, since that contrast is already expressed by the mention of belonging to Israel. The closest parallel to this designation is the '*Hebraioi*' in Acts 6:1. The reference to the tribe of Benjamin shows that Paul's family was proud of the age of its genealogy. Mordecai from the book of Esther and the patriarch Jehuda ha-nasi were also fellow members of the tribe, and the same would also apply to Jehuda's great-great-grandfather Gamaliel I, Paul's teacher. So Paul was in excellent company. We have no comparable information about members of the Greek-speaking Diaspora.

Finally the 'according to the Law a Pharisee' also indicates Paul's real mother-country. After elementary school the education described in Galatians 1:13f., which was distinguished by the 'advance in Jewish teaching' in which Paul surpassed 'his contemporaries among his people' and which made him 'so extremely zealous for the traditions of the fathers', leading him to become a Pharisaic scholar, took place in Jerusalem. Before 70 that was the only right place for a strict Jew – as Paul was – to study the Torah. Far too little notice is taken in German scholarship of this fact that Paul was a Pharisaic *talmid hakham*. If we did not by chance have these three words, *kata nomon Pharisaios* ('according to the Law a Pharisee'), from Paul's pen, historical criticism would dismiss Luke's 'I am a Pharisee, the son of Pharisees' as a typically Lukan invention. It is also more than probable that Paul studied under Gamaliel I, who was at that time the leading Pharisaic teacher. (Anyone who studied theology in Marburg between 1920 and 1950 went to Rudolf Bultmann's lectures.) Unfortunately we know all too little about Gamaliel (as about most Pharisaic teachers before 70); it is questionable whether he was the grandson of the great Hillel and even whether he really belonged to Hillel's school. Gamaliel's grandson Gamaliel II, the first 'patriarch', was the first to follow the views of the Bet Hillel in his teaching. So the controversy whether Paul was a Hillelite or Shammaite is an idle one. Indeed we have no idea whether the dispute between the schools was the decisive factor in the Jerusalem establishments among which Saul/Paul moved. Again, I know theologians who in Marburg liked to go to Rudolf Otto's lectures as well as to Bultmann's.

However, this has taken us far beyond the basic question whether Paul studied in Jerusalem. There remains an argument of Georg Strecker's which is shared by many (or most) German scholars:

> In view of the vigorous Jewish school activity in the Diaspora it is very improbable that Paul could not have received a Pharisaic education outside Jerusalem. (1979: 232, n.10)

Here Strecker refers to Matthew 23:15, to the conversion of the kings of Adiabene and, concerning 'Diaspora Pharisees generally', to Schoeps's book on Paul (1959). But this is piling error on error. Paul himself is the only example cited by Schoeps; Matthew 23:15 does not refer to Diaspora Pharisees but to Palestinian Pharisees, who travelled 'round the world' from their mother-country, while the key word 'Pharisee' does not appear at all in the account of the conversion of King Izates of Adiabene. Izates had been converted by a Jewish merchant who dissuaded him from circumcision because of political dangers. A second Jewish traveller, Eleazar, who observed the Law strictly and required circumcision, may have been a Pharisee, but he was a Galilean and not a Diaspora Jew. The king sent his sons and brothers to Jerusalem to be educated, and later they fought against the Romans on the walls of Jerusalem (Josephus, *Antiquities* XX 3–4 (34–48)).

The Pharisees were a Palestinian holiness movement of laymen whose aim was the ritual sanctification of everyday life in the Eretz Israel, such as was required of priests in the sanctuary.

For Paul, the dispute that broke out in Antioch over eating together with pagan Christians who were ritually impure (Galatians 2:11–21) amounted to a controversy with his past. That is why he had to put up such energetic opposition. As any Gentile was thought to be as unclean as a dead body, it was impossible to observe the Torah strictly in a Gentile environment. When Felix sent some priests to the imperial court in Rome they took figs and nuts with them to eat on the journey so that they did not become unclean (Josephus, *Life* 13–14). If one could only observe the Torah completely in the Holy Land, how could one really study it seriously in the uncleanness of a foreign country?

Abroad there was the threat not only of ritual impurity but also of fatal false teaching. So Abtalyon, Hillel's teacher, admonished:

Wise men, take heed to your words, that you do not incur
the punishment of exile and are banished to a place of bad
water, and the pupils who come to you drink and die.
(mAboth 1:11)

Finally, we have no knowledge of any 'intensive Jewish school
activity in the Diaspora' at the turn of the century – Alexandria
apart. There may indeed have been Jewish-Hellenistic wisdom
schools in major cities, but we have no information about them,
and it is difficult to believe that they had any great effect.

If on the basis of Paul's report that he was a Palestinian Jew,
Pharisee and pupil of the scribes, we must follow van Unnik in
accepting that Luke is right, that does not mean that we should
see him as the purest kind of Palestinian Jew.

First of all it is not as certain as van Unnik supposes that Paul
came to Jerusalem in his earliest childhood. Luke himself sets
alongside each other Paul's ability to speak Greek and Aramaic
in the same way as he does his being a citizen of Tarsus and
growing up in Jerusalem. In so doing he demonstrates the double
character of his hero, mentioning the ability to speak Greek first
(Acts 21:37–40).

Against putting Paul's move to Jerusalem so early is the fact
that Paul has such a masterly control of Greek that he is hardly
likely to have learned it as a second language. His use of the
Greek Bible is also so sovereign that we may assume that he grew
up with it; later he used a version revised on the basis of the
original text in Isaiah, Job and I Kings. In my view these revised
texts could very well be the result of his own scribal work (against
Koch 1986: 81). Paul knew large parts of holy scripture off by
heart, as do numerous Orthodox Jews and quite a number of
Swabian pietists even today. This was a basic presupposition of
his oral teaching. He did not give any written lectures as we do
today, nor could he interrupt his oral lecture to look up a quotation from a scroll of scripture. He had the freedom to quote
texts of scripture literally, to abbreviate them or to combine them.
How could he say of himself as a former Pharisee that he was
blameless as to the righteousness which is in the Law, if, as argued
by Koch (1986: 92), he had only a superficial knowledge of the
Torah?

In short, Paul's mother-tongue was Greek and he was at home

in the Greek Bible because it had been familiar to him from his earliest childhood.

THE PHARISAIC STUDY OF THE LAW IN JERUSALEM

In Acts 22:3, Luke hints at a second stage of education, to be distinguished from elementary school, a stage which began about the age of 15: 'at the feet of Gamaliel, educated according to the strict manner of the law of our fathers'. This is a reference to study of the Law in the school of the best-known Pharisaic head. The term 'at the feet of . . .' and the formula 'the strict manner of the law of our fathers' show that Luke was familiar with the Pharisaic-scribal milieu.

Paul himself mentions this in Galatians 1:13f (see p. 34). This report *can* only refer to the study of the Law as practised by the Pharisees. Moreover, the zeal for the Law which is attested by Paul and Luke was a typically Palestinian phenomenon between the time of the Pharisees and AD 70. Just as nowadays a gifted and ambitious student will want to study at a first-class college and with the best teachers, so Paul's zeal could find fulfilment only where the most famous authorities were teaching and where according to God's commandment the Torah was at home, i.e. in Jerusalem. One could paraphrase 'in Judaism' with 'in the Law'; the 'advanced' of the young Saul is a reference to his progress in the study of the Torah. The numerous contemporaries whom the brilliant young *talmid hakham* surpassed in the study of the Law were his fellow students.

The great unknown is the question of what Pharisaic study of the Law looked like in the first half of the second century in Jerusalem, and what 'theology' was taught there at that time. This unknown fact is what makes it so difficult to discuss the complex theme of 'Paul and Palestinian Judaism' (Sanders 1977) convincingly. We cannot simply transfer the reports about the rabbis which have been handed down to us in written sources since the third century to the school in Jerusalem. It is amazing how little we learn in rabbinic sources about Pharisaic teachers before AD 70. The later 'sages' no longer liked the designation *perushim*, 'the separated ones'; the new scribal elite used the proud name *hakhamim*, 'the wise', for itself. The so-called rabbinate and its institutions, especially ordination, which was a qualification for

the office of judge and gave a person the right to use the title
rabbi, came into being only after 70. At the same time there was
a rigorous suppression, indeed censorship, of older traditions,
connected with the catastrophes of the two Jewish wars.

Over against this it should be noted that the spiritual face of
Jerusalem before its destruction was a rather pluralistic one; alongside the Pharisees and the groups of scribes who led them was
the aristocratic-conservative party of the Sadducees and Boethusi-
ans. The Essenes, too, had a settlement in Jerusalem. In addition
there were political and religious 'radicals', members of the baptist
movement, apocalyptic enthusiasts and Greek speakers who had
returned from the Diaspora to synagogues of their own. Nevertheless, despite this plurality, by the end of the second century BC
the Pharisees already had the greatest influence on the people.
Against the hypotheses of Morton Smith (1956) and Neusner
(1972) we should not underestimate their significance. Similarly
there continue to be many contacts between Pauline theology, the
elements of which Paul acquired during his study in Jerusalem,
and later rabbinic literature. The first 640 pages of Billerbeck's
Volume III bear eloquent witness to this (1922–8). It tends to
be criticized today, but first its critics must write a better
commentary.

This is not the place to enumerate all the ingredients in Pauline
thought which come from the Pharisaic school and from Jewish
Palestinian thought. My view is that they relate to by far the
greater part of Pauline theology – even if they are presented in
excellent Greek.

However, it would be completely wrong to look for analogies
to the letters of Paul one-sidedly only in rabbinic writings, as we
must remember the spiritual plurality in Jerusalem before 70. A
mere glance through Billerbeck brings out the numerous parallels
to apocalyptic texts, primarily to Syrian Baruch and IV Ezra,
which come from the Pharisaic sphere. IV Ezra is the Jewish
writing which contains the closest parallels to Paul with its rigorous views on law and salvation.

The Essenes were another influential group. That their elitist
and esoteric movement exercised spiritual attraction is evident
from the report by the Pharisee Josephus, who will also have
studied Essene doctrine as a teenager (*Life* 7–12).

Again I can be brief. Paul is akin to the Qumran writings in
his basic eschatological dualistic attitude, his sense of an imminent

end and of the concealed presence of salvation, the eschatological gift of the Spirit, which makes it possible to interpret scripture in terms of the eschatological present, the predestination bound up with God's election and the inability of human beings to secure salvation by themselves – a feature which was controversial in contemporary Judaism.

The contacts with Essene theology even extend to details of terminology like 'God's righteousness', 'children of light', 'sinful flesh', or the association of justification with purification. Whereas we find no parallels for the *erga nomou* (works of the law) in rabbinic literature, *ma'ase tora* appears once in a messianic anthology and twice in the up to now unpublished letter *miqsat ma'ase hattora* of the Teacher of Righteousness (Qimron and Strugnell 1985). The letter ends: 'and may this be reckoned to you (by God) as righteousness, if you do what is right before him for your own good.'

What I have said about Jerusalem before 70 also applies to the Pharisaism of that time. It was more pluralistic and at the same time had a more marked eschatological and dualistic stamp than the much later rabbinic texts suggest. Prophetic prediction was more related to the present, the apocalyptic and mystical element came more strongly to the fore, and there was more openness towards charismatic and enthusiastic movements. The spiritual awakening of the Maccabaean period still had an effect: its consequence was a tendency towards a rigorous strengthening of the Torah. The spiritual climate in Jerusalem was thus rather different from that in Jabneh, Usha, or Tiberias.

GREEK-SPEAKING JERUSALEM AND THE FORMATION OF GREEK SYNAGOGUES

So far, however, I have been describing only one of the worlds of the 'wanderer between two worlds'. Jerusalem had become a cosmopolitan city, which in splendour and renown could stand comparison with the chief cities of the Roman Empire, and had a strong attraction for Diaspora Jews; its importance depended on the fact that it was the unique place of the perpetual worship of God and the great festivals. Jerusalem was conceivably the greatest religious pilgrimage centre of antiquity, which year by year attracted hundreds of thousands of visitors. At the same time it was the eschatological centre, the goal, of the homecoming

MARTIN HENGEL

Diaspora and of the pilgrimages of the nations, the metropolis of
the messianic kingdom, the true navel of the world. That was
reason enough for returning there.

Inscriptions are the main source of information for Jerusalem
as a 'Hellenistic' city. Around one-third of the roughly 250 texts
from the time of the Second Temple are in Greek and about 8
per cent are bilingual. I would guess that at least 10–15 per cent
of the inhabitants spoke Greek as their mother-tongue. In addition
there was the endless stream of pilgrims from the Diaspora.

The Jewish 'Hellenists' had long since organized themselves
into their own synagogue communities which brought together
compatriots, like the synagogue of the 'Libertini', the freedmen
from Rome. Presumably these communities had their own teaching staff, since a *didaskalos* (teacher) appears three times on
inscriptions.

Most illuminating is the only synagogue inscription from Jerusalem that we possess, which is at the same time the earliest. It is
by Theodotus, son of Vettenus, descendant of a priest who
returned from Rome and, like his father and grandfather, ruler of
the synagogue (see p. 32). The beginning of the building of his
synagogue, which also had a hospice for pilgrims from the Diaspora, went back as far as the Herodian period. As the institution
of the synagogue spread in the mother-country only at a late stage
and as a result of Pharisaic initiatives – the priestly nobility had
no interest in creating competition for the Temple – I assume that
this foundation, too, had a Pharisaic background. This is clear
from its task: the reading of the Law and the teaching of the
commandments.

The reading of the Law was supplemented here by the teaching
of the commandments. As the oral torah of the Pharisees went
far beyond the simple wording of the Torah, it was necessary to
instruct the festival pilgrims precisely in the specific individual
commandments.

The young Paul was at home in this environment of Pharisaic
Hellenists; he studied the Torah in the school on the Temple
Mount and at the same time improved his Jewish-Greek education,
since as a Greek-speaking *talmid hakham* he must have felt it important to instruct Jews who came to Jerusalem from the Diaspora
in the true – Pharisaic – understanding of the Law. Nowhere did
so many Greek-speaking Jews and Gentile sympathizers from all
over the Empire gather together so constantly as in Jerusalem.

The 'teaching of the commandments' in Greek, which included preaching in the synagogue, also called for linguistic competence, so the higher Jewish Hellenistic school must also have passed on basic training in rhetoric, though this need not necessarily have represented the rhetoric of the contemporary Atticistic school. God's truth sought the appropriate 'convincing form'. This included the diatribe, of which Paul was so fond. This vivid style, which contained so many elements of discussion and was not patterned on prior literary models, was cultivated in the synagogues of Jerusalem.

In other words we must attach more importance to 'Jewish Greek education' in Jerusalem in the period after Herod. This has consequences for our understanding of the pre-Christian Paul. His 'higher education' in Jerusalem also reveals the 'wanderer between two worlds'. Despite his study of Pharisaic scribal learning he keeps his spiritual home in the Greek-speaking synagogue: you might say that he 'proclaimed circumcision' there. In other words, he saw his task as being that of a teacher communicating the Pharisaic understanding of the Law to the Diaspora Jews who streamed to Jerusalem in large numbers. Therefore he acquired the basic knowledge of a Jewish-Greek rhetoric aimed at synagogue preaching which was distinct from the literary style of the Greek schools.

This background explains his conflict with the Christian group of 'Hellenists', a conflict which turned him into a persecutor.

THE PERSECUTOR

Pauline chronology has become a rather controversial matter. However, I see no reason to depart from the older consensus. If we count back between fourteen and seventeen years from the Apostolic Council we arrive at AD 31–4 for Paul's conversion. My conjecture for the crucifixion of Jesus is AD 30. So I lean towards an early date for the Damascus event. The opening of 1 Corinthians 15, according to which Paul's vision of the Risen Christ is the last one, makes an interval of many years improbable. This brief interval of between eighteen months and three years makes speculations about supposed 'pre-Pauline tradition' very difficult. Only in Jerusalem can we look for a 'Hellenistic community' *before* Paul. It is possible that the young Sha'ul even experienced Jesus' death – although only from a distance as a Greek-speaking

Jew. Whether one can allow 2 Corinthians 5:16 as evidence for this is an open question; in that verse the key phrase is the adverbial 'know after the flesh' (*kata sarka ginōskein*). He, Paul, had known Christ in a 'fleshly', sinful way – that *could* refer to a brief encounter with Jesus in Jerusalem, but applies primarily to his 'knowledge' as persecutor. This brings us to our last question: why did Sha'ul in particular become the inexorable persecutor of this new movement?

Paul stresses only his own initiative (and thus his guilt) and mentions the basic reason: 'as regards zeal, a persecutor of the church' (Philippians 3:6). *He* persecuted the community as a Pharisee, in the firm conviction that he was acting zealously and therefore in obedience to the Law of God. The same thing is expressed in Galatians 1:13f.; the Galatians know his earlier conduct in obedience to the Law, that he 'persecuted the church of God violently and tried to destroy it', and that he surpassed many of his contemporaries in his progress in the study of the Law. Evidently here he acted on his own initiative, or at least took further measures instituted by others with the aim of making a clean sweep. But that means that he was no longer a young student but already had authority as one who had 'progressed' (*proekopton*). My conjecture is that he already had a teaching function in a Greek-speaking synagogue.

Luke's evidence is ambiguous. On the one hand he gives 'the young man Saul' only a subordinate role at the stoning of Stephen (Acts 7:58). In the persecution that follows, however, Saul is the driving force. He arrests Christians in their homes and as judge votes for the death penalty (Acts 8:3; 9:1; 22:4, 19; 26:10f.). Here it is presupposed against historical reality that Jerusalem courts could carry out death penalties. The mild advice of Gamaliel (5:39) seems to have been forgotten. Luke is evidently exaggerating in order to heighten the drama in his account; the persecutor is depicted in terrifying colours in order to make the Christian missionary shine out all the more clearly. Modern conjectures which seek to make Sha'ul an ordained rabbi, a member of the supreme court, or even a widower, because ordained rabbis had to be married, introduce later conditions. In the light of Galatians 1:13f. Luke's *neanias* (young man) is to be taken seriously. Paul may have been between 25 and 35 at that time; he was not only just a *talmid*, but already had some responsibility.

A further contradiction in Luke's account is that he does not have the leaders of the Christian community, the twelve apostles, affected by the 'great persecution'. They remain in Jerusalem as though nothing has happened. The solution to this riddle has widely been recognized: contrary to what is implied by Luke, who wants to avoid any appearance of a division of the ideal community in Jerusalem, there were from the very beginning two groups of communities which held separate services for linguistic reasons: the 'Hebraioi' as the majority led by the Twelve, and the minority of the 'Hellenistai'. The 'seven' of Acts 6:5, all of whom have Greek names, were the leaders of the latter. Their first two representatives, Stephen and Philip, were missionaries impelled by the Spirit. Luke avoids the difficulty that up to this point in his narrative only the Twelve had proclaimed the gospel by making Stephen at first only do 'wonders and great signs among the people' (6:8), and it was this which aroused bitter opposition from members of the Hellenistic synagogues, including the Jews from *Cilicia*.

That the latter appear here is a first cautious reference to the person of the most important hero, who takes a subsidiary role on the stage at the very end of the Stephen drama in 7:58. The accusation against the first martyr is that he spoke 'blasphemies against Moses and God' (6:11), or 'words against this holy place and the Law' (6:14).

Despite all the differences between Luke's inconsistent account of the persecution and Paul's own comments there are some essential points of contact.

(a) The activity of Stephen and the resistance against him occur – leaving aside the disruptive introduction of the Sanhedrin (6:12) and of the high priest – in the very milieu in which Paul is also working. Only the Hellenists appear by name as those who are affected by the following pogrom of Christians: first Philip and then the Jewish-Christian 'Hellenistai' from Cyprus and Cyrenaica who are driven out of Jerusalem.

(b) In Luke the charge is of blasphemous attacks on the foundations of Israel's election, the Temple and the Torah. These accusations stir up the people and bring about the intervention of the supreme authority; however, the judgment ends in tumult and with an execution which has the characteristics of lynch law. Presumably the original account of the martyrdom did not speak of an orderly trial before the Sanhedrin; rather, the whole process may have been played out within the context of a Hellenistic synagogue community in Jerusalem. The introduction of Saul in 7:58 rests on a historical reminiscence.

(c) Paul certainly stresses the fact of his massive activity as a persecutor, but mentions only the motive we already know, that he persecuted the community out of zeal, *kata zēlos*. This does not so much stress emotion as the objective fact of 'zeal for the Law'. In Galatians 1:13, too, there is a connection between the 'violent persecution' and the 'zealot for ancestral traditions' who surpassed his colleagues. This is the 'zeal for God and his Law' which was foreshadowed by Phinehas (Numbers 25) and Elijah (I Kings 18), and had been part of the ideal of radical groups since the time of the Maccabees. A 'zealot' was ready to use force against the law-breaker in order to turn God's wrath away from Israel. Such zeal could hope for reward similar to that which Phinehas received for his action:

> Then Phinehas stood up and interposed, and the plague was stayed. And that has been reckoned to him a righteousness from generation to generation for ever. (Psalm 106:30–1)

Paul's zeal is directed against the severest transgressions of the Law, precisely those of which Stephen, too, was accused.

(d) The apostle says twice that he 'sought to destroy' the community or the new faith: in Galatians 1:13, 'how savagely I persecuted the church of God and tried to destroy it' (*eporthoun autēn*); and in Galatians 1:22f. the communities in Judaea had only heard that 'he who once persecuted us is now preaching the faith he once tried to destroy' (*hēn pote eporthei*). Luke uses the same verb in Acts 9:21: when Paul proclaimed Jesus in Damascus, 'all who heard him were amazed. . . . Is not this the man who destroyed [*ho porthēsas*] those in Jerusalem who call on this name?' The verb *porthein* has a harsh ring: destroy, devastate, raze to the ground; one cannot claim here in defence that Paul attacked only the faith, not the persons, of the Christians. *Diōkein* like *porthein* means more than just a polemical discussion. Presumably, it was only the legal situation that prevented there being any executions. Zeal for the Law also included spontaneous action bypassing the course of law. The *kata zēlos* in Philippians 3:6 and the twofold *porthein* in Galatians 1 belong together. This is a matter of brute force. Even if Luke is exaggerating, there is a good deal of room for all kinds of force, extending to the synagogue punishment of thirty-nine strokes, and even lynch law cannot be excluded.

But which was the community that Paul was seeking to annihilate? He mentions no place and assumes that the Galatians know what he means. The words *ediōkon tēn ekklēsian tou theou* at first sight suggest the whole of the 'primitive church'. At least, the general term would be more comprehensible if he were referring to the church of Jerusalem rather than to that of a single, peripheral community.

But does not Galatians 1:22f. tell against any activity at all of Paul as persecutor in the Holy City? That is not my view.

> Next I went to the regions of Syria and Cilicia and remained unknown by sight to the congregations who are in Christ in Judaea. They only heard it said, 'He who once persecuted us now proclaims the faith that at that time he sought to destroy' and they praised God for me.

It needs no special explanation that Paul, the Hellenist and pupil of the scribes, was not known personally (*kata prosōpon*) to the communities newly formed in Judaea, since Judaea here includes the whole of Jewish Palestine. It is his activity in Jerusalem itself that is problematic; if, as Luke tells us, he sat in judgement over Christian men and women and threw them into prison, he can hardly have been totally unknown to them – though we should not overlook the fact that Paul is speaking of knowing personally.

Would we not therefore do best to understand Galatians 1:23 as a reference to the persecuted community in Damascus? That is the key to the question. If we once accept the hypothesis that the troubles in Jerusalem were limited in their impact to the Greek-speaking synagogues of Jerusalem, there would be no reason to believe that the Hebraeoi would have been affected in any way by what happened. They would therefore never have got to know Saul by sight at this time. Later on, they would have heard of the 'Hellenists' who had been driven out: 'He who once persecuted us now proclaims the faith that at that time he sought to destroy.' Moved by the miracle of the conversion of the one who had persecuted them, 'they were praising God for me'. This reaction of the Hebraeoi shows that Hebrews and Hellenists were not after all separated by too deep a divide.

What we need to assume is that the persecuted Hellenists of Jerusalem fled to Damascus and that it was therefore this same community, whom he had previously driven into exile, that Paul now sought to destroy; he had indeed 'smitten' them before. This assumption clarifies various difficulties: first, it has never been obvious how it should be that a mere two or three years after the Passover at which Jesus was crucified, Damascus should already have had a significant independent Christian community of its own; second, if there was such a community at all, why should this one in particular be singled out for attack? Surely, it is far more likely that the 'zealot for the Law' was sent to Damascus because the exiled Hellenists were continuing their agitation in this Gentile trading city, with its substantial Jewish community. It is possible even that an instruction of the Spirit in the style of the Damascus Document and of Amos 5:26 played a role here. Given Luke's tendency to exaggerate, we need not necessarily accept that Saul had really been sent out by the high priest. It would be enough to believe that he had been sent out by the Jewish-Hellenist synagogues as *shaliach has-sibbur*. The reluctance of Paul to come back to the Holy City was surely then caused not by any rejection of Peter, James and the Twelve; rather, he could not return there because he was in mortal danger as an apostate. This is probably one of the main reasons why, with the exception of his visit to Peter mentioned in Galatians 1:18–20, he avoided the Holy City for many years, especially as he had been given a quite different commission: 'to preach him among the Gentiles' – and that could only happen outside Judaea.

THE THEOLOGICAL REASONS FOR THE PERSECUTION AND PAUL'S CONVERSION

This last point is the most difficult. The psychological interpretation of Paul's conversion does not take us further. Paul does not give any indication that he had been influenced by the Christians whom he persecuted nor do we know anything of discontent with the Law or of inner struggles – on the contrary, he had a good conscience: 'as to the righteousness of the Law blameless'. No one who is afflicted by depression talks like that.

The vision of the Messiah struck him like lightning, and the overwhelming event was grounded for him solely in God's saving counsel (Galatians 1:15); God's action of electing grace works like

48

the word of creation in Genesis 1 as *creatio ex nihilo* (Romans 4:17; 2 Corinthians 4:6). The conversion represents a reversal of all previous values: 'but what for me was gain I regarded as loss for Christ's sake' (Philippians 3:7). Here it becomes clear that Paul's theological thought is governed by this radical reversal of previous values. The Pauline *theologia crucis*, the question of the Law and justification at the judgement, are not 'subsidiary craters'[3] formed on the basis of later conflicts; they directed his course from the beginning.

We can also begin from these 'values' in seeking the theological motives of the persecutor. He saw what was most holy in Israel threatened by the proclamation of the Jewish Christian Hellenists. Here enthusiastic sectarians had arisen who shook basic foundations of the tradition of the fathers, disseminated fatal 'heresies' and seduced members of the community directly to 'apostasy' in order to carry out a successful mission for their own conventicle. Faced with the 'blasphemous words against this holy place and the Law', the 'orthodox' believer could only react with 'zeal for the Law' and defend God's honour with force.

The reasons which led to the stoning of Stephen and those which shortly afterwards made the young Sha'ul a persecutor *kata zēlos* will thus have been very much the same. But we should beware of excessively radical theses. We may not assume that the Christian Hellenists in principle denied the significance of the Torah for salvation or that they already carried on an active mission to the Gentiles apart from the Law only a year or two after the death of Jesus. This would go against the earliest situation of the new eschatological community, was impossible in Jerusalem and moreover would anticipate Paul's new revolutionary theological insight. Conjectures of this kind are plausible only if we ignore the chronology. Paul aside, the primitive Church was led to a mission to the Gentiles without the Law step by step.

Rather, we should continue to note how close we are in time to the activity of Jesus. The Hellenists' criticism of Torah and Temple will have been a development from the preaching of Jesus whether in the concentration of the commandments on the love command or in the antitheses of the Sermon on the Mount, the rejection of the *paradosis* of the Pharisees or the questioning of ritual commands relating to purity.

The same is even more true of criticism of the Temple. A messianic threat against the Temple played a part in the trial of

Jesus (Mark 14:58; Matthew 26:61), and the 'cleansing of the Temple' is also to be understood as a messianic act. The execution of Jesus caused further offence. His death 'for the many' (Mark 10:45) put in question the expiatory effect of Temple worship: the sacrificial cult in the sanctuary seemed to have become obsolete. This attitude made the 'Hellenists' more radical than the conservative 'Hebrews'.

Further offence was caused by the proclamation of the crucified Messiah: Deuteronomy 21:22f. puts the one who is hanged upon the tree under a divine curse. Must not the proclamation of a crucified blasphemer as the Messiah of Israel itself have looked like blasphemy? When Paul stresses around twenty years later that the crucified Messiah is a stumbling block (*skandalon*) to the Jews, he is also describing his own earlier sense of offence. His interpretation in Galatians 3:13 can be explained similarly. The Pharisaic *talmid* Sha'ul really did see the crucified Jesus as the one who had been rightly accursed by God. He countered the Hellenists' criticism of the Torah which limited the significance of individual commands and groups of commands with the text from Deuteronomy 27:26 which he quotes in Galatians 3:10: 'Cursed be every one who does not abide by *all* things written in the book of the law, and do them.' The agitators seemed to be accursed lawbreakers, those who proclaimed an accursed criminal who had led the people astray – was that not reason enough, like Phinehas in zeal for the Torah, to bring down a just punishment on their enemies or to drive them out? Who would blame the passionate hothead for such zeal for God's cause? That was what had to be done. Yet then everything was turned upside down: the crucified Messiah who met him before Damascus with the question 'Saul, Saul why do you persecute me?' (Acts 9:4) became the ground and content of his life. What had previously been a scandal came to the centre of his new existence, and his Pharisaic theology orientated on the gift of the Torah became the *theologia crucis*, the message of the Messiah who had come, 'who died for us while we were still sinners' (Romans 5:8). And in that way it became testimony to the fatherly love of the God of Israel and of the Gentiles, the God 'who justifies the godless' (Romans 4:5).

NOTES

1 Translated by John Bowden. For a more extended treatment of the issues, see M. Hengel (1991) *The Pre-Christian Paul*, London and Philadelphia.
2 I have found only one later example in the great Aphrodisias inscription.
3 The phrase was coined by Schweitzer 1930: 220 and has been taken up by Sanders 1977: 409–15.

BIBLIOGRAPHY

Billerbeck, P. (1922–8) and H. Strack, *Kommentar zum Neuen Testament aus Talmud und Midrasch*, Munich.
Broshi, M. (1975) 'La Population de l'ancienne Jerusalem', *Revue Biblique* 82: 5–14.
Hachlili, R. (1979) 'The Goliath Family in Jericho: Funerary Inscriptions from a First Century A.D. Monumental Tomb', *Bulletin of the American Schools of Oriental Research* 235: 31–65.
Hengel, M. (1975) 'Zwischen Jesus und Paulus', *Zeitschrift für Theologie und Kirche* 72: 151–206.
Koch, D.-A. (1986) *Die Schrift als Zeuge des Evangeliums*, Tübingen.
Meyer, E. (1923) *Ursprung und Anfänge des Christentums*, Vol. 3, Stuttgart and Berlin.
Mommsen, T. A. (1901) 'Die Rechtsverhältnisse des Apostels Paulus', *Zeitschrift für die neutestamentliche Wissenschaft* 2: 81–96.
Neusner, J. (1972) 'Josephus's Pharisees' in *Ex Orbe Religionum* (Festschrift G. Widengren) (Studies in the History of Religions 22), Leiden: 224–44.
Qimron, E. and Strugnell, J. (1985) 'An Unpublished Halakhic Letter from Qumran', *Biblical Archaeology Today*, Israel Exploration Society, Jerusalem: 400–7.
Ramsay, W. (10th edn, 1908) *St Paul the Traveller and Roman Citizen*, London.
Sanders, E. P. (1977) *Paul and Palestinian Judaism*, London.
Schoeps, H.-J. (1959) *Paulus. Die Theologie des Apostels im Licht der jüdischen Religionsgeschichte*, Tübingen.
Schweitzer, A. (1930) *Die Mystik des Apostels Paulus*, Tübingen.
Smith, M. (1956) 'Palestinian Judaism in the First Century', in M. Davis (ed.) *Israel's Role in Civilisation*, New York, 67–81.
Stegemann, W. (1987) 'War der Apostel Paulus ein römischer Bürger?', *Zeitschrift für die neutestamentliche Wissenschaft* 78: 200–29.
Strecker, G. (1979) 'Befreiung und Rechtfertigung. Zur Stellung der Rechtfertigungslehre in der Theologie des Paulus', in *Eschaton und Historie*, Göttingen, 229–59.
Van Unnik, W. C. (1973a) 'Tarsus or Jerusalem', in *Sparsa Collecta* (Novum Testamentum Supplement 29), Leiden, 259–320.
Van Unnik, W. C. (1973b) 'Once again Tarsus or Jerusalem', ibid.: 321–7.

Wilkinson, J. (1974) 'Ancient Jerusalem and its Water Supply and Population', *Palestine Exploration Quarterly* 106: 33–51.

3

JEWISH PROSELYTIZING IN THE FIRST CENTURY

Martin Goodman

For all students of the religious history of the Roman Empire the emergence and spread of Christianity must be a great challenge to explanation and understanding. Among a welter of significant factors which contributed to this phenomenon, one, it seems to me, stands pre-eminent. Other religions spread either because worshippers moved or because non-adherents happened to find them attractive. Christianity spread primarily because many Christians believed that it was positively desirable for non-Christians to join their faith and accrete to their congregations. It is my belief that no parallel to the early Christian mission was to be found in the ancient world in the first century. There is no space here to describe the differences, which seem to me to be crucial, in the activities of contemporary pagan priests or philosophers. Nor is there room to elucidate the possible internal motivation for mission within the early Church. The aim of this chapter will be purely negative. Many scholars have claimed that the idea of a mission to convert was inherited by the early Jesus movement from contemporary Judaism.[1] I feel that the evidence for such a claim is flimsy and may fruitfully be re-examined.

I should make it clear that I do not doubt either that Jews firmly believed in their role as religious mentors of the Gentile world or that Jews expected that in the last days the Gentiles would in fact come to recognize the glory of God and divine rule on earth. But the desire to encourage admiration of the Jewish way of life or respect for the Jewish God, or to inculcate general ethical behaviour in other peoples, or such pious hope for the future, should be clearly distinguished from an impulse to draw

53

non-Jews into Judaism. In the following pages I shall look in some detail at the evidence which has previously been put forward to commend the view that Jews in the first century actively sought proselytes.

PROSELYTES WITHIN JUDAISM

The argument tends to begin from the simple fact of the existence of proselytes (e.g. Feldman 1986). It is indeed worth noting that familiarity with the concept of conversion has bred disregard among modern historians of the peculiarity of such an institution. Jews constituted a nation which at some time before the Hellenistic period accepted the principle that it was open to anyone to integrate himself or herself into its political and social community simply by acceptance of Jewish religious customs. The potential flexing of communal boundaries entailed by such a notion is quite astounding. It is in marked contrast to the jealous preservation of the rights of individual citizens by Greek city-states and the exclusion of outsiders from such rights. The difference was particularly marked because, like Romans but unlike Greeks, Jews accepted the notion that their *politeia* was not fixed to any particular locality.

We have evidence of at least some such converts during the Hellenistic period and early Roman Empire. Josephus described the women of Damascus as converts in AD 66 (*Jewish War* II 20, 2 (559–61)) and provided a detailed description of the conversion of famous royal proselytes from Adiabene (*Antiquites* XX 2, 3–4 (34–48)). Acts 6:5 refers to a proselyte of Antioch. The semi-technical use of the term '*prosēlytos*' in the Septuagint (see pp. 62–3) suggests that the right of such converts to be considered as part of the house of Israel was widely recognized by Jews. And while there is no evidence that converts made up any great proportion of the Jewish population, the lack of such evidence cannot be decisive in assessing how many proselytes there were.

Furthermore, both Josephus and Philo seem in general to have assumed that proselytes are to be welcomed. Philo's ethical maxim that proper nobility is not an accident of good birth (*On the Virtues* 35 (187)) may have implied that anyone could acquire the virtues enshrined in the Jewish Law. The author of 2 Maccabees 9:17 rejoiced that the wicked king Antiochus Epiphanes on his death-bed promised to become a Jew. Similarly Josephus was clearly proud of the converts in Adiabene. Jews were happy to accept committed converts, as Josephus stated explicitly (*Against Apion* II 28 (210)) (cf. Cohen 1987).

JEWISH MISSIONARY ACTIVITY: THE EVIDENCE

It is likely enough, then, that Jews welcomed sincere proselytes in the first century. But passive acceptance is quite different from active mission. The evidence alleged to show that Jews took *positive* steps to win proselytes is commonly culled from a variety of sources which I shall outline here in brief.

I begin with the least convincing arguments. The activities of the earliest Jewish believers in Jesus have been adduced as indirect evidence that some Jews who did not believe in Jesus were doing the same thing (Georgi 1987: 101). But this prejudges the possibility of unique circumstances in the early Church which might have led to such missionary behaviour. It is likely that texts of the early Church which appear to attack Jews as competitors for the souls of converts refer in fact to followers of Jesus who, in the eyes of their opponents, clung too hard to Jewish customs. The missionary zeal of these Jewish Christians may have come not from their Judaism but from their belief in Christ.

Second, it has been argued that the probable growth of the Jewish population in this period, as evidenced by the remarkable spread of Jewish settlement in the Diaspora, the size of some of the communities there, and the increase in the population of Palestine apparent from archaeological survey of settlements, is in itself evidence of Jewish proselytizing (cf. Feldman 1986: 59). This seems dubious on two counts. On the one hand ancient writers explained the Jewish Diaspora by the overpopulation of the home country (Philo, *Moses* II 42 (232)) and Jewish fertility by the Jews' strange ideological opposition to abortion, infanticide and contraception (cf. Tacitus, *Histories* V 5); to this one could add the Jewish concept of charity, unique in the ancient world, which made it a religious duty to prevent the children of the poor from dying in infancy, so that the main natural inhibition on population growth was at least partially stifled.[2] The theory that a massive surge of proselytes to Judaism accounted for this population growth is not impossible, but it runs up against the curious fact that no ancient Jewish writer claimed that such widespread conversion had taken place, although it would have been an obvious source of pride. On the other hand, even if proselytes did comprise a high proportion of first-century Jews, this does not imply that such converts were actively sought.

But the case for a Jewish mission to win proselytes is based on better arguments than these, and in the next few pages I shall attempt to present as strongly as possible the best reasons often proposed, before offering counter-arguments in the second section of the chapter.

In certain circumstances some Jews may have insisted on Gentiles' conversion. In the most dramatic instances, whole populations of Gentiles are said to have been incorporated within the Jewish nation by the militant Hasmonaean dynasty. Thus the Idumaeans of southern Palestine were encouraged and perhaps forced by the Hasmonaeans to convert *en masse* in the 120s BC, and some of the Ituraeans of the northern part of the country were compelled to submit to circumcision in 104–103 BC according to Josephus (*Antiquities* XIII 9, 1 (257–8); 11, 3 (319)).[3] Both the Bible and the Apocrypha record with some glee how Gentiles at moments of Jewish glory converted to Judaism out of fear of the Jews (cf. Esther 8: 17). Like Achior the Ammonite, such Gentiles saw the power of the Lord, believed and were converted (Judith 14:10). More generally, even Jews as lax in their religious observance as members of the Herodian dynasty insisted that their Gentile marriage partners should be initiated into Judaism before marriage. All Jews accepted the metaphor of the nation as a family into which outsiders had to be adopted to be accepted, and when a fiancé refused to take up Jewish customs, the wedding was liable to be cancelled (cf. Josephus, *Antiquities* XX 7, 1 (139)). It is also possible, although not certain, that at this period, as later, some Jews still expected that their slaves would submit to circumcision as stipulated in Genesis 17: 12–13: this would at any rate be desirable if the slave was to be used for domestic purposes, since only if the slave was considered in some sense Jewish (or at least not an idolater) could the danger of pollution to food be avoided.

Since it is possible that Jews thus sometimes insisted on conversion when they had the power to enforce their will, it has been suggested that they used persuasion when that was the only weapon available to them. Undoubtedly proselytes were often instructed in Judaism by some Jew before conversion; the name of the teacher of the royal family of Charax Spasinou, Ananias, was preserved by Josephus (*Antiquities* XX 2, 3–4 (34–42)). There is no evidence that any such teachers travelled abroad specifically in order to deliver such teaching. The traveller Eleazar who insisted that the king of Adiabene, Izates, should be circumcised if he wanted to follow Jewish law is often portrayed as a missionary, but Josephus (*Antiquities* XX 2, 4 (44)) made it clear that his intention in coming to Adiabene was not to convert anyone but simply to pay his respects to the royal family. But a considerable literature has survived which, it has been claimed, may reflect the arguments and methods used by such missionaries to win converts, if such missionaries did in fact exist.

A partial list of such literature can conveniently be found in Dalbert (1954); to the texts there discussed could be added, among others, the romantic story *Joseph and Asenath*. This literature is somewhat heterogeneous. The writings of Demetrius the Chronographer comprise a rather dry analysis of the time-periods given in the biblical narrative. Philo the Elder, Eupolemus and Artapanus rewrote the biblical stories in prose with considerable embellishments. Ezekiel the Tragedian did much the same with the narrative of the Exodus but in his case produced his reinterpretation in dramatic form. Ps.-Hecataeus and Ps.-Aristeas wrote glowing accounts of Judaism as a way of life and of Jews as a people, presenting themselves in the guise of non-Jewish writers. The Jewish authors of parts of the corpus of Sibylline Oracles similarly slipped comments about Judaism into the oracles they forged. Finally, at least three authors attempted to produce a version of Judaism that would fit more or less comfortably with contemporary Greek philosophy. Of these, the author of the Wisdom of Solomon made the fewest concessions to the rigours of philosophical analysis, Philo made the most. Aristobulus, who wrote in the second century BC, lay somewhere between the two (see Schürer 1986: 470–704).

All these writings have in common that they were composed in Greek by Jews. They survive, often only in very fragmentary form, only through the interests of the Christian Church; they were almost entirely ignored by the Jewish tradition until the Renaissance. Why should anyone believe that they were originally composed with a Gentile audience in mind? After all, it seems fairly likely that the greatest literary production of Greek-speaking Jews, the translation of the Bible into Greek as the Septuagint, was intended for use by Jews in their own liturgy, and this is also probable for the revisions of the Septuagint by Aquila and others.

None the less the Septuagint may point to at least a secondary intention by the authors to bring Judaism to the attention of a Gentile audience, for there is evidence that at least one Gentile writer, the anonymous author of a rhetorical treatise *On the Sublime*, may have come across at least the opening of the text of Genesis (see commentary in Stern 1974: 361–5). It has even been argued that the survival of writings like those of Philo through a non-Jewish tradition may imply that they were originally intended for non-Jews (Georgi 1987: 368). At the least it can be asserted that there is no *proof* that such literature was *not* meant for outsiders alone.

If Gentiles read such literature, were they expected to react by considering conversion to Judaism? Perhaps. At any rate, that they would be expected to develop a friendly attitude towards Jews and Judaism seems clear: a work like the third Sibylline book unabashedly praises the Jews and their mode of worship.

But if Jews did write such propaganda literature in order to win proselytes, how did they expect to make sure that their propaganda was read or heard? In a time before mass printing, books would spread only in single, rare copies. Enthusiasts would have to employ slaves to produce their own copies. Perhaps, then, it has been suggested, the literature enshrines material that was disseminated more widely by oral means. It has been alleged that Jews invited pagans into their synagogues to hear displays of preaching along the same lines as the extant writings. Georgi has drawn attention to Philo's statement that 'each seventh day the synagogues stand wide open in every city' as 'schools of good sense' and other virtues, while Philo's denial that Jews on the sabbath attended performances in the theatre has been taken to suggest that a comparison between synagogues and theatres was possible.[4] Josephus wrote of the Jews of Antioch that they had brought into their rites (*thrēskeiai*) in the first century AD many Greeks and (presumably by this means) made them 'in some sense part of themselves' (*Jewish War* VII 3, 3 (45)). Not enough survives of first-century synagogues to tell whether they allowed easy access to casual outsiders to listen from the street, but it is possible: in Caesarea in AD 66 one synagogue was down an alleyway next to pagan houses, though in this case not conversion but antagonism resulted (Josephus, *Jewish War* II 14, 4 (285–6)).

If Jews were really eager to win converts, the easiest way to increase their number might be to remove some of the more onerous requirements laid upon proselytes. It has been vehemently argued by, among others, McEleney (1974) that some Jews in the Diaspora were prepared to allow some male Gentiles to be treated as Jews even without undergoing circumcision. It is certain that an uncircumcised Jew was not a logical impossibility. Later rabbis discussed haemophiliacs for whom the operation would endanger life and could therefore be forgone (bPesaḥim 96a). When other rituals, including the bringing of an offering to the Temple, were also required of converts, the question also arose of the religious status of a proselyte who had fulfilled some of the initiation procedures but not (yet?) all of them (Nolland 1981: 173–94). Philo in one passage referred to a small group of Jews – 'extreme allegorists' – who believed that *only* the inner meaning of the Torah matters and that its actual observance was therefore irrelevant (*On the Migration of Abraham* 16 (89)). Such Jews might perhaps forgo circumcision for their sons and stress instead a moral allegory such as that propounded for the operation by Philo himself (*Questions and Answers on Exodus* II 2). Finally, Epictetus wrote in the early second century as if the ultimate sign of dedication to Judaism by a convert was baptism, and the same seems also to have been implied by the (probably Jewish) author of *Sibylline Oracles* IV 164, who wrote in c. AD 80, although this latter passage may refer not to a baptism for converts but just to a bath for purification.

If Jews were so keen to win converts, they will have been eager also to lure pagans away from their customary worship. A pragmatic willingness to partake in other cults was not standard for Jews, although it was not entirely unknown in this period as in others.[5] As such, any Jewish mission for converts was likely to provoke opposition from the Gentile society in which it operated. Evidence for resentment against Jews on these grounds is not to be found in pagan writings composed before AD 96, and I have argued elsewhere (Goodman 1989b) that before that date Romans at least were actually ignorant of the Jewish notion that a Gentile could become Jewish. But modern authors have pointed out that Jews were expelled from the city of Rome in 139 BC and AD 19 and have asserted that this was as a punishment for seeking proselytes (e.g. Stern 1974: 357–60; 1980: 70). In the former case one of the Byzantine epitomators of the first-century writer Valerius Maximus implied that the Jews' crime was that they 'tried to transmit their sacred rites to the Romans'. In the latter case Cassius

Dio (LVII 18, 5a) is said by John of Antioch to have written (in the early third century AD) that the Jews were 'converting many of the natives to their ways', an explanation which is missing in the earlier historians Josephus and Tacitus, who related instead a curious story of the duping of an aristocratic Roman lady proselyte by unscrupulous Jews intent on her money. It is not impossible that Tacitus was ignorant and that Josephus (*Antiquities* XVIII 3, 5 (81–4)) hid the truth because it embarrassed him in his apologetic aim of reconciling the Romans to the Jews.[6]

The case for believing in a mission to win proselytes may reasonably be ended with two of the most striking categories of literary evidence. First, Horace, *Satires* I 4, 142–3, *veluti te / Iudaei cogemus in hanc concedere turbam*, has been interpreted to mean that 'like the Jews, we will compel you to join our throng' (see Stern 1974: 323). Second, and most strikingly, Matthew 23:15, which reads 'Woe to thee, scribes and Pharisees, that you cross land and sea to make one proselyte', seems to imply that scribes and Pharisees did indeed travel in such a way to win converts to Judaism.

THE ABSENCE OF A JEWISH MISSION: A REINTERPRETATION

This last text, from the gospel of Matthew, has often been taken as the starting-point for discussions of the Jewish attitude to mission in the first century AD, and it seems fitting to begin with this passage my scrutiny of all the arguments and evidence for such a mission which have been laid out above.

What reason, then, not to believe the plain meaning of Matthew 23:15? Few scholars would wish to construct too elaborate an argument on one of Matthew's statements about Pharisees, since his discussion of them is notoriously tendentious and polemical and the undiscriminating collocation 'scribes and Pharisees' in the woes in this gospel may be attributed to his muddled views as a redactor.[7] The saying here ascribed to Jesus *may* belong to the earliest (i.e. Palestinian) stratum of the tradition about him, since it uses various Semitisms including the Aramaic term 'Gehinnom' (Jeremias 1958: 17–18, n. 4), but the fact that it is omitted by Luke suggests that it reflects the special interests of Matthew, whose own preconceptions about the desirability of winning converts for Christ may therefore be reflected in the ascription of parallel aims to the despised Pharisees. However this may be, it is overwhelmingly likely that the phrase made sense to Matthew's audience at the end of the first century and that they accepted that Pharisees could be particularly eager to gain one proselyte.

But what does this phrase mean? The expression is decidedly odd. Why 'land and sea'? And why 'one proselyte'? Is the reader expected to supply the term to make it '*even* one proselyte'? It has been suggested that Matthew had in mind a particular instance of a Gentile converted by a Pharisee, which is possible (so Munck 1959: 266). Even an isolated case, however, would be sufficient to show that some Jews were interested in seeking converts in the first century. And that is what Matthew 23:15 clearly must mean if the term *prosēlytos* is understood in its customary sense. But this, as I shall show below, cannot be taken for granted. I shall suggest instead that Matthew is here attacking Pharisees for their eagerness in trying to persuade other Jews to follow Pharisaic *halakhah*.[8]

It seems clear that the *prosēlytos* to whom Matthew referred became a Pharisee or a follower of Pharisaic teaching as a result of the Pharisees' efforts. He becomes 'twice the son of Gehinnom' that the Pharisee is, which is not an expression which Matthew was likely to use about Jews *qua* Jews. Is the conversion of Jews to Pharisaism something that Pharisees would have found desirable in the first century? There is little explicit evidence, but it seems at least possible. Pharisees believed that they alone could interpret the Torah correctly and it would seem obvious that, like the prophets of old calling the people to repent, they should feel a duty to teach the rest of the Jews how to live righteously and bring divine blessings on to the community. Similarly the members of the Qumran sect, if they were celibate, as is probable, may have adopted a missionary stance in order to survive for their divinely ordained mission, since no children could be born within the group. The only figure given in any ancient text for the size of the Pharisees' sect is Josephus' reference to the 'more than six thousand' individuals who identified themselves as Pharisees at the end of the first century BC when they refused to take an oath to Herod (*Antiquities* XVII 2, 4 (41–5)). There is no evidence that there were any more followers of the sect than that number, even though they were widely influential, persuading the people about prayers and sacrifices (Josephus, *Antiquities* XVIII 1, 3 (15)). It is reasonable to suppose that they might wish as many Jews as possible to 'become Pharisees', although precisely how such a conversion would be marked (other than by the self-description of the convert) is unclear.

That Matthew should find such missionary behaviour by Pharisees objectionable is also unsurprising. For much of the first century the followers of Jesus may have been competing against Pharisees and other interpreters of Judaism to win Jews as converts to Christianity. More of a problem is the implication that Pharisees sought followers outside Palestine, for which there is no other firm evidence: the Diaspora Jew St Paul claimed to be a Pharisee, but he may have been trained in Jerusalem rather than Tarsus, and Josephus, who said that he was a Pharisee when in Rome, made no explicit mention of Pharisaic teachers outside the land of Israel. But the teachings of the rabbis, who were in some ways the successors of the Pharisees after AD 70, did in time spread to Babylonia and elsewhere and eventually were to become normative among Jews of the western Diaspora as well. In any case, the same objection applies whatever interpretation of the term *prosēlytos* is preferred, since there is also no other evidence for Pharisees seeking to convert Gentiles to Judaism outside Palestine.[9]

In sum, the passage makes good sense – even better sense – if *prosēlytos* has the meaning I have suggested rather than that traditionally attributed to it. Is such a meaning possible? There are a number of factors in its favour. First, it should be noted that the term is very rare in the first century except in quotations from the Septuagint. It was hardly used by Philo and never used by Josephus. Apart from the passage in Matthew, the only book of the whole new Testament where it is found is Acts, where it occurs three times (Acts 2:11; 6:5; 13:43). It was clearly *becoming* a technical term among Jews for a converted Gentile, and had been doing so since the time of the Septuagint translation of the third and second centuries BC (see Allen 1894), but its meaning was not yet confined to this sense alone.

An examination of Philo's use of the term may illustrate this continuing flexibility. In referring to Gentile converts to Judaism Philo preferred to use the word *epēlus*. *Prosēlytos* appears only when it is already found in the passage of the Septuagint which Philo was quoting (Daniel 1975: 221–12). In the Septuagint itself *prosēlytos* undoubtedly *usually* means a Gentile convert: the Hebrew word *gēr* which means 'immigrant' or 'resident alien' in the earlier layers of the Pentateuch and 'Gentile who has become Jewish' only in the latest layer, was always translated by *prosēlytos* in the Septuagint when it has the latter meaning (except once, when it was transliterated as *geiōras*), whereas other terms, such as *paroikos*, were usually used for those places where *gēr* appears in the Hebrew with one of its earlier meanings (Meek 1930). But 'Gentile convert' cannot have been the *only* acceptable meaning of *prosēlytos* for the Septuagint translators for, just occasionally, this term also was used to mean a resident alien (e.g. Leviticus 19:10; 24:16).

This latter use is striking in the Greek of Exodus 22:20, where *prosēlytoi* is found, as a translation of *gērim*, to refer not to Gentiles but to the Israelites in Egypt. Philo evidently found such a usage strange but not impossible, since he did not choose to substitute one of the other Septuagintal translations of *gēr* at this point, as he could have done. In *Questions and Answers on Exodus* II 2 he commented that what makes a *prosēlytos* is not circumcision (which, he therefore implied, is what one might have expected), since the Israelites were not circumcised until they began their wanderings in the desert; what matters is turning to God for salvation. He made the same observation at *On the Special Laws* I 9 (51), pointing there to the etymology of the word, which suggests that the *prosēlytos* 'comes to' a holy life from a different one. This sense of *proserchesthai* as the approach to something sacred can also be found in the general use of the verb in the gospel of Matthew (Edwards 1987), and in Josephus, *Jewish War* II 8, 7 (142), where those who join the sect of the Essenes are described as *tous prosiontas*, a participial form of the same verb.

What I suggest, therefore, is that *prosēlytos* in the first century had both a technical and a non-technical sense, and that in that latter sense it could quite easily be applied to Jews. This usage is precisely parallel to that long ago noted for the term 'God-fearer' in this period, which often, sometimes apparently as a semi-technical term, referred to Gentiles but which was also, perhaps metaphorically, used to describe Jews (Feldman 1950). If this argument is accepted, then it will no longer be possible to use Matthew 23:15 as a proof-text – often *the* proof-text – for a mission by Pharisees and other Jews to win converts to Judaism from the Gentile world.

So too with the other literary 'evidence'. The text in Horace,

Satires I 4, 142–3, *veluti te / Iudaei cogemus in hanc concedere turbam*, need not refer to Jewish eagerness to proselytize at all: Horace certainly portrayed the Jews as prone to use pressure to achieve their ends but he implied nothing about Gentiles being compelled to become Jewish or about the corollary of such conversion, that such converts learn to despise their own gods. The Jewish crowd was notorious in Roman politics, at least in the previous generation when Cicero referred to them (*In Defence of Flaccus* 28, 66) as prone to use mass intimidation to get their way when lawsuits were in progress, and that may be all that is at issue here (Nolland 1979).

It is unlikely that any of the residual arguments for a Jewish mission in the first century would ever have been proposed if such a mission had not already been presupposed. The mass conversions to Judaism said by Josephus to have been forced by the Hasmonaeans were obvious political gambits which may have owed something to the example set by the Roman republic in the spread of Roman citizenship over Italy: the notion of an indefinite expansion of citizenship in this way is found in the ancient world only among Jews and Romans and, since the latter had found it strikingly advantageous in the centuries immediately preceding the Hasmonaean dynasty, it would not be all that surprising if the Jewish monarchs, who were eager to maintain contact with the Romans, followed suit.[10] Certainly a Gentile observer such as Timagenes (cited by Strabo) accepted such conversions as standard political incorporation of a neighbouring people (Josephus, *Antiquities* XIII 11, 3 (319)). If the Hasmonaeans wanted a theological justification – and it is quite possible that by the 120s BC they had so far assumed the characteristics of a normal Hellenistic state that they saw no need for one – they could find it in the notion that the land of Israel must be purified by the exclusion of idolatry (cf. Deuteronomy 12: 1–3). Despite the location of Pella just east of the Jordan, such an attitude would best explain the treatment of the inhabitants of that place: because they did not promise to go over to the national customs of the Jews, their city was destroyed (Josephus, *Antiquities* XIII 15, 4 (397)). It was the same notion as lay behind the enthusiastic exclusion of Roman military standards from polluting the land when the Syrian legate Vitellius wished to march through with his legions against the Nabataeans in AD 37 (Josephus, *Antiquities* XVIII 5, 3 (121)). So too the Galileans who were intent on the enforced circumcision of two of Agrippa II's Gentile courtiers whom they caught in their territory in AD 67 argued that 'those who wished to live among the Jews' must needs be circumcised (Josephus, *Life* 23 (113)). If this distinction was generally made by Jews, it provides of course an argument against any universal mission, since it suggests that Gentiles are welcome to remain uncircumcised provided that they live outside the Holy Land. As for the conversion of the Idumaeans, it is true that biblical Edom was not part of the biblical land of Israel, but in Maccabaean times the story of the relationship between Jacob and Esau (ancestor of Edom) was rewritten in the book of Jubilees to emphasize both their fraternal origins and the justified domination of the latter by the former. In any case the area inhabited by Idumaeans by the 120s BC was north of biblical Edom and in fact lay within the southern part of the old kingdom of Judah.[11]

The assumption by Jews that marriage partners should convert before union seems to have been general by the first century. As evidence can be cited the very public insistence to this effect by the women of the Herodian family. Against such a view, it has been argued that the term *memigmenon* at Josephus, *Jewish War* II 18, 1 (463) must refer to Jews who have intermarried with the Gentile population. That many intermarriages without conversion took place is highly probable – the papyri from rural Egypt may provide examples.[12] But it must be assumed that many Jews viewed such liaisons with distaste, for the actions of the Herodians would otherwise be inexplicable. It is, however, hard to see how such insistence on conversion for marriage can be seen as missionary. It might even be suggested that opportunities for mission were lessened by such a custom since a Jew could not seek to convert his or her partner after marriage, as was permitted among Christians (II Corinthians 7: 12–14). That Jews in general preferred to portray themselves as marrying only within the fold was common knowledge (cf. Tacitus, *Histories* V 5: *discreti cubilibus*). When an outsider was allowed in, he or she would have to be initiated into the community; such behaviour reinforces the group's boundary and solidarity, it does not open it up to the outside (cf. B. Wilson cited in Towler 1974:125). In other words, it is striking that the conversion of the Gentile partner was apparently devised at some time between the period of Ezra, who does not seem to have conceived of such a solution to the problem of foreign wives, and the first century AD, but, though of immense practical importance, the innovation in no way attacked the basis of Ezra's ideal Israel as a pure nation separated from the pollution which enveloped it. All this needs emphasis because it is a priori probable that in antiquity, as now, the majority of conversions to Judaism took place to facilitate a marriage. It is noteworthy that the story of Asenath in *Joseph and Asenath* seems to portray her as the paradigm of the proselyte, but that the main theme of the story is that she cannot marry Joseph while she is heathen whereas she can and does so as soon as she has been initiated into Judaism.

Little need be said about the other group on whose circumcision Jews may have insisted, namely their male slaves. It has been suggested above (see p. 56) that this may have been partly for domestic convenience, and it is likely that almost all slaves owned by Jews, at least in Palestine, will have served primarily as domestic servants since that was their normal function in the Near East. Such insistence – if indeed it was already standard at this period, which is debatable (see p. 56) – must be understood in a similar way to conversion for marriage. The slave became by force a member of the family group and circumcision established him as part of that group. Such an attitude reveals nothing at all about Jews' expectations and hopes for those whose economic circumstances did not bring them into this sort of close social relationship with a Jewish family.

What explanation should be offered for the fragments of the large literature which, it is claimed, was produced to win converts to Judaism? The argument, it will be recalled, was roughly as follows (see p. 57). Some Jews wrote a number of religious tracts in Greek during the first century AD and the two centuries before. Such works would have been more or less readily comprehensible to non-Jews. Since the main burden of such writings was praise of Judaism and the Jewish God, it is assumed that those Gentiles who read such material were expected or hoped to become proselytes. The fallacies in this assumption are evident and have been demonstrated by others since the pioneering work of Tcherikover (1956). It is more than likely that most if not all the Jewish literature in Greek was composed primarily for Greek-speaking Jews. This has already been pointed out for the Septuagint translation of the Bible (see pp. 57–8), but the same assertion applies also to all the Jewish texts which both proclaim their Jewishness and stress the need to keep the Law. There is no evidence at all of any Gentile interest in, for example, the Wisdom of Solomon or the fourth book of Maccabees. It is highly unlikely that any non-Jew would be interested in the dry chronological calculations of Demetrius. Even those writings masquerading under Gentile authorship, such as the work of Ps.-Hecataeus and Ps.-Aristeas, may have been intended primarily for Jews: Jews steeped in the surrounding Greek culture as well as their own religious traditions will have taken comfort from such testimony by respected Gentiles to the truth of their faith, much as more recent rabbis appeal on occasion to modern science as support for the wisdom of traditional Jewish customs.

It is of course *possible* that some of these works were read by Gentiles as well as by Jews, and that this was intended by their authors, even though the only Gentile known to have taken any interest in any of these writings before Christians adopted them was the polymath Alexander Polyhistor, who collected such material in the first century BC for his own work *On the Jews*. But, if so, it is hard to see what Gentiles were to make of such literature. The status of Gentiles in the cosmic order was referred to on occasion, particularly in the *Sibylline Oracles*, but this question was decidedly not the main focus of the bulk of these works. On the contrary, their main theme was the excellence of Judaism. When the writings urged specifically Jewish customs, such as the observance of the sabbath, they tended to be pseudonymous: thus, the fact that Orpheus was portrayed by a Jewish forger as approving of rest on every seventh day, or that Phocylides was shown approving of Jewish morality, was likely to be comforting for a Jew who was impressed by Orpheus and Phocylides but was not likely to persuade a Gentile to become Jewish. By contrast, those writings which were openly Jewish often urged not conversion to Judaism but a more general ethic. The themes which crop up in, for instance, the *Testament of Abraham* are moral ones: charity, hospitality, the avoidance of adultery and homosexuality, the shunning of infanticide and so on (cf. Collins 1983: 137–74 on 'the common ethic'). Even in a work like the third book of the *Sibylline Oracles*, where the fact that it was the Jewish cult that was being praised was only thinly disguised and one could argue that such a disguise was a necessary part of the oracular form, there was no suggestion that Gentiles should immediately rush to convert, or, indeed, that the covenant of Judaism (including circumcision) had anything to do with them – at least, until the final reckoning at the end of days (Collins 1985: 165–6).

Literature intended to persuade Gentiles to abandon their social customs and enter a new society in Judaism would need to be far more direct than this. It is only because some modern scholars assume (wrongly) that Jews sought proselytes of some sort that they have sometimes attributed to such writings an intention to attract proselytes who would observe only a select few of the commandments (McEleney 1974: 323–4). For Josephus, the matter was simple: those proselytes who found it beyond their endurance to keep the laws properly were considered to be apostates (*Against Apion II* 10 (123)).

And yet, as has been seen (see p. 59), many have argued that one religious duty in particular was often waived by Jewish missionaries in their eagerness to win proselytes. It was possible, so it is claimed, for Gentile males to become Jewish without undergoing circumcision. Why this particular duty rather than any other? To be sure, circumcision is a painful business and cases are recorded from the ancient world of this being the sticking-point for would-be converts: Izates of Adiabene hesitated to undertake an act which might prove disastrously unpopular with his subjects (Josephus, *Antiquities* XX 2, 4 (38–9)). But the main reason for modern scholarly interest in this particular religious duty is the emphasis laid upon it by St Paul in his attacks on 'those of the circumcision' and his insistence that it was not required for entrance into the Church (McEleney 1974: 328–41). The operation is no more painful or dangerous than that in other initiation rites; indeed, it could be argued that the discomfort caused constitutes part of its efficacy for initiation. Many peoples other than Jews practised (and practise) the same custom. It seems naive to suggest that dropping this one requirement could bring a flood of proselytes to join the Jewish fold. The physical discomfort would be negligible compared to the social problems faced by the new convert.

But in fact the evidence for uncircumcised proselytes is anyway minimal and should be discounted.[13] Epictetus, assuming baptism as the main sign of initiation (ap. Arrian, *Dissertations* II 9, 20), may simply have been confused or taking a part of the initiation ceremony to stand for all. The rabbinic texts said to consider the possibility of a proselyte who has not (yet?) been circumcised discussed the case only as part of a gradual unveiling of a complex theoretical argument. An examination of Philo's allegorical method and its application to the significance of circumcision makes it highly implausible that he suggested the abolition of this law any more than any other. It needs to be recognized how far-reaching such an abolition would be. Circumcision was the symbol of the Jew (for outsiders as well as for Jews themselves), however many other peoples did it and regardless of the occasional Jew who, for whatever reason, did not carry out the Law. The attitude of Metilius, the Roman garrison commander in Jerusalem in AD 66, can be taken as indication of the importance of the rite. He was prepared, he said, to become Jewish (*ioudaizein*) 'even as far as undergoing circumcision' (Josephus, *Jewish War* II 17, 10 (454)).

One final claim needs to be countered, namely that the expulsion of the Jews from the city of Rome in 139 BC and AD 19 was in retaliation for the vehemence of their proselytizing (see p. 59). Neither case is as well documented as is often assumed. The affair in 139 BC was referred to only by Valerius Maximus, an author of the late first century BC whose remarks survive only in two Byzantine epitomators, Julius Paris (c. AD 400) and Nepotianus (c. AD 500). Since the two accounts differ, they are clearly not preserved verbatim, and the confused nature of the reference to Jupiter Sabazius in Julius Paris has been well clarified by Lane (1979; see Stern 1974: 357–60 for the passage). According to Nepotianus, the Jews were banished, along with astrologers, for 'trying to transmit their sacred rites [*sacra*] to the Romans'; private altars were therefore removed by the Roman authorities from public places, and they were expelled from the city. Various peculiarities about this story have been noted. One is that it is not clear who these Jews could be. There is no other evidence for a Jewish community in Rome in the second century BC. The suggestion has been made that these Jews were the deputation from Simon the Maccabee mentioned in the first book of Maccabees, but this does not fit in with the required date. More significant, however, is the odd description of the Jews' alleged crime. It seems difficult to imagine a new convert being recommended to set up altars of any kind. Jews did countenance the setting up of a temple at Leontopolis in this period by priests who had come from Jerusalem, but no Jews are recorded as having approved of the use of private altars in this way. What was at issue here, then, if the account is not totally confused, was something rather less than the conversion of proselytes. I suggest that the Jews were accused not of teaching Romans to despise their native cults, which would be the most obvious and objectionable effect of conversion, but

simply of bringing in a new cult into public places without authority, a practice which the Romans traditionally deprecated, as they
had shown recently in their opposition to the spread of the cult
of Bacchus. What may have happened is that some Romans,
impressed by Jews, chose to express their admiration in conven-
tional Roman fashion by the setting up of altars within the city.
How pleased Jews might be about this it is impossible to say, but
they would certainly distinguish it quite clearly from the conversion of Romans to Judaism.

As for the expulsion of AD 19, it has already been noted that
neither Tacitus not Josephus gave missionary activity as an explanation (see p. 60). The suggestion that Josephus might be prepared
to hide the truth is somewhat implausible: if the Jews' missionary
activity was well known, Josephus would have been better advised
to try to justify such behaviour than to try to pretend it did not
happen. It seems to me better to explain the motive for the
expulsion, which is first found in a fragment of Cassius Dio's
history preserved not in the manuscript traditions but in a solitary
quotation (not necessarily verbatim?) by the seventh-century
Christian writer John of Antioch, in terms of a new Roman
awareness of the possibility of proselytism since the end of the
first century, and perhaps as evidence for a real proselytizing
mission in *his* day, the third century AD (see p. 74).

On examination, then, the evidence for an active mission by
first-century Jews to win proselytes is very weak. I think that it
is possible to go further and to suggest that there are *positive*
reasons to deny the existence of such a mission. Unlike all other
contemporary religions before Christianity, Judaism was a way of
life, which could even be cited in contrast to living like a Greek
(W. C. Smith 1978: 72). Conversion to such a new life and to the
new social group which went with it was a major undertaking.
One would expect much negative comment about such proselytizing in the anti-Semitic literature which survives, but it is not to
be found before the end of the first century AD (cf. Goodman
1989b). One would also expect riots and expulsions from the
other great centres of Jewish life, giving proselytizing as justification, but, again, only in the city of Rome is this said to have
happened, and even there the evidence seems doubtful. One would
expect a great deal to be said about such a mission in the works
of Philo and Josephus if Jews wished all Gentiles to take so
momentous a step. But in fact these authors have little about

proselytes and nothing about a mission to win them. Indeed, Josephus is explicit that those outsiders who only flirt with Judaism will not be accepted as proselytes (*Against Apion* II 28 (210)). A full commitment was needed, and if this diminished the number of conversions no contemporary Jewish author expressed any regret. It should be recognized that the suggestion that Josephus deliberately hid the fact that Jews believed that they had a mission to convert the world (e.g. Delling 1970: 51) is a major, and most implausible claim. How could he hope to escape undetected with such a lie?

Furthermore, the ambiguous status of proselytes in the eyes of Jews is itself evidence that the winning of more was not seen as a religious duty. That the Jews were remarkable in espousing the whole notion of permitting converts to enter the body politic has been noted above (see p. 54), but this should not prevent awareness of the limitations in the openness to outsiders thus expressed. If Jewish attitudes to proselytes are compared not to those of contemporary pagans but to those of the early Church, those limitations will rapidly become clear.

In the early Church, a convert to Christ was in essence equal to his or her fellows. There is no evidence of prejudice against those who had formerly been in darkness, except in so far as they needed to heed the teachings of the more enlightened. In the early years, of course, all Christians had been converts. By contrast, a proselyte to Judaism became in religious terms a member of a clearly defined, separate and, in a few cases mostly concerned with marriage, less privileged group within the Jewish commonwealth. That this was so was doubtless due to the dual function of conversion as entry into a political and social as well as into a religious entity, but it is significant that the distinct definition of proselytes as a particular *sort* of Jew was retained throughout antiquity. It was even possible to describe the descendants of the Idumaeans who had converted to Judaism as 'half-Jews' (Josephus, *Antiquities* XIV 15, 2 (403)).

It would be wrong to suggest that a negative attitude towards proselytes predominated in the Jewish texts of the first century – in so far as converts were discussed at all, it was usually with sympathy and sometimes with admiration. But even the possibility of such ambivalent attitudes is enough to show how unlikely the picture is of a Jewish mission to win converts. If Gentiles wished to come to (*proserchesthai*) Israel, the commandments and God, they were welcome, but the etymology of the word 'proselyte' implies movement by the Gentile concerned, from darkness into light, not the changing of the Gentile's nature as simple repentance might be termed, and not a bringing in by the body of the Jews as the model of mission would require. The role of the Jews was simply passively to bear witness through their existence and piety; how the Gentiles reacted to such witness was up to them.

JEWISH ATTITUDES TO GENTILES

This *laissez-faire* attitude was much facilitated by the general variety and frequent tolerance of Jewish attitudes in this period towards those Gentiles who had not converted. For a truly missionary philosophy it is necessary to believe that the unenlightened are in some way damned. It is not easy to find clear evidence of first-century Jews asserting that those who do not become proselytes will suffer such a fate.[14]

Speculation by Jews about the fate of Gentiles either immediately after death or at the expected end of the world was very varied. Some texts implied apocalyptic destruction (2 Baruch 82:3) – perhaps only for unrighteous Gentiles (2 Baruch 72:4); others implied eventual subjugation to a redeemed Israel; yet others expected Gentiles to participate in the kingdom. Most Jewish texts had nothing to say on the matter: in a period of great trauma for Israel the status of non-Jews was hardly a pressing matter. But enough can be culled from the evidence to show that the notion that only by conversion could Gentiles be removed from the multitude of the damned would not often have received the assent of first-century Jews.

It is true enough that Philo wrote that the proselyte who had left the country of idolatry had come to his true homeland in Judaism (*On the Special Laws* IV 34 (178)), implying perhaps that all other pagans are in exile (or perhaps, more sophisticatedly, that proselytes must in some sense have been born as potential Jews (cf. bShabbath 146a)). It is also true that the tendency of many Jews in this period was to shy away from social contact with the Gentile world; it is a tendency that seems to me to have been based more on instinct than on theology or religious law, as can be seen from the symbolic extension of food taboos to exclude more and more non-Jewish food from the kosher diet, but it was justified in religious terms by the (correct) feeling that Gentiles

JEWISH PROSELYTIZING IN THE FIRST CENTURY

were always prone to idolatry, from which Jews were so strongly excluded by their law. But Jews in the first century did not even agree among themselves whether life after death was possible for Jews, so the idea that they should have had any clear notion on the availability of such post-mortem existence for Gentiles seems implausible.

From those Jews who did refer to the expected fate of Gentiles there is plenty to suggest that the future of at least some unconverted Gentiles was deemed to be safe enough. At places Philo described the achievement of wise and virtuous Gentiles with approval (*On the Special Laws* II 12–13 (44–8)). Quite what a Gentile was reckoned to have to do in order to be deemed wise and virtuous was perhaps debated. The Jewish texts in Greek discussed above (see p. 57) urged a general morality: sexual continence (especially avoidance of homosexuality), charity, hospitality and so on. The most common theological demand was a recognition by Gentiles that there is only one God, but this could usually be achieved with singularly little action by the Gentile concerned simply by the avowal that the divinities he worshipped were all aspects of the single divine nature (cf. Ps.-Aristeas 16, 189). Some Jewish texts encouraged further worship specifically at the Jewish shrine (e.g. *Sibylline Oracles* III 565) but this was rarely felt to be incompatible for Gentiles with continued pagan practices: thus the Septuagint version of Exodus 22:27 urged Jews not to revile the gods of others, an attitude echoed both by Josephus (*Antiquities* IV 8, 10 (207); *Against Apion* II 33 (237)) and by Philo (*Moses* II 38 (205); *On the Special Laws* I 9 (53); *Questions and Answers on Exodus* II (5)). Josephus urged that everyone should be allowed 'to reverence the god according to his own inclination' (*Life* 23 (113)). Artapanus, an Egyptian Jewish author of the mid-second century BC, could even commend the utility of pagan cults (Eusebius, *Preparation of the Gospel* IX 27, 4).

This Jewish attitude was not just a question of theory. The Jewish merchant Ananias who taught the royal family in Charax Spasinou and Adiabene to revere the god (without converting to Judaism) presumably thought this would be pleasing to God and of advantage to them (Josephus, *Antiquities* XX 2, 3 (34–5), 4 (41)). The same must surely be true of the Jewish treatment of the pagan priestess in Phrygia, a certain Julia Severa, who, also in the first century, was granted an honoured position in a synagogue without becoming Jewish. The evidence for a formally recognized group of Gentiles designated as 'God-fearers' does not predate the third century AD, but the theological preconceptions which were then to encourage the emergence of such a defined status for honoured non-Jews were already established in the first century. That theology was of great simplicity. Gentiles stood outside the special covenant made between God and Israel. They had none of the burdens of the covenant. They might win divine favour by freely offering worship, but such worship was not required of them. Their only duty, in the eyes of Jews, was a general morality.

CHRISTIANITY AND JEWISH ATTITUDES TO MISSION

Jews thus lacked an incentive for proselytizing, and it could be argued that in theological logic arguments against winning converts could even have been brought forward. If many Jews believed at this time that the imminent arrival of the last days could best be facilitated by the righteous behaviour of Jews (cf. bSanhedrin 97a), it might seems a retrograde step to produce more Jews who, through human nature and the difficulties inherent in full observance of the Jewish way of life, were liable to add to the number of Jewish sinners. But such arguments are found only in later periods and even then have an air of justification after the event – no one seems to have urged the corollary, that producing children should also be avoided.

The lack of a proselytizing movement in first-century Judaism seems to me all the more striking when it is contrasted not just with the early Church but with developments within Judaism later in antiquity. At some time in the second or third century some Jews seem to have begun looking for converts in just the way they were apparently not doing in the first century. The evidence, which is extensive but oblique, has been discussed by me in detail elsewhere (Goodman 1989a), but presentation of one strand here may usefully bring out the new mood among some rabbis. In Sifre to Deuteronomy 313 (on Deuteronomy 32:10), a rabbinic text probably compiled in the late second or early third century AD, the patriarch Abraham was described as being so good a missionary that he caused God to be known as king of earth as well as heaven, and this prowess in winning proselytes was one of the main features of the career of Abraham singled out for praise in later rabbinic writings. By contrast, it was Abraham's piety as a convert, not a converter, that was stressed by Philo, Josephus and other writers of earlier periods.[15] What might appear to be an exception on closer inspection proves the rule. Josephus wrote that Abraham went to Egypt 'intending, if he found their doctrine more excellent than his own, to conform to it, or else to rearrange them to a better mind should his own beliefs prove superior' (*Antiquities* I 8, 1 (161)). But what he taught was not, it seems, Judaism, or anything like it. The burden of his teaching emerges unexpectedly as arithmetic and astronomy (*Antiquities* I 8, 2 (167)), while the Jew Artapanus in the second century BC envisaged Abraham, as the bearer of culture, teaching the Egyptian Pharaoh astrology (Eusebius, *Preparation of the Gospel* IX 18, 1).

The missionary hero in search of converts for Judaism is a phenomenon first attested well after the start of the Christian mission, not before it. There is no good reason to suppose that any Jew would have seen value in seeking proselytes in the first century with an enthusiasm like that of the Christian apostles. The origins of the missionary impulse within the Church should be sought elsewhere.

NOTES

1 For an extreme example of the argument that the first Christians imitated Jewish missionaries see Georgi; 1987: 83–228. This study was completed in 1989. I have benefited from much secondary literature that I have not had space to cite here. I am grateful to Paula Fredriksen and Ed Sanders for help and advice.

2 See my arguments in Goodman 1987: 61. Note, however, that rabbinic references to Jewish foundlings (e.g. mKiddushin 4:22) suggest that some Jews may have adopted the standard Gentile custom of exposing unwanted children.

3 Kasher 1988: 46–77, 79–83, argues vehemently and ingeniously that the allegation that the Hasmonaeans used force was fabricated by Gentiles as anti-Hasmonaean propaganda. But I am unconvinced by his assertion, which is necessary for his argument, that Josephus included such propaganda in his history out of lip-service to his Roman masters. Josephus was proud of his own Hasmonaean lineage (Josephus, *Life* 1 (2–4)).

4 Philo, *On the Special Laws* II 15 (62); *Moses* II 39 (211); cf. Georgi 1987: 85, 113–14.

5 Note, for example, Herod's attendance at a Roman state sacrifice on

the Capitol in Rome at the start of his reign (Josephus *Jewish War* I 14, 4 (285)), despite his portrayal of himself as a Jew.

6 Thus Georgi 1987: 92–3. For the texts, see Stern 1974, Stern 1980.

7 Precisely what group was designated by the word *grammateis* in the gospel of Matthew is not clear. See Garland 1979: 41–6.

8 This interpretation was floated by Munck 1959: 267 in one paragraph, but (so far as I know) it has never been fully argued.

9 Baumgarten 1983: 414, n. 10, argues that Eleazar, who converted the king of Adiabene, Izates, may have been a Pharisee because he was described by Josephus (*Antiquities* XX 2, 4 (43)) as *akribes* ('accurate') in the Law. But *akribeia* in Josephus' writings cannot always be equated with Pharisaism: in Josephus, *Against Apion* II 31 (227) the Spartans are said to have observed *their* laws *akribōs* (as noted by Baumgarten himself, 1983: 413, n. 6).

10 See M. Smith 1978. If Kasher 1988: 46–8 is correct to emphasize against Josephus' account the remark of Strabo, *Geography* XV 2, 34, that 'the Idumaeans are Nabataeans [*sic*], but owing to a sedition they were banished from there, joined the Judaeans and shared in the same customs with them', there would be no need to explain Hasmonaean motives in forcing conversions since the whole story of such conversions was fabricated. But see my reservations, above, note 3.

11 On the attitude of the book of Jubilees, see Mendels 1987: 75–81.

12 See Tcherikover and Fuks 1960: 2–3, on CPJ II, no. 144. On the Josephus passage, see M. Smith 1987: 182, n. 33. On intermarriage, see in general ibid., 65–6.

13 See Nolland 1979 for the following arguments.

14 See discussion by Sanders 1976: 11–44. On Jewish expectations of the fate of Gentiles in the messianic period, contrast Sanders 1985: 18–20 to Fredriksen 1988: 149ff., 166ff.

15 Philo, *On Abraham* 13–14 (60–7); Philo, *On the Virtues* 39 (212–19); Josephus, *Antiquities* I 7, 1 (154–7).

BIBLIOGRAPHY

Allen, W. C. (1894) 'On the meaning of προσήλυτος in the Septuagint', *Expositor* (series 4) 10: 264–75.

Allen, W. C. (2nd edn, 1907) *A Critical and Exegetical Commentary on the Gospel of S. Matthew* (International Critical Commentary), Edinburgh.

Baumgarten, A. (1983) 'The Name of the Pharisees', *Journal of Biblical Literature* 102/3: 411–28.

Cohen, S. J. D. (1987) 'Respect for Judaism by Gentiles According to Josephus', *Harvard Theological Review* 80: 409–30.

Collins, J. J. (1983) *Between Athens and Jerusalem: Jewish Identity in the Hellenistic Diaspora*, New York.

Collins, J. J. (1985) 'A Symbol of Otherness: Circumcision and Salvation in the First Century', in J. Neusner and E. S. Frerichs (eds) *'To See*

Ourselves as Others See Us': Christians. Jews, 'Others' in Late Antiquity, Chico, Calif.

Dalbert, P. (1954) *Die Theologie der Hellenistich-Jüdischen Missionsliteratur unter Ausschluss von Philo und Josephus*, Hamburg.

Daniel, S. (ed.) (1975) *Philo, De Specialibus Legibus*, Paris.

Delling, G. (1970) *Studien zum Neuen Testament und zum hellenistischen Judentum*, Göttingen.

Edwards, J. R. (1987) 'The use of προσέρχεσθαι in the Gospel of Matthew', *Journal of Biblical Literature* 106: 65–74.

Feldman, L. H. (1950) ' "Jewish Sympathisers" in Classical Literature and Inscriptions', *Transactions of the American Philological Association* 81: 200–8.

Feldman, L. H. (1986) 'The Omnipresence of the God-fearers', *Biblical Archaeology Review* 12, 5: 58–63.

Fredriksen, P. (1988) *From Jesus to Christ: the Origins of the New Testament Images of Jesus*, New Haven, Conn.

Garland, D. E. (1979) *The Intention of Matthew 23* (Supplement to Novum Testamentum 52), Leiden.

Georgi, D. (1987) *The Opponents of Paul in Second Corinthians*, Edinburgh.

Goodman, M. D. (1987) *The Ruling Class of Judaea: the Origins of the Jewish Revolt against Rome, AD 66–70*, Cambridge.

Goodman, M. D. (1989a) 'Proselytising in Rabbinic Judaism', *Journal of Jewish Studies* 38: 175–85.

Goodman, M. D. (1989b) 'Nerva, the *fiscus Judaicus* and Jewish Identity', *Journal of Roman Studies* 79: 40–4.

Jeremias, J. (1958) *Jesus' Promise to the Nations*, trans. S. H. Hooke, London.

Kasher, A. (1988) *Jews, Idumaeans and Ancient Arabs: Relations of the Jews in Eretz-Israel with the Nations of the Frontier and the Desert*, Tübingen.

Lane, E. N. (1979) 'Sabazius and the Jews in Valerius Maximus: a Re-examination', *Journal of Roman Studies* 69: 35–8.

McEleney, N. J. (1974) 'Conversion, Circumcision and the Law', *New Testament Studies* 20: 319–41.

Meek, Th. J. (1930) 'The Translation of Gêr in the Hexateuch and its Bearing on the Documentary Hypothesis', *Journal of Biblical Literature* 49: 172–80.

Mendels, D. (1987) *The Land of Israel as a Political Concept in Hasmonean Literature: Resource to History in Second Century BC Claims to the Holy Land*, Tübingen.

Munck, J. (1959) *Paul and the Salvation of Mankind*, trans. F. Clarke, London.

Nolland, J. (1979) 'Proselytism or Politics in Horace, Satires I, 4, 138–143?', *Vigiliae Christianae* 33: 347–55.

Nolland, J. (1981) 'Uncircumcised Proselytes?', *Journal for the Study of Judaism* 12, 2: 173–94.

Sanders, E. P. (1976) 'The Covenant as a Soteriological Category and the Nature of Salvation in Palestinian and Hellenistic Judaism', in

R. Hamerton-Kelly and R. Scroggs (eds) *Jews, Greeks and Christians: Religious Cultures in Late Antiquity*, Leiden.

Sanders, E. P. (1985) *Paul, the Law and the Jewish People*, London.

Schürer, E. (1986) *The History of the Jewish People in the Age of Jesus Christ*, Vol III. 1, ed. G. Vermes, F. Millar and M. Goodman, Edinburgh.

Smith, M. (1978) 'Rome and the Maccabean Conversions – notes on I Macc. 8', in E. Bammel, C. K. Barrett and W. D. Davies (eds) *Donum Gentilicium: New Testament studies in honour of David Daube*, Oxford.

Smith, M. (1987) *Palestinian Parties that Shaped the Old Testament*, London.

Smith, W. C. (1978) *The Meaning and End of Religion*, London.

Stern, M. (1974) *Greek and Latin Authors on Jews and Judaism*, Vol. I, Jerusalem.

Stern, M. (1980) *Greek and Latin Authors on Jews and Judaism*, Vol. 2, Jerusalem.

Tcherikover, V. A. (1956) 'Jewish Apologetic Literature Reconsidered', *Eos* 48: 169–93.

Tcherikover, V. A. and Fuks, A. (1960) *Corpus Papyrorum Judaicarum*, Vol. II, Cambridge, Mass.

Towler, R. (1974) *Homo Religiosus: Sociological Problems in the Study of Religion*, London.

4

HISTORY AND THEOLOGY IN CHRISTIAN VIEWS OF JUDAISM

Judith Lieu

INTRODUCTION

In his still influential study of 'The relations between Christians and Jews in the Roman Empire (AD 135–425)' M. Simon pinpointed the heart of the issue in the following terms: 'The problem of Jewish expansion and of the spread of its influence is bound up with that of anti-Semitism' (Simon 1948/64: 395). These words, written in the postscript fifteen years after the first publication of the book, were reaffirming, against the rejection by some of the term 'anti-Semitism', his earlier assertion – 'the most compelling reason for anti-Semitism was the religious vitality of Israel' (p. 232). In his own context Simon was forcefully countering the prevalent view which saw the Judaism of the period as turned in on itself and, as far as any external impact went, moribund – 'strangers in a pagan world'.[1] His arguments for the religious vitality of Judaism were sufficiently persuasive to have become increasingly familiar in modern discussions of the world of early Christianity. Perhaps equally significant is Simon's interpretation of the Christian polemic in terms of 'anti-Semitism' or anti-Judaism; this is rarely found in earlier discussions of Christian-Jewish polemic in the patristic period whereas now it is regularly proposed as in this judgement by Hruby: 'the attitude of the church fathers to Jews and Judaism is synonymous with anti-Jewish polemic and with Christian anti-Judaism' (Hruby 1971: 6). Simon himself saw no difficulty in defending the term 'anti-Semitism', even while acknowledging that, in contrast to its modern form, it had relied neither on a theory of race nor on an

economic basis (p. 203) and while also firmly distancing himself
as a historian from any attempt 'to connect the Nazis' anti-Jewish
persecutions too closely with Christian teaching' (p. 397). This
last quotation comes from the 1964 postscript: the issue of modern
anti-Semitism rarely surfaces in the first publication of the book,
and then only in contrast with that of the first centuries or when
labelling the attempt to present an 'Aryan' Christianity rid of its
Jewish heritage as a renewal of the 'Marcionite' heresy (p. 238).

It is in this area that scholarship has become more nuanced,
and perhaps more self-critical; it might be better to speak of
'Christian' scholarship, for many of those who work in this area
come from a Christian theological background and have contemporary theological concerns which infuse their historical interests
– a good example is Wilken's introduction to his study of Cyril
of Alexandria where he speaks of his theological interest in anti-
Judaism and of his growing current contacts with contemporary
Judaism: Wilken 1971: ix. A consequence is that the choice of the
term 'anti-Semitism' (as opposed to 'anti-Judaism'), particularly in
the title of a book about the early Church or, even more, about
the New Testament, has become something of a polemical issue
determined by more than merely the recognition that the term is a
nineteenth-century coinage with a specific, outmoded, conceptual
background. Indeed, since the mid–1970s there has been an
explosion of literature in the subject, and few authors are able to
avoid at least a sidelong glance at the continuing heritage of the
earliest Christian attitudes to the Jews.

A further landmark for English-speaking scholarship was Rose-
mary Ruether's study of the 'theological roots of anti-Semitism'
with the arresting title *Faith and Fratricide* (1974); while the main
part of the book focuses on the New Testament and patristic
periods, her concluding chapter demands a fundamental rethinking
of Christian identity and theology. Her key contention behind this
demand is that anti-Judaism is neither superficial nor peripheral to
Christian thought but that from the New Testament period
onwards it was inseparable from developing Christian self-identity
and that its continued vitality within Christian tradition provided
the fertile ground for the Nazis' adoption of a racial and secular
anti-Semitism. Her presentation of a straightforward continuity
within the Christian tradition (but not so much from earlier *pagan*
'anti-Semitism') has provoked valid criticisms of over-generaliz-
ation and of a lack of attention to detail, and has been followed

by more careful analyses; equally contentious has been her isolation of Christology, the Christian proclamation of Jesus as the promised Messiah, as the reverse side of anti-Judaism and so as the heart of the problem – 'Is it possible to say "Jesus is the Messiah" without, implicitly or explicitly, saying at the same time "and the Jews be damned"?' (p. 246). Other scholars have sought to show that disputes between Jews and Christians about the status of Torah or about the interpretation of the (Hebrew) scriptures were more fundamental than those about the messianic status of Jesus. Yet it is significant that despite all the acknowledged weaknesses of the book, it continues to provoke respect, discussion and, most notably, responses which bring together the historical and the contemporary theological dimensions of the problem (for example, Davies 1979). Another inescapable part of the contemporary picture is the growth of attempts by Christian as well as by Jewish theologians to struggle with the understanding of God and of the justice of God in the light of 'Auschwitz'.

It is in this context that historical setting and theological evaluation – both of the modern interpreter and of the original source – combine in an unresolved tension. In her survey Ruether paid only limited attention to the particular social setting of the different Christian writers. However, as in the broader study of the New Testament and early Church, this concern has come to be a significant feature of recent study. As of course already argued by Simon, it was the presence of contemporary Judaism that sharpened the polemic of early Christian writers; but this can be given a more local and specific focus, as it has already by Wilken for Cyril of Alexandria (1971) and more recently for John Chrysostom (1983). Inevitably this leads to a further question: how does the pressure of the immediate situation relate to the continuing heritage of a writer's (or preacher's) words? Melito of Sardis has been labelled the 'first poet of deicide'; the virulence of his attack against Judaism may well owe more than a little to the vitality of Judaism in his home city as now attested by archaeology (Kraabel 1971). How far should this awareness colour our assessment of him in view of the later legacy of the charge of deicide (although not on the authority of Melito)?

For many the issue is more pressing when we go back to the New Testament; in the Fourth Gospel Jesus declares the Jews to be children of a father who is the devil and who was a murderer from the beginning (John 8:44; there is probably a covert reference to Cain). With its 'evangelical' authority that charge too has had a long legacy – it is taken up by many later church writers – and, together with the overall presentation of the Jews in that Gospel, has earned John the label 'the father of the anti-Semitism of the Christians'. Recent study has proposed conflicting interpretations of the gospel's attitude to the Jews; for some the hostility reflects the sharpness of polemic and pain occasioned by the recent radical break between Jews and Christians within John's own community, itself reflected in the references to exclusion from the synagogue (John 9:22; 12:42; 16:2). For others the 'Jews' of John 8 are a cover for 'Judaizers' (see below) in the Johannine community – they are Jews who had believed in Jesus (as in 8:31) but whose faith is found wanting; it is an internal hostility and has nothing to do with the 'real' Jews. For others again the 'Jews' are but representatives of the 'world' which, within the characteristic dualism of the Gospel, represents for the author the ultimate hostility to God and to believers. Not only are scholars undecided as to the appropriate interpretation of John's words in their original context, they are equally undecided whether such an interpretation, particularly the second or third, would properly absolve the Gospel of the charge laid against it. Yet it is clear that concern prompted by the contemporary situation overshadows if it does not inspire the historical-critical task – 'through careful study, Christians can isolate what genuine forms of anti-Judaism really colour the major writings and, by examining their historic genesis, neutralise their potential for harm' (Davies 1979: xv – here speaking of the New Testament but the sentiment could be repeated of the later texts).[2]

THE FATE OF JUDAISM IN EARLY CHRISTIAN THOUGHT

This discussion may well seem to have taken us away from our proper concern with the situation under the Roman Empire. Yet the last two paragraphs indicate both that there is a considerable 'unfinished agenda' in the analysis and interpretation of the Christian witnesses to the role of Judaism in the religious interaction of the Roman Empire, and that the setting of a significant part of that analysis and interpretation combines both historical and theological worlds, in the modern period no less than in the early Church.

That this is true of the early Church needs little demonstration. The picture of Judaism after the end of the first century AD as passive if not moribund and as playing no active religious role in relation to Christianity has found its way into 'histories' of Judaism and of the period generally. Whether or not modern scholars espousing this view were gullibly seduced by the patristic sources, this is certainly what those sources would have their readers believe. Yet that image drew its conviction from theological necessity and is effectively refuted not simply by modern archaeological discoveries (see T. Rajak in this volume) but by the very same sources themselves. The sheer variety and impact of the polemic against Judaism and against those who succumb to its attractions betray the authors' actual experience even though it may be at variance with the image they want to project (so Simon 1948/64: *passim*). For these early Christians it is now the Church that has replaced the Jews as the heirs to God's promises, the Church that is properly 'Israel' (or the 'new Israel'), the Church that is the covenant partner with God. The reverse side of this must be that the Jews are no longer God's people, that they have lost God's election, often by their own wilful rejection of it. Here we need not pause over the many variations and different nuances on this theme, for example, how much value is given to Israel's past history 'before Christ': its overall tenor is plain and could be richly documented (see Hruby 1971: 27–54). Nor can we pause to speculate how an alternative tradition of interpretation might have developed, namely the early Christian conviction that they too were entering into God's covenant promises (1 Peter 2:4–10; Romans 9–11).

What did happen was that 'history' itself appeared to validate this Christian perception of the rejection of the Jews through the destruction of Jerusalem in AD 70, through the loss of Temple and sacrificial cult, and through the apparent 'confirmation' of this loss after the failure of the Bar Kochba revolt. Of course Jewish tradition was also able to interpret the defeat as punishment but without according it ultimate finality, and even the Christian writer Hegesippus apparently saw it only as the punishment for the murder of James the brother of Jesus (in Eusebius, *Church History* II 23, 18). However, Origen represents the Christian consensus when he says that the Jewish nation had to be overthrown and God's invitation to blessedness transferred to others, and attributes this 'to what they had dared to do against our Jesus'

(*Against Celsus* II 8; IV 22). For many writers the time-gap between the crucifixion and the destruction of Judaism becomes eclipsed, but Origen acknowledges it as forty-two years graciously given by God for repentance. Both the dispersion of the Jews, 'their scattering to all nations of the whole world', and their unceasing suffering since are the consequence of their sin against Jesus (Eusebius, *Demonstration of the Gospel* I 1, 6); like many other writers Eusebius here ignores the antiquity of the dispersion and ties the scattering to the loss of Jerusalem as divine punishment. In the same way we can accord Tertullian no historical integrity when he says the Jews began to have synagogues in the dispersion when they did not believe in Jesus (*Against the Jews* 13). For these authors, that the Jews have ever since continued to suffer, 'wandering, banished from their soil and sun, having neither man nor God as king' (Tertullian, *Apology* 21, 5), is part of the same theological necessity and obviously would not reflect the self-perception of Tertullian's Jewish neighbours with their long-established history in North Africa or elsewhere. Small wonder then that Christian authors provide a model which effectively excludes the Jews from active participation in the history of the Empire – something in which they are aided by rabbinic sources' lack of historical interest.[3]

The consequences of this theological conviction can be seen in the violent (literary) reaction to the Emperor Julian's plans to rebuild the Temple in Jerusalem – for this would undermine a central pillar of the Church's own self-understanding (e.g. Ephraem, *Hymns against Julian* IV 20–1; see Wilken 1983: 138–48 who argues that this was part of Julian's conscious intention). On the other hand, the fact that the Jews continued to exist, even after the Christianization of the Empire had seemed to prove the victory of the Church, demanded an explanation and provoked Augustine's influential declaration that they must continue as a testimony to Christian truth (*City of God* XVIII 46; *Against Faustus* XVI 21; Blumenkranz 1958: 230–3).

The continuing existence of the Jews posed a very real problem to these early Christian writers. Given their prolific literary activity, it is not surprising that they can be an invaluable source of information about contemporary Judaism – and they have long been used as such. Yet this information invariably comes from contexts in which the authors had quite different concerns of their own. So, for example, Origen attests the continued payment of the *fiscus iudaicus* until at least the middle of the third century, as well as the authority accorded by the Romans to the ethnarch 'as if he were a king'; he also mentions the blind eye turned towards sentences of death passed by Jewish courts according to their law. He does so, in his discussion of the History of Susannah (*To Africanus* 14), to demonstrate the freedom that the Jews as a captive people might be allowed, and we may trust him when he says he speaks from first-hand knowledge. Jerome offers a dramatic description of the anguish of the Jews, permitted on one day of the year to come and weep over the destruction of their city and Temple (*Commentary on Zephaniah* I 15–16). Schürer closed the first volume of his 'History of the Jewish People in the time of Jesus Christ' with a long quotation of this description together with its grim ascription of the suffering to their killing of the servants of God and of the Son of God (Schürer 1901: 705f.).[4] Yet when Jerome speaks of the broken-down women and old men who come as demonstrating '*the wrath of God*' in their bodies and clothing, when he asks whether any who see it can doubt it is a '*day of distress and anguish, a day of calamity and misery*' and again when he speaks of them as weeping over '*the high pinnacles*' of the Temple, from which they killed James – an echo of the interpretation found in Hegesippus – he draws his vocabulary from the text on which he is commenting, Zephaniah 1:15f. When he goes on to say (17–18) that after the destruction of Jerusalem '*their blood was poured out like soil over the whole area and their bodies remained unburied like dung over the face of the earth*' he is again quoting his scriptural text, just as he is when he says that they suffered this '*because they had sinned against the Lord*'. Contemporary reality (assuming that the Jews were still with limited exception excluded from Jerusalem) is serving, and at the same time is coloured by, the needs of the exegesis of the 'Old Testament'.

Such exegesis, particularly of the prophets, although directed at an internal or 'home' audience plays a significant role in Christian anti-Jewish polemic; the prophecies of doom are regularly interpreted as directed against the Jews; those of hope and promise are seen as finding their fulfilment in the Christian Church. Undoubtedly this makes what is said about the Jews tendentious, but not necessarily pure fantasy: it is in Jerome's commentary on Ezekiel that we hear of the Jewish traditions, for which he, probably following their practice, uses the Greek term *deuterōseis*,[5] although he dismisses them as 'myths'; he also reports that 'the Hebrews say' that the Babylonian teachers wear parchments around their foreheads on which is written the decalogue – it may have been the case that phylacteries were rarely worn in Palestine in his time although the inclusion of the decalogue goes against the evidence (*On Ezekiel* XI 36; VII 24). Augustine's report, in commenting on Deuteronomy 11:20, that *mesusoth* were not in frequent use may well be right, although this is undoubtedly coloured by his assertion, as he considers contemporary elaborate houses, that the injunction that they be fixed to the doorpost *could* not be followed literally (*Questions on the Heptateuch* V 17); that the injunctions of the Law could not be followed literally is of course even more a theological statement about the Christian understanding of the Law's true significance. On the other hand, when Eusebius says the Jews no longer have a king, leaders, chief priests, prophets, Pharisees or Sadducees, or others of old revered by them (*On Isaiah* I 81), he is guided by his 'text', Isaiah 22:2–3, 'all your rulers have fled together'. By contrast, Origen, this time commenting on the New Testament, on Matthew 23:2–3, declares that one can see 'even now among the Jews' scribes and Pharisees sitting on the chair of Moses (*Commentary on Matthew* IX). We cannot assume from this that Origen is deliberately referring to contemporary rabbis as Pharisees or even witnessing to the historic link between them; again it is his text that guides him, and as his exegesis develops it soon becomes clear that he is as much concerned with those within the Church who teach only a literal interpretation of the scriptures as he is with the Jewish teachers whose characteristic method, in his view, this is.

Each of these authors offers valuable information about the situation, life, or beliefs of the Jews of their day. This is particularly true of Origen and Jerome, both of whom had contacts with contemporary Jewish teachers, to whom they are often indebted for exegesis of the scriptures;[6] none the less, their indebtedness apparently did little to soften the harshness of their polemic against the Jews or against those influenced by them. On the other hand, other authors also must have been aware of well-established Jewish communities in their midst and yet betray much less direct knowledge. Tertullian's anti-Jewish polemic is particularly virulent but he offers only a few hints of contemporary Jewish communities in Carthage, and these mainly as illustrations of some other point;[7] when he is writing against the Jews they become for him the people of the Old Testament who rejected and persecuted the prophets that spoke of the coming of Jesus, and who eventually rejected both him and the Church. It has been well argued that his polemic is sharpest not in his work against the Jews but in his attack against Marcion, the second-century 'heretic' who rejected the Old Testament and drove a wedge between the creator God there encountered and the Father revealed by Jesus Christ. Marcion's views were undoubtedly attractive to many and provoked a barrage of refutations; forced to justify the Church's retention of the Jewish scriptures while rejecting the literal observance of many of the precepts within them, and in order to preserve the consistency and unity of God's character, the early Christian writers presented the initial recipients of those scriptures, the Jews, as consistently blind to God's word, unable to see in their own scriptures the promised coming of Christ, needing the injunctions of the Law to control their many vices, or perceiving only its literal meaning, which even then they disobey (see Efroymson in Davies 1979). Thus it is that the Jews of Christian polemic are so often a uniform, stylized type, trapped within the Old Testament, first within the charges brought against the people by the prophets, and secondly within the regulations which they can only interpret literally and yet cannot observe literally, in the past because of their own character, in the present because of the loss of the Temple. So, for example, in the fourth century, contemporary Jewish claims to celebrate the Passover validly are 'proved' fraudulent, for the Temple is laid waste, they no longer have any priests, the stipulated victim is not to be found, God rejects animal sacrifice (eg. Isaiah 1.11), and the people are in any case deserted by God! (Zeno of Verona, *Tractates* I 19: 28; 51). It is this theologically moulded 'scriptural' mask that gives rise to the false impression that the authors are blind to the real face of contemporary Judaism.

CONFLICT AND CONTACT

In none of this intertwining of historical experience and theological rationale, of the interpretation of the past and the realities of the present, can we ignore the encounter between Judaism and Christianity as a meeting not of two strangers, but of two who were irrevocably bound up with each other. Of course the problems of identity, definition and distancing were not fully reciprocal; Judaism was more of a problem for Christianity than Christianity for Judaism, although the latter probably engaged in more debate and polemic than the surviving Jewish sources betray. Yet the question of boundary, relationship and opposition is nowhere clearer than in the existence of what, in the absence of a better term, we must call Judaizing. As Simon already argued, it was often the vitality and so the attraction of contemporary Judaism that provoked the strength of the reaction and of what he termed anti-Semitism. It is equally often pointed out that many of the attacks against 'the Jews' are in reality directed against 'Judaizing Christians' – Christians adopting Jewish beliefs or practices. As we have already seen, this is hinted at in Origen's exegesis of Matthew 23 and even more clearly in his interpretation of Matthew 16:5–12 where those who eat 'the bread of the Pharisees' are those Christians who do not recognize that the Law is spiritual or discover the things of which the Law is a shadow (*On Matthew* XII 5). Reflecting this awareness of the true provocation of the polemic, Chrysostom's sermons *Adversus Iudaeos* ('Against the Jews') have recently been translated under the more eirenic title *Against Judaising Christians* (Harkins 1977). Here particularly the relation between reality and theological perception, or between different perceptions, needs careful disentangling.

The (theological) perception of the early Christian writers (at least outside the New Testament) is of two separate entities, Judaism and Christianity, which have been separated virtually from birth. It is a model implicitly adopted by Simon when in Part 2 of his book he discusses the polemics under the heading of 'The Conflict of Orthodoxies'; for him the conflict is the aspect of Jewish–Christian relations 'involving the *orthodox* members of each group' (p. xiii; my italics). The other, equally significant, aspect comes under the heading 'Contact and Assimilation' (Part 3) or 'contacts resulting in *syncretism*' (p. xviii; my italics). This image of 'orthodoxy: conflict versus contact: syncretism' is the same as that projected, for example, by Jerome in his argument against the continuing observance of the Law by converts to Christianity from Judaism. In a passage whose lack of clarity suggests he is not speaking from personal knowledge, he introduces the Ebionites 'who pretend that they are Christians'; in an attempt to identify them he goes on to speak of a contemporary heresy 'throughout all the synagogues of the East among the Jews', called 'of the Minaei' or, popularly, 'the Nazaraeans'. They believe in Christ as Son of God, in the virgin birth, his suffering under Pilate and his resurrection. For all this, 'while they wish to be both Jews and Christians, they are neither Jews nor Christians' (*Letters* 112, 13). We need not here pursue the question how this report relates to others about the Ebionites, Nazaraeans, or other 'Jewish Christian' groups, nor how the statement that 'even today they are cursed by the Pharisees' relates to the application and history of the so-called 'benediction against heretics' or *birkath ha-minim*. The most revealing point is that for Jerome neither they nor anyone else can be both Jew and Christian, but that, if we can trust Jerome, this is precisely how they did see themselves and indeed, if they were to be found in the synagogues despite being cursed by contemporary 'Pharisees', how they actually lived.

In a different setting, the Christians of Antioch who observed the sabbath, joined in Jewish fasts and festivities, and respected the awe and sanctity of the synagogue 'were not marginal renegades who came to church only infrequently – they appear to be regular members of his [John Chrysostom's] congregation who thought they could remain members of the Church while observing Jewish rites and customs' (Wilken 1983: 175–6). For Chrysostom, however, the Jews are bent on bringing destruction to the Christian flock, and those who succumb are 'mixing what cannot be mixed' (*Against the Jews* IV 3, 6).[8] Such testimonies could be multiplied,[9] although it is hard to determine when we are being persuaded by the rhetoric of the speaker to see a more substantial threat than numbers justified. Origen warns Christians listening to him on a Sunday against bringing up what they had learnt the previous day in the synagogue (*Homilies on Leviticus* V 8); yet when he interprets Exodus 12:46, 'in one house shall it [the Passover] be eaten', as a prohibition against 'eating' in church and in the synagogue of the Jews or, equally, in church and in the synagogue of heretics (*Selections on Exodus* 12, 46), we may suspect he is guided as much by text and rhetoric as by contemporary, contrary practice.

Behind these perceptions lies a complex reality. What Chrysostom, Origen and others testify to is ordinary Christians participating in Jewish life. By contrast, Jerome's appeal to the Ebionites belongs to a series of descriptions of groups with apparently fixed identities, and with beliefs (for example, a 'low' christology) or practices (observance of all or part of the Jewish Law) which in the patristic writers' eyes betray too close a convergence with Jewish belief and practice. Sometimes such groups are presented as close to the Jews, sometimes as bitterly hostile. From the time of Irenaeus they are categorized as 'heretical', and, like other heretical sects as seen through Christian eyes, soon acquire names implying a specific allegiance or origin – Symmachians, Nazaraeans, Ebionites – genealogies (usually going back to apostolic or immediately post-apostolic times) and other marks of a fixed identity, namely specific beliefs and adherence to particular (sectarian) writings.[10] They figure not only in catalogues of heresies but also in other settings as sources or illustrations of particular views (their millenarian beliefs: Jerome, *Commentary on Zechariah* III 9; *Commentary on Joel* III 7–8) or practices (being both circumcised and baptized: Augustine, *Against Cresconius* I 31, 36), and as a threat to other Christians (Augustine, *On Baptism* VII 1, 1). In modern scholarship these groups are commonly labelled 'Jewish Christian', a confusing term since it can also be applied to the earliest stages of Christianity in general, to patterns of Christian theology with Jewish roots or parallels, or to Christians of Jewish birth. Patristic sources are more likely to label them by 'sect' or to call them 'Judaizers' (so Jerome in the references just given where they are associated with 'the Jews': 'the Jews and our *iudaisantes*').

A different group – or a different perception – appears in the shadowy figures who feature in rabbinic literature as the 'sinners of Israel' (*poshe'e yisrael*); it has been forcefully argued that since these people are sometimes treated more openly than informers, those who deny Torah or resurrection, or than those who separate themselves from the community, they represent 'Jewish Christians' who continued to observe sabbath, festivals, circumcision and certain dietary and purity laws (Marmorstein 1935). Similarly, while a simplistic identification of the 'heretics' or *minim* of rabbinic sources with Jewish Christians is now widely rejected, it still seems likely that they included some Jewish Christians. This does not mean, however, that we can readily identify them with the same 'Jewish Christian' groups as those of the Christian heresiological writings.

The perceptions or presentations of the Christian writers offer little clarity and lead naturally into the terminological confusion of modern scholarship. Even the evidence we have cited suggests first that some people within the churches were attracted by Judaism for a variety of reasons, many probably not 'theological' in terms of the arguments explored earlier in this discussion, and shared in certain public aspects of Jewish life. How they perceived their activities or were viewed by other Jews within the synagogues is left to our imagination, but our imagination should be coloured by the fact that Judaism had long had a fascination for outsiders within the Graeco-Roman world and that visitors to the synagogue were rarely repulsed even when active proselytism was not favoured.[11] It is usually assumed that these 'Judaizers' – although the term is probably too specific for this group – were of Gentile origin (as of course were the majority of Christians). In fact the genealogical model, so loved by the anti-heretical writers of the early Church, is frequently transferred to this group so as to speak of a continuous tendency to 'judaize' from the opponents of Ignatius (to whom we shall return) to those of Chrysostom (see p. 89), although such an interpretation introduces a uniformity that not even the sources attempt.

Despite the superficial 'concreteness' of the descriptions of the second group, namely 'Jewish Christians' with fixed, theologically grounded identities and presumably independent structures, the traces that they have left are hardly less elusive than those of the first group. It has been left to modern scholarship to try to re-create the reality behind the conflicting descriptions given by the church fathers and to determine which writers betray any genuine knowledge; it is a matter of unresolved debate whether members of such groups were of Jewish or Gentile birth, and whether some can be traced back in historical continuity to the more positive attitudes towards the abiding validity of the Jewish Law ascribed in the New Testament to Peter or to James, while others are products of later 'syncretizing' tendencies. The church fathers may have done most to mislead by combining a genealogical model with an institutional model of 'counter-churches'; although they apply that model even more determinedly to gnostic groups, the gnostic literature from Nag Hammadi does little to support such clear 'gnostic' self-consciousness and suggests that often the 'gnostics' were still within the Church, while maintaining a critical distance from some of its institutions. In our case an agreed definition, identification and analysis of comparable 'sectarian' Jewish Christian literature has yet to be achieved.[12]

IMAGE AND REALITY

Fortunately it is not our task here to attempt to clarify the picture any further. It is enough that the picture that has emerged so far is one of considerable complexity. In each case we must ask not so much how clear are the boundaries between Christianity and Judaism, but more particularly who is drawing them and for whom. We may illustrate the question by turning to one of the earliest post-New Testament sources, Ignatius of Antioch. Travelling from that city, where he was bishop, to Rome, where he was to be martyred (soon after 110 AD), Ignatius wrote letters to six churches on his route; some of these he had visited, while from the others he had received delegations and news. The burning concern with unity which infuses these letters has as its reverse side a polemic against false belief. The dominant point of conflict is the reality of Jesus Christ's humanity and death, dominant perhaps in reality but also because of its consequences for any understanding of Ignatius's own, eagerly anticipated, martyrdom. However, in two letters, those to the Magnesians and the Philadelphians, the problem is of 'Judaism'.

We may leave aside here two important questions; first whether Ignatius is reflecting the situation in Antioch, which he knew somewhat better, or the situation in the churches of Asia Minor to whom he writes; secondly whether there is but one heresy in these churches, which combines Judaizing elements with a docetic christology, or whether the problem in Magnesia and Philadelphia is 'simply' that of Judaizing.

Writing to the church at Magnesia, which he had not personally visited, he says, 'If up to now we live according to Judaism, we confess that we have not received grace'; 'It is impossible to speak of Jesus Christ and to judaize. For Christianity did not put its faith in Judaism but Judaism in Christianity' (*To the Magnesians* 8, 1: 10, 3). He warns the Philadelphians, of whose situation he did have personal experience, 'if anyone interprets Judaism to you, do not listen to him; for it is better to hear Christianity from a circumcised man than Judaism from an uncircumcised' (*To the Philadelphians* 6,1). For Ignatius there are two separate and contrary entities, *Ioudaismos* and *Christianismos*. The former term we meet already in the Maccabaean literature (2 Maccabees 2:21; 8:1; 14:8; 4 Maccabees 4:26), perhaps representing a significant step in combining life and beliefs within a single term; *Christianismos* appears first in Ignatius (also *To the Romans* 3, 3) and may well be modelled on *Ioudaismos* by antithesis. If we ask what 'Judaism' actually means for Ignatius we get a remarkably circumscribed answer, particularly when we recall that Antioch was the home of a large and flourishing Jewish community of whom he must have had some knowledge. *To the Philadelphians* 6, 1 (just quoted) depends for its irony on an assumption that Judaism is irreversibly characterized by circumcision.[13] Not surprisingly, the other characteristic is sabbath: those who 'converted' from Judaism to Christianity either the prophets or the first disciples no longer sabbathized (*sabbatizontes*) but lived 'according to the lord's [day]' (*kata kuriakēn zōntes*) (*To the Magnesians* 9, 1).[14] Again Ignatius does not elaborate what he means by this and it is left to modern scholarship to draw links with his emphasis elsewhere on the communal meetings of the Church, which he accuses his opponents of avoiding, and to speculate how the assertion relates to their teaching or practice. For Ignatius Judaism and Christianity are two separate systems with typical 'phenomenological' characteristics – for Judaism, the same characteristics as were most noted by the pagan world, circumcision and sabbath. The only relationship between the two is a one-way passage which virtually renders Judaism obsolete. Such is the separation that the prophets belong to Christianity and not to Judaism (*To the Magnesians* 8, 2) – there can be no common ground between the two.

So Ignatius; yet it is equally clear that this does not represent the real situation which he was addressing. As is also the case with his docetic opponents, the problem he is addressing is one within the Church; at Philadelphia he found himself in an exegetical debate with other members of the Church about the Old Testament where he failed to prove his point (8, 2). Inevitably then modern scholars speak of the problem within these churches (or perhaps in reality at Antioch) as one of 'Judaizing', although interpretations of the character of this Judaizing vary greatly; it was members of the Church who were appealing to the scriptures, 'intepreting' or accepting interpretations of Judaism, and perhaps 'sabbathizing'. It was a situation of weak or poorly defined boundaries, whether those were the boundaries between the Jewish and Christian communities or, more probably, the internal boundaries within the Christian community which encompassed a broad range of possible belief and practice. This, however, is not Ignatius's perception; for him 'Judaizing' is 'Judaism' and is incompatible with Christianity. To put it anachronistically, Ignatius is working with the model of orthodoxies – orthodoxies which, despite his well-articulated theology of the Church, are determined by visible social and structural characteristics; the members of the churches, however, were living within a different pattern but not one that merits the term 'syncretism' or assimilation.

Only in very broad terms can we see a continuity of problem and response between Ignatius and Chrysostom; certainly the situation of the latter cannot be read into that of the former – we do not know what the Christians of Magnesia were doing on the sabbath, if anything. Not only were Judaism and Christianity not the homogeneous entities the polemical writers present, but the situation of both the Jews and the Christians changed radically through the centuries and so too must have the varying patterns of relations between them. Clearly this is not to imply that at any point during this period the boundary between Judaism and Christianity was imaginary. Even though we must avoid reading back into the first and second centuries later conceptions of orthodoxy, none the less Ignatius's perception represents the dominant and formative perception of the developing self-consciousness of the Church, as it was expressed in literature, liturgy, creed and structures. External factors too reflected and confirmed the same reality; the Christians knew that it was as Christians that they were persecuted, while they were denied the privileges of protection they saw enjoyed by the Jews. Even here not everyone may have shared the same perception; Christian writers warn their audience against accepting the protection of the synagogue during persecution (*Martyrdom of Pionius* 13). If some accepted such protection rather than apostasizing into paganism it was presumably because for them Judaism was an acceptable spiritual home (see Jerome, *On Famous Men* 41); they would not have agreed with Origen's exegesis of the three servants whose questions prompt Peter to deny Jesus, as first the Jewish synagogue, secondly the Gentiles, and thirdly the heretics (*Commentary on Matthew* CXIV on Matthew 26:69–75). Here, however, the numbers appear to be very small compared with the anxieties about and supposed evidence of Judaizing.

Rather, we see here as throughout, that the relationship between Jewish and Christian groups in the Roman Empire, and between 'Judaism' and 'Christianity', was a complex, contradictory and rarely stable one. An attractive rhetorical conclusion would be that the theological relationship projected by the church fathers is simple, consistent and unchanging! It may be truer to say that the dialectic between practice (?history) and theology shares in the same complexity.[15]

NOTES

1 For example, Schürer (1901: 703), 'So sind die Juden immer mehr das geworden, was sie ihrem Wesen nach waren: Fremdlinge in der heidnischen Welt'.

2 For John see E. Grässer, 'Die Juden als Teufelssöhne in Johannes 8,37–47', in Eckert 1967: 157–70, and the discussion on pp. 210–12; the same question could be asked of Matthew or of Luke Acts. For a patristic source compare Harkins 1977: x, 'Even if he [Chrysostom] was motivated by an overzealous pastoral spirit, many of his remarks are patently anti-Semitic. For these objectively unChristian acts he cannot be excused even if he is a product of his times.'

3 It is not a very big step from the sentiments of Eusebius or Tertullian to the historical statement that after the disasters of the revolt against Rome the Jews became increasingly 'strangers in the Gentile world' quoted above.

4 This has been retained in the new edition (1973) although with a counterbalancing note of hope and has been quoted by other 'histories' since.

5 See F. Millar in this volume, pp. 114–15. Jerome also uses the term elsewhere as do other writers of the period.

6 See Lange 1976; Krauss 1892–4.

7 For example, in *On Fasting* 16 where he speaks of Jews having left their 'Temples', praying in open air when they fast; *To the Nations* I 13 about those who follow Jewish festivals, sabbath, '*cena pura*', etc. It has also been argued that Tertullian shows contact with Jewish Haggadah.

8 Harkins follows Chrysostom (I 4, 7) when he speaks of the 'demi-Christians' (1977: xxxix).

9 Simon 1948/64: 306–38; Wilken 1983: 66–83.

10 See Klijn and Reinink 1973 for a full analysis of the texts.

11 See Goodman in this volume.

12 Work, and so the literature, in this area is now growing fast, and so this paragraph has inevitably included gross simplifications. For some of the debate see *Aspects* 1965, and for a more recent bibliography, Manns 1979.

13 Unless we are to speculate about 'Judaizers' who advocated a Judaism without the requirement of male circumcision. This is not impossible but the antithesis seems to be more the expression of Ignatius's perception of the two entities and the one-way relation between them than a report of the 'heretics'' views.

14 Or perhaps 'the lord's life'; there is no noun with the feminine

adjective 'lord's'. 'Day' provides a better contrast with the reference to sabbath, although the main emphasis is a way of life.

15 This paper was completed while on leave with the support of A. v. Humboldt Stiftung at the Institut für Antikes Judentum und Hellenistische Religionsgeschichte at the University of Tübingen.

BIBLIOGRAPHY

Aspects du Judéo-Christianisme (1965) (Colloque de Strasbourg 23–5 avril 1964), Paris.

Blumenkranz, B. (1958) 'Augustin et les Juifs – Augustin et le judaïsme', *Recherches Augustiniennes* 1: 225–41.

Davies, A. (ed.) (1979) *AntiSemitism and the Foundations of Christianity*, New York.

Eckert, W. (1967) *Antijudaismus im Neuen Testament?*, Munich.

Efroymson, D. (1979) 'The Patristic Connection', in Davies 1979: 98–117.

Harkins, P. (1977) *Saint John Chrysostom. Discourses against Judaising Christians* (The Fathers of the Church 68), Washington DC.

Hruby, K. (1971) *Juden und Judentum bei den Kirchenvätern*, Zurich.

Klijn A. F. J. and Reinink, G. J. (1973) *Patristic Evidence for Jewish Christian Sects* (Supplement to Novum Testamentum, 36), Leiden.

Kraabel, A. T. (1971) 'Melito the Bishop and the Synagogue at Sardis: Text and Context', in D. G. Mitten, J. G. Pedley and J. A. Scott (eds) *Studies Presented to George M. A. Hanfmann*, Mainz, 77–85.

Krauss, S. (1892–4) 'The Jews in the Works of the Church Fathers', *Jewish Quarterly Review* 5: 122–57; 6: 82–99, 225–61.

Lange, N. de (1976) *Origen and the Jews: Studies in Jewish Christian Relations in Third-Century Palestine*, Cambridge.

Manns, F. (1979) *Bibliographie du Judéo-Christianisme*, Jerusalem.

Marmorstein, A. (1935) 'Judaism and Christianity in the Middle of the Third Century', *Hebrew Union College Annual* 10: 223–63.

Ruether, R. (1974) *Faith and Fratricide*, New York.

Schürer, E. (1901) *Geschichte des jüdischen Volkes im Zeitalter Jesu Christi* I, Leipzig; revised English edn by G. Vermes and F. Millar (1973), Edinburgh.

Simon, M. (1948/64) *Verus Israel*, 2nd edn with postscript 1964, Paris; cited by page according to the English translation by H. McKeating, (1986) Oxford.

Wilken, R. (1971) *Judaism and the Early Christian Mind*, New Haven, Conn.

Wilken R. (1983) *John Chrysostom and the Jews: Rhetoric and Reality in the Late 4th Century*, Berkeley and Los Angeles.

5

THE JEWS OF THE GRAECO-ROMAN DIASPORA BETWEEN PAGANISM AND CHRISTIANITY, AD 312–438

Fergus Millar

INTRODUCTION: AURELIUS SAMOHIL

In the year 383 in Catania in Sicily a Jew named Aurelius Samohil bought a tomb in which to lay the remains of himself and his wife, and recorded the fact for posterity in an inscription in Latin, with an introductory line in Hebrew, while adorning the stone with two incised representations of menorahs. The text, written in a rough approximation to Latin, runs as follows:[1]

> Shalom to Israel, amen, amen; Shalom Shmuel [Hebrew], I, Aurelius Samohil have bought [this] tomb [*memoria*] for myself and my wife Lasiferina, who died on the 12th day before the Kalends of November, on Friday [*diae Veneris*], on the eighth day of the month, in the consulship of Merobaudes for the second time and of Saturnus. She lived 22 years in peace. I adjure you by the *honores* of the *patriarchae*, and similarly adjure you by the Law [or the Light – *licem*] which the Lord gave to the Jews, that no one should open the tomb and put in another body over our bones. But if anyone were to open it let him give 10 pounds of silver to the *fiscus*.

The inscription is perhaps even more remarkable than it may appear at first sight; and it also raises more problems than are immediately apparent. What is clear is that Aurelius Samohil proclaims himself unambiguously as a Jew, with a proud attachment to Jewish religious tradition. When he records that the Lord (*dominus*) gave *licem* to the Jews, he almost certainly means the Law (*lex*); though he might have meant 'the light' (*lux*). What is clear at any rate is that he is living by a combination of a secular dating-system and calendar and a Jewish one. 'Friday' is expressed as 'di(a)e Veneris', 'the day of Venus', the term which would evolve into 'venerdi'/'vendredi'. But the month referred to must be Marheshvan. It cannot be certain that he knew Hebrew himself; but at the very least he was in a position to have some appropriate Hebrew words inscribed.

Who are the *patriarchae* to whose *honores* he refers? He may well mean the biblical patriarchs. But the inscription might alternatively be evidence of the extension to Sicily of the influence of the contemporary Jewish patriarchs in Palestine, to whom imperial legal pronouncements (see p. 117) first refer in 392, as *clarissimi et illustres Patriarchae* (*Cod. Theod.* XVI 8, 8). If Aurelius Samohil is referring to them, that in its turn raises the much wider question of the nature of Diaspora Judaism in the late Roman period. Are we to think of a relatively integrated and homogenous Jewish world, in which all or most of the communities in the provinces of the Roman Empire observed a Judaism closely resembling that 'rabbinic' Judaism of Palestine, which was just giving birth to the 'Palestinian' or 'Jerusalem' Talmud – or which the Talmud presents to us as 'the' Judaism of late Roman Palestine? And if so, was this integration achieved by active contacts and supervision from Palestine? There is in fact one item of Roman legal evidence, an instruction sent in 399 by Arcadius and Honorius to (Valerius) Messalla, Praetorian prefect of Italy and Africa, which implies that the *patriarcha* was sending emissaries (*apostoli*) to collect money in this area, that is to say, the Latin-speaking west (*Cod. Theod.* XVI 8, 14). How far such *apostoli* exercised any religious authority or influence is of course a more complex question.

But the Roman legal evidence also raises another possibility: for it shows that among the numerous and varied Greek terms used to designate the officials of individual Jewish Diaspora communities, the term *patriarcha* also figured.[2] So Aurelius Samohil *may* simply have been referring to such local Jewish officials.

The most remarkable fact about the inscription, however, is that it is both the longest Hebrew and the longest Latin documentary text known from the Jewish Diaspora of this period. It is beyond question that the best-attested language of the Diaspora Jewish communities is Greek, and we need not doubt that the

Bible in Greek translation was very commonly used in the synagogues of the Diaspora (Colorni 1964), just as it could be even in the Greek-speaking communities of Palestine itself (jSotah 7.21b; Schürer 1986: 142). That does not prove that the Hebrew Bible was unknown in the Diaspora (for biblical scrolls in Hebrew in use in Rome in the 380s see p. 115); nor does it prove that Hebrew or Aramaic was nowhere spoken or used. At least for the Greek provinces, the recent publication of a *ketubah* written in Aramaic in Antinoopolis in Egypt, and securely dated to AD 417, must completely reopen the question of the use of Semitic languages in the Diaspora; and perhaps all the more so because it contains such a high proportion of transliterated Greek, indicating the use in the text of the language of daily life (Sirat *et al.* 1986).

Aurelius Samohil could at any rate have a line of commonplace expressions inscribed in Hebrew. But the fact that he could express himself as an observant Jew in Latin is far more significant. As we will see, there is very clear evidence for the existence of Jewish communities in many parts of the Latin-speaking west in this period, from Africa to Italy, Spain and Gaul. Though they may well have begun typically as immigrant communities of Greek-speakers, it is very likely that by now many of their members used Latin in ordinary life. The story of the conversion of the Jewish community of Minorca in 417 (see pp. 119–20) clearly presupposes the use of Latin equally by the Jews and by the surrounding Christians. But what of the Bible itself? The Christians seem to have had Latin translations of books of the Bible since the second century. Might the synagogue service ever have been conducted in Latin? And what of religious disputation, teaching, or writing? Augustine's story of Jewish opinions being asked on a point of biblical interpretation at Oea in North Africa seems to imply the use of Latin at least to discuss the text (see p. 115). But whether there was a Jewish Bible in Latin remains wholly uncertain (Colorni 1964: 73f.). The social, intellectual and religious history of the Jews in the Latin-speaking environment of the western half of the Later Roman Empire remains a largely unexplored field. Fortunately we have some evidence, however scattered, which allows rather more direct access to the Judaism of the Diaspora in the Greek-speaking part of the Empire.

THE DIASPORA IN A GREEK ENVIRONMENT

The Diaspora of the eastern part of the Empire has certainly left far fuller evidence, both documentary and archaeological, than is available for the west; and some of this evidence needs to be set out, to establish a framework, before we look at the much more complex issue of the relations between religious groups. But as it happens, some, though not all, of the archaeological evidence itself also illustrates with the greatest clarity the effects of religious conflict, above all in the fifth century.

We may begin with the well-known synagogue at Stobi in ancient Macedonia, in the south of present-day Yugoslavia. A substantial inscription of the late second or early third century records that a private house was made over to the Jewish community, and converted for use as a synagogue. If the conditions of its use were broken, a very large fine was to be paid to the *patriarchēs*: this was surely not the *nasi* or *ethnarchēs*, far away in Palestine (the forerunner of the fourth-century *patriarcha*), whose rise to power had hardly begun (Goodman 1983: 111f.). More probably, legal evidence suggests (p. 98), this will have been a local official. Later the synagogue was replaced by a more elaborate one. But before the end of the fourth century this synagogue was to be destroyed, and replaced by a Christian basilica built directly on the site (Schürer 1986–7: 67–8).

A very similar story is revealed by the Belgian excavations at the great city of Apamea in Syria. For near the centre of the city, not far from the famous Great Colonnade which runs north-south, and some 120 m south of the main east-west street, the excavators discovered the mosaic floor of a late fourth-century synagogue, with nineteen mosaic inscriptions recording the names of those who paid for the laying of the mosaic in and around the year 391 (J. C. Balty 1981: 139f.; J. Balty 1986: 6f.). The mosaics are strictly geometric and non-representational; the inscriptions, all in Greek, show a number of Hebrew names in transliteration: 'Nemeas' (Nehemiah), 'Phineas', 'Eisakios', 'Saoulos'. They also illustrate the complexity of office-holding within Diaspora communities, revealing *archisynagōgoi*, *gerousiarchoi*, *presbyteroi* and a man described as *(h)azzan* or *diakonos*. One of the donors was Ilasios son of Eisakios, '*archisynagōgos* of the Antiochenes' – the Jewish community of Antioch to the north, of which more later (p. 115). It would be difficult to find better evidence of a Jewish community established at the heart of the Greek city – except that, once again, a Christian church was built exactly on the site of the synagogue in the fifth century, to be enlarged and adorned in the sixth (Napoleone-Lemaire and Balty 1969).

A very similar progression is visible at Gerasa in Jordan, where the mosaics of a fourth- or fifth-century synagogue – this time with representational elements depicting the story of Noah – underlie a Christian church which seems to have been constructed in AD 530–1.[3] But here we are in a bilingual Greek/Aramaic setting, almost in the Holy Land itself; and it is better to turn to a contrasting case, the vast synagogue of Sardis in western Asia Minor (Seager and Kraabel 1983; Schürer 1986–7: 21–2). In this instance the building which eventually became a synagogue was not originally built as such, but comprised one part of a complex of buildings in the centre of the city, including a bath-house and a gymnasium. The section which by the third century had come into use as a synagogue consisted of a large basilica-like hall with a forecourt; its dimensions far surpass those of any other ancient synagogue, for the main building is some 80 m by 20 m, and the forecourt some 20 m². It seems to have reached its completed form as a synagogue in the fourth century, as coins trapped under the mosaic floor show. Some marble revetment also dates to this period, and some adornment still seems to have been added in the fifth and perhaps the sixth century. Some of the dedicatory inscriptions from the mosaic floors and the marble revetments of the walls have been published in full (Robert 1964), and others reported (Hanfmann 1967: 27–32); the entire corpus is now being prepared for publication by Professor J. H. Kroll. Taken as a group, they clearly support the impression of a firmly Jewish community which is also integrated in the wider city. A number of donors describe themselves as *theosebēs*, 'God-worshipper' – a term which we can now be confident meant a Gentile attached to a Jewish community without being a full convert (Reynolds and Tannenbaum 1987: 48f.). Others are labelled as *bouleutēs*, 'town-councillor', an indication of high social standing even in a period when this role was frequently an unwelcome burden. Perhaps most striking is the mosaic inscription which reads 'Vow of Samoe, *hiereus* and *sophodidaskalos*'. In the context *hiereus* (priest) can only mean that he was a *cohen*; *sophodidaskalos* should mean 'teacher of wisdom', perhaps to be thought of as a translation of *talmid hakham*. Whether we should think of such a person as a 'rabbi', and if so how we should (once again) conceive of the relations between the 'rabbinic' Judaism of Palestine and that of the Diaspora, are questions to which we will come back (see pp. 110–11 and 113–15).

The Sardis synagogue, however, tells a different story from those of Stobi, Apamea, or Gerasa, for it seems to have remained in use as a synagogue until the seventh century. But all of them will serve to remind us that we have to see the religious history of the later Roman Empire at various different levels, one of which is the elementary one of street-level coexistence, or conflict, between groups professing different beliefs. Jewish synagogues (not to speak of Samaritan ones, see Crown 1986; Rabello 1987), Christian churches and pagan temples coexisted as visible structures within the bounds of provincial towns. The temples of course had long been there. But visible, recognizable synagogues were quite a new feature, and churches even more recent. Dura-Europos on the Euphrates may provide a model for the earlier period; when the town was destroyed by the Persians in the 250s, it already had a Christian church and a synagogue – but both had been constructed within existing houses like the first version of the synagogue at Stobi (Rostovtzeff 1938: ch. 4; Kraeling 1967 and 1979; Gutmann 1973). How visible and recognizable as structures synagogues in pagan towns typically were in the classical period remains unclear, though the Alexandrian mob in AD 38, for instance, had had no difficulty in finding those in the city and forcibly setting up pagan ornaments in them (Philo, *Against Flaccus* 41–52). But the few archaeologically known synagogues of the fourth century were more elaborate and explicitly Jewish structures than any attested before; and churches, constructed as such, were a wholly new and revolutionary feature of the urban landscape. There are slight traces of such purpose-built churches before the conversion of Constantine in 312; but it was the wave of church-building, mainly in basilica form, immediately after that, which began the transformation of the ancient city (Krautheimer 1967; Milburn 1988: 83f.).

THE CONVERSION OF CONSTANTINE AND ITS CONSEQUENCES

The conversion of Constantine to Christianity in 312 is both an undeniable historical fact and (it could be argued) a significant turning-point in the nature of the state. For it was from that moment that religious conviction came to structure the activities the state in a quite new way; above all the Christian emperors came, step by step, to define the rights of their subjects differentially, in terms of their attachment to different religious groups. The year 312 was *not*, however, the moment when Christianity became 'the official religion of the Roman state'. There was as yet no such thing; and what happened in that year was simply to make Christianity (whether 'Catholic' or Arian) the religion of successive emperors, other than Julian (AD 361–3).

It is curious that, in spite of many discussions of various aspects (e.g. Alföldi 1948; MacMullen 1984; Barnes 1989), it remains very difficult to analyse or sum up the impact of the Christian beliefs of Constantine and his successors on the pagan cult-practices of the Empire. What is certain is that a few prominent temples in the Greek east were destroyed by imperial action already under Constantine (Eusebius, *Life of Constantine* IV 55–6); that large amounts of treasure and ornaments were looted from temples (*Life of Constantine* IV 54); and that a succession of imperial pronouncements were directed against sacrifice, divination and magical practices (*Life of Constantine* II 45; *Cod. Theod.* XVI 10, 1f.). But it is equally certain that for more than half a century the vast majority of pagan temples remained open, and that cults and sacrifices continued. A new, more emphatically Christianizing phase, to which we will return later (see pp. 116–21), opened only in the 380s, to reach a sort of culmination in the 430s.

The significance of the period from 312 to the 430s in the history of Diaspora Judaism is, first, that it was a unique phase of overt coexistence, competition and conflict between fundamentally different religious systems. This coexistence was first of all, as already indicated, a literal coexistence within the bounds of countless towns, large and small. Second, it was an uneasy coexistence, where competition might take peaceful forms, as in Jerome's marvellous story of how the hermit Hilarion secured by the application of holy water the victory of a Christian racing-chariot in games held at Gaza: so much faster was the Christian-owned chariot that their opponents hardly glimpsed the horses' backs as they sped by (Jerome, *Life of Hilarion* 20). But it was also a coexistence which could at any time break out into communal violence, sometimes prompted by, and often going beyond, the explicit wishes and intentions of the emperors. Far too little has been made, in the religious history of the fourth century, of the evidence for local Christian attacks on temples (the evidence is collected by Fowden 1978). Such attacks had already begun under Constantine (ruling in the east 324–37) and continued under Constantius (337–61); see now the important paper by Barnes 1989. The response was a wave of pagan violence unleashed by the arrival on the throne of a self-professed and militant pagan, Julian, in 361. Julian himself explicitly intended not to create Christian martyrs. His pagan subjects, however, had other ideas, and had local scores to settle. To take only two examples, at Heliopolis in Phoenicia a Christian deacon, Cyrillus, had taken part in the smashing of idols as early as the reign of Constantine; when Julian came to the throne the local pagans killed and disembowelled him (Theodoret, *Church History* III 3). Then, under Constantius, at Arethusa in Syria the bishop Mark went about the conversion of pagans 'with more spirit than caution' and destroyed a magnificent temple; under Julian he was publicly tortured, thrown into a sewer and tossed in the air, to land on the upturned styluses of the local pagan schoolboys (Sozomenus, *Church History* V 10).

The main significance of this very clear evidence for underlying communal-religious tensions for the position of Judaism is its relevance to similar conflicts in the period of overt Christian militancy in the 380s and after, of which more below. But it should be noted that Ambrose of Milan, in his famous *Letter* 40 of 388 (one of the prime testimonies to the Christian anti-Jewish militancy of that period) claims that under Julian not only pagans but also Jews had been active in destroying Christian churches:

And to be sure if I were to talk in terms of the law of peoples [*iure gentium*] I would say how many basilicas of the Church the Jews burned in the time of Julian's rule: two at Damascus, of which one has barely been repaired, but at the expense of the Church not the Synagogue; the other basilica lies in squalid ruins. Basilicas were burned in Gaza, Ascalon, Berytus, and almost everywhere in that area, and no one sought revenge. A basilica was also burned at Alexandria by pagans and Jews.

Nearly all of Ambrose's cases relate to the borders of the Holy Land. But the future was to show that street-level conflict, involving Jewish communities, could break out anywhere. Indeed we know that it already had; for almost the earliest of the long series of legislative acts by Christian emperors concerning the Jews were pronouncements by Constantine forbidding Jews to stone or otherwise attack Jewish converts to Christianity.[4]

PAGANISM, JUDAISM AND CHRISTIANITY

That brings us closer to a different level of religious coexistence, contact, or conflict, namely the questions of individual conversion to or from paganism, Judaism, or Christianity; of actual dialogues, discussions, or debates conducted across the boundaries of religious systems; and of theoretical or theological expositions of any of these religious systems, either as such or in explicit contrast with any of the others.

To treat these questions adequately would be to write the entire religious and intellectual history of the period. But it may be possible to keep to the very broadest lines, beginning with the last-mentioned level, conscious religious self-definition in contrast with other systems, returning finally to the street-level coexistence and conflict in the half-century from the 380s to the 430s.

It might immediately be objected that to talk of 'paganism' at all, as a definable religious system, as an ' –ism', is to apply a wholly inappropriate and misleading category. This view could be defended for the Classical period proper, though even that was marked by profoundly different philosophical views of the gods and by explicit discussions such as Cicero's *On the Nature of the Gods*, or later by Porphyry's views on sacrifice as expressed in his *On Abstinence from Living Things*. But by the fourth century the challenge of Christianity had long since forced those who observed the cults of the gods into explicit philosophical reflection on their system of belief and practice – which we therefore may appropriately call paganism; obvious fourth-century examples are Iamblichus, *On the Mysteries* (ed. des Places, 1966), and Sallustius, *Concerning the Gods and the Universe* (ed. Nock, 1926). As a parallel and related development, explicit criticism of Christianity (well surveyed by Wilken 1984), had begun in the second century with Celsus' *Alēthēs Logos* ('True Word'), to culminate in the Emperor Julian's *Against the Galileans*. Pagan attacks on Judaism as a religious system could also be found in the Classical period; most of those which are known are so because they were quoted and answered in Josephus' *Against Apion*, written in Rome in the

AD 90s (Troiani 1977). Celsus had also related Christianity very firmly to its Jewish context. But with one exception which proves the rule, serious pagan attention to Judaism as a religious system is not well attested in the period of religious coexistence with which we are concerned. All the available evidence is collected and discussed in the second volume of the *magnum opus* of the deeply regretted Menahem Stern, *Greek and Latin Authors on Jews and Judaism* (1980). It may of course be that a pagan literature of this period which did discuss Judaism has been lost; but if so it has left no trace. The exception proving the rule is of course the Emperor Julian himself, who is an exception precisely because he was born and brought up as a Christian; he then converted secretly, and only declared himself as a pagan in 361 (Bowersock 1978; Athanassiadi-Fowden 1981). We are not concerned here with the details of his plan to rebuild the Temple in Jerusalem, except to note that it is beyond question, as recorded by both pagan and Christian sources, that work did start on this project, and was then interrupted by fires which Christians took to represent divine intervention (see Blanchetière 1980). What is significant in this context is Julian's complex three-way analysis of Judaism, Christianity and paganism, as expressed most fully in his *Against the Galileans* (Wilken 1984: ch. 7). To summarize drastically, Julian saw Judaism as a traditional culture and set of religious observances, which had its own values, but could never claim the cultural level and achievements of Classical civilization; but it was precisely the traditional observances of Judaism which the Christians had reprehensibly rejected, while on the other side abandoning the cults of the pagan gods. What was more, traditional Judaism had once manifested a feature which made it comparable to and compatible with paganism, namely a Temple at which sacrifices were offered: 'I wished to show that the Jews agree with the Gentiles [i.e. pagans], except that they believe in only one God. That is indeed peculiar to them and strange to us; since all the rest we have in a manner in common with them – temples, sanctuaries, altars, purifications and certain precepts' (*Against the Galileans* 306B, Loeb trans.).

In Julian's conception of a revived paganism, sacrifice was to be the central act; and in seeking to underline the actual or potential compatibility of Judaism and paganism he offers what *may* be one of the very few attested observations of contemporary Judaism by a (now) pagan observer. For just before the passage quoted above he asserts that sacrifice is not entirely absent from Judaism even now:

> No doubt some sharp-sighted person will answer, 'The Jews too do not sacrifice.' But I will convict him of being terribly dull-sighted, for in the first place I reply that neither do you [the Christians] also observe any one of the other customs observed by the Jews; and, secondly, that the Jews do sacrifice in their own houses [?], and even to this day everything that they eat is consecrated; and they pray before sacrificing, and give the right shoulder to the priests as the first-fruits; but since they have been deprived of their temple, or, as they are accustomed to call it, their holy place, they are prevented from offering the first-fruits of the sacrifice to God.
>
> (*Against the Galileans* 305D–306A, Loeb trans.)

What exactly Julian means to refer to here is not immediately obvious; for it seems certain that no regular sacrifices, conducted by priests on an altar, persisted, or even could have persisted, after the destruction of the Temple (Guttman 1967). The inability of the Jews to sacrifice without a Temple is remarked on frequently by Christian authors, with considerable complacency,[5] and represented of course the central reason for Julian's proposed restoration. The most likely explanation, as Dr William Horbury points out to me, is that Julian is thinking of the eating of the Paschal Lamb, as conducted by Jews in their houses, if *en adraktois* is the right reading, and if that is what it means. For the Pesach meal really does embody a direct transference into a domestic context of an element derived originally from the Passover sacrifice in the Temple.[6] If what Julian says here is indeed an observation, and an accurate one, the fact is worth some emphasis. For as we have seen, there is almost nothing to suggest that contemporary paganism was marked by curiosity about Judaism; while, as we shall see in more detail below (see pp. 116ff.) such attention as Christians ever paid to the realities of the Judaism occupying the same space and time as themselves is shown mainly in two contexts: in legislation of an increasingly repressive kind, and in records of assaults on Jewish synagogues.

Julian's *Against the Galileans* remains by far the most explicit reflection deriving from this period on the interrelations and contrasting histories and values of the three religions. Only

Augustine's *City of God* might challenge comparison within in this respect (see p. 112). But Julian owed his capacity to enter as a pagan into the nature of the Judaeo-Christian tradition to his own upbringing as a Christian. It is in that sense that, as a pagan, he must count as the exception proving the rule. Moreover, although he did note also other features of contemporary Judaism, such as mutual Jewish charity (*Letter* 22 Loeb; Stern 1980: no. 482), the Judaism which most deeply attracted him was one which no longer existed, and which, whether by divine intervention or not, he proved unable to revive.

FOURTH-CENTURY JUDAISM

Various sources allege (see Avi-Yonah 1984: 193–4) that Julian's initiative had been greeted with great enthusiasm by the Jews of the Diaspora, who rushed to participate in the rebuilding of the Temple. That may indeed be so, but our greatest difficulty in trying to map the broad lines of the interrelations of paganism, Judaism and Christianity in this period is precisely that there is so little testimony by Jews which, explicitly or implicitly, looks outwards to the great conflicts and fundamental changes which were taking place around them. As Rokeah (1982) has argued for a slightly earlier period, the religious debates between Christians and paganism involved Judaism; but the Jews are not known to have participated explicitly. Although our topic is the Judaism of the Diaspora, we ought not necessarily to exclude the 'rabbinic' literature of Palestine. For, first, the question of the relations or non-relations of Palestinian Judaism to the Diaspora is precisely one of the large open issues which remain to be decided. And, second, the Jewish community of the Holy Land itself lived in a Graeco-Roman world from which pagan practices had by no means disappeared, and which was also increasingly invaded by Christian churches and congregations, as well as by streams of curious and devout pilgrims (Hunt 1982a). One of these was Jerome; and it is unfortunate in the context of an enquiry about Diaspora Judaism that, of all the Christian writers of this period, the one who engaged in much the most active exchanges with Jewish teachers did so in the Holy Land; none the less one clear revelation of his reports of these exchanges is that the 'rabbinic Judaism' of the Holy Land was itself a bilingual activity which could be described and expressed in Greek (see p. 114).

By contrast, as the long and fruitless debate as to whether the *minim* mentioned in rabbinic writings were or were not Christians itself shows (Simon 1964/1986: ch. 7), explicit observation of other religious systems is not a prominent feature of these works. So, for instance, the tractate Abodah Zarah in the Palestinian Talmud, like the tractate of the Mishnah on which it comments, is not *about* the nature of pagan worship, but about how to conduct a Jewish life in a largely pagan context. It is very interesting indeed to see how entirely pagan is the context from whose impurities protection was deemed to be necessary, whether it was the presence of idols, or the question of buying goods sold at a pagan fair (jAbodah Zarah 1:4). Even the impact of pagan imagery and popular tradition makes itself felt (jAbodah Zarah 3:1, trans. J. Neusner):

> Said R. Jonah: 'When Alexander of Macedon wanted, he could swing upward, and he would go up. He travelled upward until he saw the world as a sphere and the sea as a dish. That is why they represent the world as a sphere in the hand [of an idol].

The reader would find it difficult to guess, reading this work, that in the contemporary Holy Land there were churches, bishops and Christian congregations. Nor is the wider history of the time more than subliminally visible, though Neusner (1987) has argued that the rabbinic works of this period do show, under the unspoken influence of Christianity, a concern with history which had been absent from the Mishnah. Talmudic writings contain no more than a couple of oblique references to Julian's project to rebuild the Temple (Avi-Yonah 1984: 197–8). Diocletian on the other hand achieves a higher profile; for instance, the terms of his persecution are presented as one possible reason out of several why Samaritan wine was considered unclean (jAbodah Zarah 5:4, trans. J. Neusner):

> When Diocletian the King came up here, he issued a decree, saying: 'Every nation must offer a libation, except the Jews'. So the Samaritans made a libation. That is why the sages prohibited their wine.

The late Roman Holy Land, with its separate religious communities, Christian, of various persuasions, pagan, Jewish and Samaritan – mutually hostile but necessarily inhabiting neighbouring streets and fields – would offer a fascinating study. And the 'rabbinic' literature of the Jewish community there *might* also in principle offer one window on the life of the Jewish Diaspora overseas; except that even bare allusions to identifiable places beyond the borders of the Holy Land are very few (Neubauer 1868 seems to be the only available survey). And moreover the criteria for the historical study of this material have not yet been established.

It would of course be still more illuminating if the communities of the Diaspora of this crucial period had left evidence through which they could speak for themselves. Was the Mishnah known to and used by them too? Did their rabbis prepare commentaries on it? Did they indeed have rabbis at all? Or are we speaking (notionally) of a quite different Judaism, necessarily that of a significant proportion of the Jewish people at that time, of which, however, all real trace has disappeared? For if the Judaism of the Diaspora in this period did produce any literature, it has been entirely lost. The most recent survey of ancient Jewish literature, in all genres and in whatever language, produces not a single case of a Jewish work which is known to have been written in the Diaspora between AD 312 and 440 (Schürer 1986–7). It has indeed been boldly asserted that the late Roman work in Latin called *Collatio legum Mosaicarum et Romanarum* ('Comparison of Mosaic and Roman Laws'), a not very perceptive comparison of Jewish and Roman law as applied to a number of separate issues, was written by a Jew living in Rome in the second half of the fourth century (Ruggini 1983: 33). Anything is possible: but it is necessary to underline just how isolated such a work, if really Jewish, would then seem.

If the Judaism of the Diaspora can speak for itself at all, it is only through the physical remains of its synagogues, some of which have been discussed above; its inscriptions, whether from synagogues or tombs, or isolated; and occasional papyri. But of the known papyri written in Hebrew characters only the *ketubah* of AD 417, mentioned above, is securely dated (Sirat 1985). This is not the place to attempt to analyse all the documentary evidence for the Diaspora which dates, or may date, to this period (it is surveyed, on geographical basis, in Schürer 1986: 1–88). But it may be worth returning to one question: were there rabbis in the late Roman Diaspora? The evidence consists first of references to persons, like the *hiereus* and *sophodidaskalos* from Sardis (see p. 101), who are recorded on inscriptions in terms which suggest a role or function comparable to that of a rabbi. Then there are the people described in the undatable Jewish epitaphs of Rome as *nomomathēs*, 'learned in the Law' (*CIJ*, no. 333), or *mathētēs sophōn*, 'disciple of the wise' (no. 508). The actual term 'rabbi' is also attested on inscriptions (Cohen 1981–2). For instance, it appears on an enigmatic and isolated graffito of the mid-fourth century from Cyrene (*SEG* XXXI, no. 1578G), which reads either 'Lord, help the rabbi' or 'Help, Lord of the rabbi' (van der Horst 1987). A 'prayer of Rabbi Attikos' (*euchē rabbē Attikou*) is also recorded on a third-century inscription from Cyprus (*CIJ* no. 736). But the term also appears in Italy, perhaps first in an inscription of the fourth century from Brusciano near Naples; it begins with the word *shalom* written in Hebrew, and is adorned with a shofar, menorah and palm-branch. The Latin text reads 'Here lies Rabbi Abba Maris the honoured one' (Miranda 1979; *SEG* XXIX, no. 968; *JIWE* no. 22). A similar mixture of (rather more extensive) Hebrew and Latin appears on the epitaph of a Jewish girl from Venosa (Venusia) for whom mourning was said by 'two *apostuli* and two *rebbites*' (*CIJ* no. 611). If *apostuli* has the normal meaning of *apostoli*, emissaries of the Patriarch, the inscription would both confirm the Patriarch's influence in Italy (see p. 98) and (presumably) date from before the *excessus* ('cessation'?) of the Patriarchs which is alluded to in a law of 429 (*Cod. Theod.* XVI 8, 29). But nothing serves to date the epitaph of the 'daughter of Rabbi Abundantius' (*filia Rebbitis Abundanti*) found at Salerno in Italy (*CIJ* no. 568), or the Latin inscription from Emerita (Mérida) in Spain mentioning 'Rebbi Se[muel?]' and 'Rebbi Ja[cob]', (*CIJ*, no. 665a). From Volubilis in Mauretania Tingitana, where a Greek inscription of the third century confirms that there was a 'synagōgē of the Ioudeoi', a Hebrew inscription which may be of the fourth century reveals a daughter of a Rabbi, MṬRWN' BT RBY YHWDH NḤ (Le Bohec 1981: nos 79–80). Few as they are, these inscriptions are invaluable, because they are firmly located in space, if less so in time. Through them, as through the inscription of 383 from Catania (pp. 97–8), the late Roman Diaspora does speak. They tend to confirm the importance there too of the study of the Law, the gradual revival of Hebrew and the coming into currency of the term 'rabbi' – or rather 'rebbi', now treated as a Latin word which can be declined and given a genitive ('rebbitis') and a plural ('rebbites'). But there our strictly Jewish evidence, so far as I can determine, stops. New evidence may one day enable the Diaspora of the late Roman world to speak for itself. But so far it does not.

THE CHRISTIANS AND JUDAISM

If we want to know more of the late Roman Diaspora, we have no choice but to see it through Christian eyes, with all the problems that that entails. The first problem in fact is whether or to what extent Christian writings allow us to see the actual contemporary Diaspora at all, as opposed to that Judaism which Christians took as being revealed to them by the Bible. For the claims of Christianity to the inheritance of the Old Testament, to the right to see the fundamental message of the Old Testament as having been the foretelling of Christ, to the assertion that Christ had indeed been the Messiah foretold, and to the status of being the 'true Israel' (the *Verus Israel* of the fundamental work of Simon 1964, 1986) all meant that Judaism was integral to Christian writing. If we look for Jews and Judaism in the overwhelming mass of the Christian writing of the period, in Greek and Latin, we shall find too much. If Jewish writing (all from the Holy Land) paid little overt attention to Christianity (though rather more to problematic features of paganism as it affected normal life), while pagan writers, Julian excepted, paid almost no attention to Judaism, Christian writers amply make up for the averted gaze of their neighbours by the centrality of Judaism for them, and (more rarely) by extensive critiques of paganism. Augustine's *City of God* of course displays both features: in books I–VII a devastating analysis of the internal contradictions of Roman paganism, and in XV–XVIII an obsessive demonstration of the underlying Christian message of the Old Testament.

Christian critiques of paganism are not our concern here, though actual Christian measures against paganism certainly are, for the evolving position of the Jews can be best seen in relation to them (see pp. 116–20). But the central problem is how to use the vast mass of Christian writing as historical evidence for the Judaism and the Jewish communities of the period. For this problem to be addressed properly, it would be necessary to consider the whole of the Christian literature of the period, and its relation to Jews and Judaism, distinguishing (a) confrontations with Judaism as a timeless system whose features are determined by the Old Testament; (b) apparent attributions of beliefs and attitudes to contemporary Jews; (c) apparent reports of contemporary Jewish customs; (d) reports or descriptions of actual episodes, dated and located in space. These last, while they may well still retain highly tendentious features, must inevitably be the most promising material on which a historian can work. They may be considered along with the legislation of the Christian emperors relating to Jews and Judaism, all of it recently presented in exemplary fashion by Linder (1987). For it was, paradoxically, in the shape of legislation of an increasingly repressive kind that Christians of the period most fully revealed a detailed attention to the realities of contemporary Jewish life, of a sort which it is a major labour to find in their theological literature.

What follows is not claimed to be the result of the type of systematic analysis of Christian literature adumbrated above, an enterprise from time to time attempted in part (Krauss 1892, 1893; see also especially Cohen 1987), but never carried through in full. It merely offers some examples of the types of material which Christian literature presents, and of the problems to which it gives rise. I ignore here of course all of the general and timeless characterizations of Judaism as a religion, which are integral to Christian writing, and turn instead to apparent attributions of belief to contemporary Jews. For instance, two extraordinarily powerful evocations of Jewish messianic and apocalyptic beliefs are presented by Jerome in his commentaries on the minor prophets. First, writing in the 390s on Zephaniah 3:8–9, he says (*CCL* LXXVIA, p. 700):

> This the Jews interpret as relating to the advent of the *Christus* whom they hope will come, and say that when all the nations have been gathered together, and the wrath of the Lord has been poured forth upon them, the world is to be consumed in the fire of his anger. And just as it was before the building of the tower [of Babel], when all peoples spoke a single tongue, so, when all have turned to the worship of the true God, they will speak Hebrew, and the whole world will serve the Lord.

In the middle of the next decade, in his *Commentary on Zechariah*, Jerome gives a rather different, and perhaps even more vivid, account of Jewish (and Judeo-Christian) expectations of the end of time (*CCL* LXXVIA, p. 885):

113

The Jews and Judaizing Christians promise themselves at the
end of time the building-up of Jerusalem, and the pouring
forth of waters from its midst, flowing down to both seas.
Then circumcision is again to be practised, victims are to be
sacrificed and all the precepts of the laws are to be kept, so
that it will not be a matter of Jews becoming Christians but
of Christians becoming Jews. On that day, they say, when
the *Christus* will take his seat to rule in a golden and jewelled
Jerusalem, there will be no more idols nor varieties of
worship of the divinity, but there will be one God, and the
whole world will revert to solitude, that is, to its ancient
state.

This passage is very notable in that the expectations attributed to
Jews and Judaizing Christians embrace both Christians and
pagans, as well as a full-scale restoration of the Temple cult. But
the specific idea, present in the earlier passage, that all survivors of
the Day of Judgement will speak Hebrew, makes no appearance. It
seems impossible to tell whether Jerome has derived these two
visions from different Jewish interlocutors in Bethlehem, and if
so whether either or both might have found subscribers in the
Diaspora – or whether he has been carried away by his all-too-
fluent command of rhetoric.

What is of course certain is that he did engage in serious
exchanges with rabbis in the Holy Land (Kelly 1975: esp. chs
14–15), and can report in detail on precisely that world of rabbinic
scholarship and exegesis which was just then producing the Jerusalem Talmud. Thus in *Letter* 121, written from Bethlehem in 405,
he can report that the *traditiones* of the Pharisees are now called
(in Greek) *deutērōseis* ('repetitions'), and that Jewish teachers
(*magistri, sapientes,* or – in Greek – *sophoi*) would give rulings on
questions such as the sabbath limits. The teaching of the 'wise',
taking place on fixed days, could be described in a set Greek
terminology: 'the *sophoi deuterousin*' – 'the *sapientes* teach the
traditiones'. Similarly, in his *Commentary on Habbakuk* (I 2,
15/17, CCL LXXVIA, p. 610) he records approaching a Jew at
Lydda 'who among them was called *sapiens* and *deuterōtēs*'. It
seems clear that his Jewish contacts could and did explain the
system to him in Greek. The question of how profound, if profound at all, was the gulf between the Holy Land and the Diaspora
presents itself once again. Fifteen years later, Augustine, writing

his *Against an Adversary of the Law and the Prophets* at Hippo
in North Africa, could also note that Jewish teaching of unwritten
traditions was called *deuterōsis* (*PL* XLII: 637): had he learned
this at second hand, or from personal observation there? He himself records that his fellow bishop at Oea in Tripolitania had been
forced by violent reactions among his congregation, especially the
Greeks, when faced with a controversial reading in Jonah, to ask
the local Jews what reading there was in their *Hebraei codices*
(*Letter* 71, 5). Is it possible that the Hebrew Bible really existed
there in *codex* (i.e. book) form rather than in scrolls? But in fact
Jerome, replying to Augustine on this point, quietly corrects him,
and speaks of the reading to be found 'in the *volumina* of the
Jews' (Augustine, *Letter* 75, 22). Equally suggestive is Jerome's
report of how in Rome in 384 he was given some *volumina* by a
Hebraeus who had borrowed them from a synagogue with the
intention of reading them – 'quasi lecturus' (*Letter* 36, 1). In this
case *volumina* clearly does mean scrolls, for Jerome has to unroll
one of them to read the relevant passage – 'volumen Hebraeum
replico' (36, 13). We need not doubt that there was at least one
synagogue, as a recognizable building, in Rome, for under the rule
of the usurper Maximus (383–8) it was burned down, evidently by
Christians (Ambrose, *Letter* 40, 25). The report of a synagogue
functioning also as a sort of lending library, and thus contributing
to intellectual dialogue with Christians, adds a different element
to the picture.

As is well known, such day-to-day contacts and mutual influ-
ences are also very well attested in the 380s at the other end of
the Mediterranean, at Antioch. For they are the subject of the
sermons delivered there by John Chrysostom as presbyter in
386–7.[7] His sermons, though inevitably hostile in tone, are not
directed against the Jews of Antioch as such, but against Christians
from his congregation who allowed themselves to be drawn into
participating in the Jewish festivals, both the season of High Festivals – New Year with its trumpets, the Day of Atonement and
Tabernacles – in the autumn, and Passover in the spring. We
should not miss the significance of this evidence that the annual
cycle of festivals was indeed observed by the synagogue community of Antioch, and in such a way as to attract the attention,
favourable or hostile, of their Christian neighbours (Rabello
1981/2). Chrysostom reverts several times to the destruction of
the Temple, to the consequent Jewish inability to sacrifice, and to

the failure of Julian's attempt to restore it. But the attractions of Judaism are strong – partly because the synagogues were revered as the place where the Law and the Prophets were kept (*Discourse* I 5, 2). Catholic Christianity was still threatened on all sides: 'here we are fighting not only against Jews but against the pagans and many heretics' (VII 3, 3, trans. Harkins).

The sense of danger and rivalry which Chrysostom expresses here was, however, already in the course of being answered by appropriate imperial action. The reign of Theodosius I (379–95) had begun with an emphatic assertion of the sole legality of the Catholic Church (*Cod. Theod.* XVI 1, 2 (380) and 3 (381)). Thereafter all non-Catholic forms of Christianity were to suffer progressive disability and oppression on the part of the state. Action against the pagan cults followed more slowly, and in many places was preceded and stimulated by local Christian violence, led by bishops and often carried out by bands of monks. Just as Chrysostom was delivering his warning sermons, his fellow citizen of Antioch, Libanius, was addressing his Oration XXX, *On behalf of the Temples*, to Theodosius: surely imperial orders, however repressive of the pagan cults, had never authorized the physical destruction of the temples, such as was now being witnessed in the east? They had indeed not done so; but within a few years orders prohibiting all forms of sacrifice or pagan cult-practices did follow (*Cod. Theod.* XVI 10, 10, AD 391; 12, 392). If the actual destruction of temples was still not specifically ordered, it was none the less just at this time (391) that imperial agents and local Christians, acting together, destroyed the great temple of Serapis in Alexandria. Similar acts of destruction followed elsewhere, following an irregular rhythm largely dictated by local Christian initiatives. If it was imperial agents who destroyed temples in Carthage in 399 (Augustine, *City of God* XVIII 54), it was the initiative taken by Porphyry, bishop of Gaza, which led to the destruction of all the temples there in the first years of the fifth century, and the use of stones from the temple of Marnas to pave the courtyard of a new church. The story is told in the biography of Porphyry by Mark the Deacon (ed. H. Grégoire and M. A. Kugener: 1930).

The fundamental change in the religious climate which began in the 380s is the essential background which must be borne in mind if we are to understand the very significant, but in many ways less drastic, change which affected the Jewish communities of the empire in the same period. The change is most clearly visible in imperial legislation; given the excellent collection, translation and analysis of the texts by Linder (1987), we may keep to the essentials. Before this period imperial attention to the position of the Jews had been largely directed to two issues: preventing the ownership, or at any rate the conversion and circumcision, of Christian slaves by Jews; and defining the limited number and nature of Jewish community officials who could enjoy exemption from service on town councils. The emperors at various times defined these officials as *patriarchae* (see p. 98), *presbyteri, hiereis* (priests), *archisynagogi* and *patres synagogarum* (e.g. *Cod. Theod.* XVI 8, 2 and 4, of AD 330), thereby, as mentioned earlier, expressing an awareness of day-to-day Jewish community life which is not so evident in other contexts. The earliest of these pronouncements, dating to AD 321, is simultaneously the earliest evidence for the existence of an established Jewish community in Cologne (*Cod. Theod.* XVI 8, 3).

In the 380s, however, new themes begin to come in. In 383, for instance, the emperors Gratian, Valentian and Theodosius declared the confiscation of the property of Christian converts to paganism, Judaism, or Manichaeism (XVI 7, 3), perfectly reflecting the anxieties which Chrysostom was to express three years later. Judaism itself, however, was at all times stated to be legal, for Jews. Thus in 393 Theodosius and his sons, Arcadius and Honorius, wrote to the *comes* of the Orient as follows (XVI, 8, 9, trans. Linder):

> It is sufficiently established that the sect of the Jews is prohibited by no law. We are therefore gravely disturbed by the interdiction imposed in some places on their assemblies. Your Sublime Magnitude shall, upon reception of this order, repress with due severity the excess of those who presume to commit illegal deeds under the name of the Christian religion and attempt to destroy and despoil synagogues.

The emperors were clearly in this instance trying to stem the tide of popular Christian feeling, as they did again in relation to Illyricum in 397 (*Cod. Theod.* XVI 8, 12). There are, however, also signs of an opposing current of popular action, from the Jewish side: in 408 Arcadius and Honorius banned the celebration of Purim by the mock crucifixion of a Haman-figure as a deliberate insult to neighbouring Christians (*Cod. Theod.* XVI 8, 18).

The ban seems to have arisen from an incident at Inmestar in Syria, between Antioch and Chalcis, when Jewish villagers were alleged to have crucified a Christian boy as a deliberate act of mockery, and hence became involved in clashes with the local Christians (Socrates, *Church History* VII 16). In the same year the emperors took measures against the disturbance of Catholic services by Donatists, heretics, Jews, or pagans (*Const. Sirmond.* 14). But one of the most significant continuing themes in imperial legislation is the (sometimes half-hearted) restraint on the destruction or seizure of synagogues and their contents by local Christians, accompanied by repeated statements of a ban on the construction of new synagogues. A pronouncement of Honorius and Theodosius II dating to 423 will best express the complexities of the situation (XVI 8, 2, trans. Linder):

> It seems right that in the future none of the synagogues of the Jews shall either be indiscriminately seized or put on fire. If there are some synagogues that were seized or vindicated to churches or indeed consecrated to the venerable mysteries in a recent undertaking and after the law was passed, they shall be given in exchange new places, on which they could build, that is, to the measure of the synagogues taken. Votive offerings as well, if they are in fact seized, shall be returned to them provided that they have not yet been dedicated to the sacred mysteries; but if a venerable consecration does not permit their restitution, they shall be given the exact price for them. No synagogue shall be constructed from now on, and the old ones shall remain in their state.

The other significant theme was the succession of pronouncements, banning Jews (and Samaritans, and later also pagans) first from the imperial service (*militia*), then from advocacy; finally, in 438 (Theodosius, *Novella* 3) Jews and Samaritans were also barred from all *honores* and *dignitates*, apparently meaning offices held in cities. Throughout, none the less, it is never implied that Judaism is itself illegal, if practised by Jews, or that synagogues do not have the protection of the law. However, that protection, as expressed in 433, might be limited and retrospective. It is moreover highly significant, as Linder (1987: 57f.), points out, that Judaism, which had earlier been described as a *religio*, then became, in 416 and after, a *superstitio*. The vocabulary of imperial rhetoric reflects a fundamental shift of attitudes.

All the issues sketched in this chapter come together in the account by the local bishop, Severus, of how in 417 or 418 the well-established Jewish community of one of the two towns on Minorca was converted under the threat of mass violence, and its synagogue destroyed and turned into a church. The account, printed twice in Migne (*PL* XX, 731–46; XLI, 821–32), and excellently discussed by Hunt (1982b), need only be touched on here. Its importance in this particular context lies not so much in its narrative of the sequence of events, vivid and moving though that is, as in its revelation of the scale, organization and public standing of the local Jewish community as it had been up to that point.

The Jewish community of the small town of Mago consisted of at least 540 persons, and possessed a synagogue situated in the town, containing silver vessels and 'sacred books' (*libri sancti*). The leading figure of the community, Theodorus, is described as having held all the offices within the town council (*curia*), and as *defensor* and *patronus* of his fellow citizens (*municipes*); he owned property also on the neighbouring island of Majorca. Within the community he functioned as a *legis doctor* – surely (cf. p. 111) yet another reference to a 'rabbinic' role. It must be relevant that Jerome uses the same expression, *legis doctor*, to describe the learned Jew from Tiberias who in the late 380s helped him with the proper names in Chronicles (*PL* XXIX, 401f.; Pavan 1965–6: 398; Kelly 1975: 158–9). Severus, however, notes that Theodorus' formal title in the Jewish community was *pater patrum*. We meet also other leading figures, with a mixture of Hebrew, Greek and Latin names (Ruben, Meletius, Innocentius, Galilaeus, Caecilianus, Florinus, Arthemisia) typical of a late Roman Jewish community. Meletius turns out to be versed in both Greek and Latin literature.

The conversion of this entire community to Christianity was inspired by the bringing to the island of relics of St Stephen, and began with Christians marching in procession to Mago from the other town, Iammo, where there were no Jewish inhabitants. On arrival at Mago they invited the Jewish leaders to a debate and then advanced on the synagogue singing hymns, to be met with stones hurled down on them by Jewish women. The studiously self-righteous narrative cannot conceal the fact that in the face of this mass threat the Jews retreated, and the Christians occupied the synagogue and burned it down. The silver ornaments were

119

returned to the Jews, but the *libri sancti* removed, in case they should suffer damage while in the protection of the Jews ('ne apud Iudaeos iniuriam paterentur').

Three days later a debate began on the site of the ruined synagogue, before a large crowd of Christians; then step by step there followed the conversion of each of the *primarii* of the Jewish community in turn. Seventeen days after leaving Iammo the Christians were able to return in triumph. When Easter was celebrated, 540 souls had been added to the Christian congregation. One final demonstration of their new faith was required: the foundations of the synagogue were dug up, and for the construction of the new basilica which was to rise in its place, the converted Jews not only contributed funds but carried stones on their shoulders.

This episode, far from the only one of its kind attested in this period (see Hunt 1982b), serves to make very clear the background of local Christian pressure on other religious groups against which contemporary emperors were issuing their pronouncements. There had indeed been a profound change of mood as against the earlier period, which might well be seen as an exceptionally favourable one for the Jewish Diaspora, when no other religious group could claim a secure dominance. Yet even this later period should not be seen as one of systematic persecution (*pace* Seaver 1952); there is moreover ample evidence of Jewish communities throughout the Roman world in the fifth and sixth centuries (Rabello 1987). There was, however, a significantly increased danger of mob violence on the part of Christians, and the legal status and the rights of Jews were substantially reduced. But the right to practise their religion remained in principle, and, often precariously, in fact. It is something of a paradox that along with the archaeological and documentary evidence, it is precisely the increasingly repressive legislative pronouncements of the emperors on the one hand and Christian records of their own hostile measures on the other which give us the best hope of recapturing the reality of a distinctive phase in Jewish history. Its beginnings are obscure, but we might see it as going back to the second century, and as coming to a sort of fruition in the fourth. That is to say that the evidence, scattered and disparate as it is, suggests that the period of unresolved tensions between pagans and Christians may have been a relatively favourable and prosperous one for the settled Jewish communities of the Graeco-Roman Diaspora. If so, then what we can dimly perceive is quite a significant chapter in the communal and religious history of the Jewish people. That it has been on the whole a neglected chapter makes the many remaining questions about the nature of Judaism in the late Roman Diaspora all the more important.[8]

NOTES

1 *CIJ* 1975 no. 650; *Année Epigraphique* 1984, no. 439; *JIWE* no. 145.
2 For example, *Cod. Theod.* XVI 8, 102, AD 329–30; XVI 8, 13, AD 397.
3 Kraeling 1938: 234–41; 318–24; 483f.; ins. nos 323–5.
4 *Cod. Theod.* XVI 8, 1 = *Cod. Just.* I 9, 3; *Const. Sirmond.* 4 = *Cod. Theod.* XVI 8, 5; 9, 1.
5 Eusebius, *Demonstratio Evangelica* ('Demonstration of the Gospel') I 3; Augustine, *Tractatio Adversus Iudaeos* ('Against the Jews') 9–12.
6 See de Lange 1976: 168f., and the review by W. Horbury 1979: 324.
7 Wilken 1983; translation and commentary on the discourses by Harkins 1979.
8 An earlier, and very different, version of this paper was given as a Martin and Helene Schwartz Lecture in the Department of Jewish Studies at Harvard University in 1987. I am grateful for comments and corrections to the editors and to Professor Jacob Neusner and Dr N. R. M. de Lange.

BIBLIOGRAPHY

Alföldi, A. (1948) *The Conversion of Constantine and Pagan Rome*, Oxford.
Athanassiadi-Fowden, P. (1981) *Julian and Hellenism: An Intellectual Biography*, Oxford.
Avi-Yonah, M. (1976) *The Jews of Palestine: A Political History from the Bar Kochba War to the Arab Conquest*, chs 7–9 (reissued (1984) as *The Jews under Roman and Byzantine Rule*), Oxford.
Balty, J. C. (1981) *Guide d'Apamée*, Brussels.
Balty, Janine (1986) *Mosaïques d'Apamée*, Brussels.
Barnes, T. D. (1989) 'Christians and Pagans in the Reign of Constantius', *L'église et l'empire au IVe siècle* (Entretiens Hardt, XXXIV), 301.
Blanchetière, F. (1980) 'Julien. Philhellène, Philosémite, Antichrétien. L'Affaire du Temple de Jerusalem (363)', *Journal of Jewish Studies* 31: 61–81.
Bowersock, G. W. (1978) *Julian the Apostate*, London.
Cohen, S. J. D. (1981/2) 'Epigraphic Rabbis', *Jewish Quarterly Review* 72: 1–17.
Cohen, S. J. D (1987) 'Pagan and Christian Evidence on the Ancient Synagogue', in L. I. Levine (ed.) *The Synagogue in Late Antiquity*, Jerusalem, 159–81.

Colorni, V. (1964) 'L'uso del greco nella liturgia del giudaismo hellenistico e la Novella 146 di Giustiniano', *Annali di Storia del Diritto* 8: 19.

Crown, A. D. (1986) 'The Samaritans in the Byzantine Orbit', *Bulletin of the John Rylands Library* 69: 96–138.

Fowden, G. (1978) 'Bishops and Temples in the Eastern Roman Empire', *Journal of Theological Studies* 29: 53–78.

Frey, J.-B. (2nd edn, 1975) *Corpus Inscriptionum Judaicarum*, Vol. I, ed. B. Lifshitz, New York.

Goodman, M. (1983) *State and Society in Roman Galilee, AD 132–212*, Totowa, NJ.

Gutmann, J. (ed.) (1973) *The Dura-Europos Synagogue: a Re-evaluation (1932–1972)*, Chambersburg, Pa.

Guttman, A. (1967) 'The End of the Jewish Sacrificial Cult', *Hebrew Union College Annual* 38: 137.

Hanfmann, G. M. A. (1967) 'The Ninth Campaign at Sardis', *Bulletin of the American Schools of Oriental Research*, 187: 27–32.

Harkins, P. (1979) *Saint John Chrysostom: Discourses Against Judaising Christians* (Fathers of the Church, 68), Washington, DC.

Horbury, W. (1979) review of de Lange 1976, *Journal of Theological Studies* 30: 324–8.

Hunt, E. D. (1982a) *Holy Land Pilgrimage in the Later Roman Empire, AD 312–460*, Oxford.

Hunt, E. D. (1982b) 'St Stephen in Minorca: An Episode in Jewish-Christian Relations in the Early Fifth Century AD', *Journal of Theological Studies* 33: 106–23.

Kelly, J. N. D. (1975) *Jerome: His Life, Writings and Controversies*, London.

Kraeling, C. H. (1938) *Gerasa, City of the Decapolis*, New Haven, Conn.

Kraeling, C. H. (1967) *The Excavations at Dura-Europos, Final Report VIII, 2: The Christian Building*, New Haven, Conn.

Kraeling, C. H. (1979) *The Excavations at Dura-Europos, Final Report VIII, 1: The Synagogue* (revised with additions; first edn 1965), New Haven, Conn.

Krauss, S. (1892) 'The Jews in the Works of the Church Fathers', *Jewish Quarterly Review* 5: 122–57.

Krauss, S. (1893) 'The Jews in the Works of the Church Fathers', *Jewish Quarterly Review* 6: 82–99, 225–61.

Krautheimer, R. (1967) 'The Constantinian Basilica', *Dumbarton Oaks Papers* 21: 115.

Lange, N. R. M. de (1976) *Origen and the Jews: Studies in Jewish-Christian Relations in Third-Century Palestine*, Cambridge.

Le Bohec, Y. (1981) 'Inscriptions juives et judaïsantes de l'Afrique romaine', *Antiquités Africaines* 17: 165–207, 209–29.

Linder, A. (1987) *The Jews in Roman Imperial Legislation*, Detroit and Jerusalem.

MacMullen, R. (1984) *Christianising the Roman Empire*, New Haven, Conn.

Milburn, R. (1988) *Early Christian Art and Architecture*, Aldershot.

Miranda, E. (1979) 'Due iscrizioni greco-giudaiche della Campania', *Rivista dell'Archeologia Christiana* 55: 337.

Napoleone-Lemaire, J. and Balty, J. C. (1969) *L'église à atrium de la grande colonnade* (Fouilles d'Apamée de Syrie, I. 1), Brussels.

Neubauer, A. (1868) *La Géographie du Talmud*, Paris.

Neusner, J. (1987) *Judaism and Christianity in the Age of Constantine: History, Messiah, Israel and the Initial Confrontation*, Chicago.

Noy, D. (1993) *Jewish Inscriptions of Western Europe* I, Cambridge.

Pavan, M. (1965–6) 'I cristiani e il mondo ebraico nell'età di Teodosio "il Grande" ', *Ann. Fac. Lett. filos. Perugia* 3: 267.

Rabello, A. M. (1981/2) 'L'osservanza delle feste ebraiche nell'impero romano', *Scripta Classica Israelica* 6: 57.

Rabello, A. M. (1987) *Giustiniano, Ebrei e Samaritani* Vol. 1, Milan.

Reynolds, J. and Tannenbaum, R. (1987) *Jews and Godfearers at Aphrodisias* (Cambridge Philological Society, Supplementary Volume 12), Cambridge.

Robert, L. (1964) *Nouvelles Inscriptions de Sardes* I: 37–58.

Rokeah, D. (1982) *Jews, Pagans and Christians in Conflict*, Jerusalem and Leiden.

Rostovtzeff, M. (1938) *Dura-Europos and its Art*, Oxford.

Ruggini, L. Cracco (1983) 'Tolleranza e intolleranza nella società tardoantica: il caso degli ebrei', *Richerche di storia sociale e religiosa* 23: 27.

Schürer, E. (1986–7) *History of the Jewish People in the Age of Jesus Christ*, Vol. III. 1–2, ed. G. Vermes, F. Millar and M. D. Goodman, Edinburgh.

Seager, A. R. and Kraabel, A. T. (1983) 'The Synagogue and the Jewish Community', in G. M. A. Hanfmann (ed.) *Sardis from Prehistoric to Roman Times*, Cambridge, Mass. and London, ch. 9.

Seaver, J. E. (1952) *Persecution of the Jews in the Roman Empire (300–438)* Lawrence, Kansas.

Simon, M. (2nd edn, 1964) *Verus Israel: études sur les relations entre Chrétiens et Juifs dans l'empire romain (135–425)*, Paris (English translation published (1986) as *Verus Israel*, Oxford).

Sirat, C. (1985) *Les Papyrus en caractères hebraïques trouvés en Égypte*.

Sirat, C., Caudelier, P., Dukan, M. and Friedman, M. A. (1986) *La Ketouba de Cologne: un contrat de mariage juif à Antinoopolis*.

Stern, M. (1980) *Greek and Latin Authors on Jews and Judaism*, Vol. 2, *From Tacitus to Simplicius*, Jerusalem.

Troiani, L. (1977) *Commento storico al 'contro Apione' di Giuseppe*.

van der Horst, P. W. (1987) 'Lord, Help the Rabbi: The Interpretation of SEG XXX 1578b', *Journal of Jewish Studies* 38: 102–6.

Wilken, R. L. (1983) *John Chrysostom and the Jews: Rhetoric and Reality in the Late 4th Century*, Berkeley and Los Angeles.

Wilken, R. L. (1984) *The Christians as the Romans Saw Them*, New Haven, Conn.

6

SYRIAN CHRISTIANITY AND JUDAISM

Han Drijvers

ANTIOCH AND EDESSA

The main centre of Christianity in Syria was Antioch on the Orontes, the former Seleucid capital, where the first Gentiles converted to the new belief. There the name Christians (*christianoi*) came into use for the first time, and from there the mission to the Gentiles started (Acts 11:19–26). Antioch, therefore, was the first place where the Christians (= 'Christus–people') stood out from Judaism as a distinct sect (Meeks and Wilken 1978: 13–36; Downey 1961: 272–8). We can assume that the new belief spread eastwards from Antioch along the main trade routes to northern Mesopotamia. So it came to Edessa, capital of the small kingdom of Osrhoene in northern Mesopotamia, through Cyrrhus, Doliche, Zeugma on the Euphrates, and Harran (Dillemann 1982: 147–55; Drijvers 1977: 864). From there the road, as part of the famous silk road, continued through Nisibis to Iran and northern India. Although the Euphrates was considered the frontier between the Roman Empire and first the Parthians and later the Sassanians, northern Mesopotamia like adjacent Armenia was usually under strong Roman influence, because it was of vital interest for every military expedition to the Persian area which always started from Antioch. Rome's power in the trans-Euphrates area was essential to the protection of the flanks of the Roman army, in particular when it retreated from Parthian territory. Many battles between Rome and Parthia were therefore fought in northern Mesopotamia beginning with the well-known and fatal battle of Carrhae-Harran in 53 BC (Oates 1968: 69; Drijvers 1977: 869–72). In other words, northern Mesopotamia and the little kingdom of Osrhoene with its capital Edessa were not isolated from the rest of Syria; there was on the contrary a continuous exchange of goods and ideas along the busy highroads from Antioch to the east and vice versa.

Antioch and Edessa are the two poles of Syrian Christianity as it developed during the first centuries AD in the Roman province of Syria. It is tempting, and would be essential for a real understanding of Christian origins and developments in this particular area, to sketch the area's culture and history in more detail, since Christianity is not an isolated phenomenon which developed *in vacuo*, but an integral part of Graeco-Roman civilization (Cameron 1986: 266–71).

Only a few aspects of Syrian culture that are relevant to the rest of this chapter will be adduced here. First of all, the Syrian area was thoroughly bilingual. Greek was widely spoken and understood, especially in the urban centres like Antioch, but Aramaic was in use too as a spoken and written language, as becomes clear from the range of bilingual Aramaic – Greek inscriptions from Palmyra. From the Edessene region we possess a few Greek inscriptions and about seventy Old Syriac ones. A Syriac deed of sale written in AD 243 at Edessa was found at Dura-Europos on the Euphrates (Millar 1971: 1–17; Schmitt 1980: 187–214; Drijvers 1972; Bellinger and Welles 1935: 95–154). Recently a number of Greek papyri and two Syriac parchments have come to light which once belonged to a family archive. The two Syriac documents written in AD 240 and 242 at Edessa can be compared to the deed of sale from Dura-Europos and contain the same kind of formulas (Teixidor 1989: 219–22). Syriac, the local Aramaic dialect of Edessa and its surroundings, which was to become the official language of Syriac-speaking Christianity, must already have had a long history before it was used for writing down Christian texts. It is of interest that all Old Syriac inscriptions from the first three centuries AD are of Gentile origin, and that some of them show traces of a literary tradition. Other remnants of a Syriac literary tradition are preserved in Manichaean hymnography and in the texts written on magic bowls.[1] Lucian of Samosata in his famous book *De Dea Syria*, on the Syrian goddess who was venerated at Hierapolis halfway between Antioch and Edessa, has stories on her cult and temple which certainly go back to a local Aramaic tradition (Oden 1977: 1–46; Drijvers 1980: 76–121). But these are scanty remains of an undoubtedly rich literary production. The

Christian supremacy of later times suppressed these other branches of Syriac literature or took them over in modified form. From its very beginning, however, Christianity used Syriac as the vehicle for its message and doctrine and monopolized this language for its exclusive use.

Edessa was called the Athens of the east because it had a famous school where philosophy and rhetoric were taught to the young. Greek works were most likely read in Greek, but the teaching was mainly in Syriac, so that there existed a continuous process of translation from Greek into Syriac and the other way round. When in the second half of the second century AD the philosopher Bardesanes lived and taught at the court of the Edessene king Abgar VIII the Great (AD 177–212), he wrote his philosophical treatises in Syriac, but they were very soon or even simultaneously translated into Greek. Bardesanes' doctrine of fate and free will shows a strong influence from the philosophy of the Peripatetic philosopher Alexander of Aphrodisias with whose works the Aramaic philosopher must have been acquainted (Drijvers 1966: 50–95; Dihle 1982: 108–10). Eusebius of Caesarea gives detailed information on this translation process in his *Church History*:

> In the same reign [i.e. of Marcus Aurelius, 161–80] heresies increased in Mesopotamia, and Bardesanes, a most able man and skilled in Syriac, composed dialogues against the Marcionites and other leaders of various opinions, and he issued them in his own language and script, together with many other of his writings. Those who knew them, and they were many, for he was a powerful arguer, have translated them from Syriac into Greek. Among them is his very powerful dialogue with Antoninus, *Concerning Fate*. (*Church History* IV 30)

Every one of the Christian works written in the region between Antioch and Edessa during the second and third centuries AD is known in a Greek as well as in a Syriac version. It is often hard to tell which version has priority, a matter of extensive scholarly discussions, but it should be emphasized that these problems are less important than they seem to be. Syriac does not represent a culture different from Greek; both languages are expressions and vehicles of the same Hellenistic civilization in Syria, the traditions of which go back to the former Seleucid empire. A similar situation existed at Palmyra in the middle of the Syrian desert, where

126

in the third century AD the philosopher Longinus stayed at the court of Queen Zenobia and undoubtedly taught and wrote in Greek, which was understood and spoken as well as the local Aramaic dialect. In Syria, language was not a cultural barrier.

Second, Syria had a very mixed population: locals, Greeks, Persians, Jews, and a range of what we would call minorities. The area displays a mixture of proper names, whose ethnic origin is often hard to decide. Dura-Europos, the fortress on the Euphrates frontier, is thoroughly typical in this respect. There was therefore a permanent interaction between the various population groups which lived densely packed within the walls of the usually small towns, where privacy was rare. The best-defined group with a well-established identity and clearer boundaries may have been the Jews, but they were as Hellenized as the rest of the population (Drijvers 1980: 190–2: Gutmann 1973: 119). The well-known synagogue of Dura-Europos, now completely restored and on view at the National Museum of Damascus, is a good example of the cultural interaction in Syria. Its wall-paintings are products of the artistic repertoire current in the whole Syrian area and do not reveal a specific Jewish style. Indeed, if the painting of King David playing for the animals had been found in another context than a synagogue, everybody would have believed him to be Orpheus (Kraeling 1956; Goodenough 1964).

CHRISTIANITY IN SYRIA

Christianity spread first near Antioch, the main administrative and cultural centre and a starting-point of military and commercial activities to the east. It may be safely assumed that the Christian belief also spread from Antioch to the east and reached the cities of northern Mesopotamia, Edessa and Nisibis, some time during the second century. The details of the Christian mission in the Syrian region are, however, completely unknown. Christianity also came to Dura-Europos, where a Christian chapel used as a baptistery has been excavated (Kraeling 1967). A Greek fragment of the *Diatessaron*, a gospel harmony composed by Tatian during the second half of the second century AD, was also discovered at Dura-Europos (Kraeling 1935). The connection with Antioch is an important one and was, so to speak, dictated by the road-system. Direct ways from Jerusalem to northern Mesopotamia through the desert did not exist. Travellers who wanted to journey from Jerusalem to Edessa or Nisibis, a centre of Judaism in northern Mesopotamia, first went to the north, then journeyed along the highways in southern Anatolia, crossed the Euphrates at Zeugma and at last arrived at Edessa or Nisibis further to the east. Ideas, like goods and travellers, move along the existing roads, and do not fly through the air or come down straight from heaven. Christianity similarly arrived at this northern Mesopotamian region and the areas further east from the Syrian metropolis Antioch; with Rome, Antioch was the main centre of early Christianity in the Roman Empire.

The various forms of Christian belief in northern Mesopotamia and in particular at Edessa deserve special attention, because it has widely been believed to represent a very special kind of Christianity. Its supposedly close links with Judaism especially are of interest, since it often has been considered to have developed in a kind of cultural enclave, untouched by Hellenism, as a scholar once characterized it (Vööbus 1958a: 4; cf. Murray 1975: 277–347; Murray 1982a: 3–16). Edessa consequently would have preserved a pure form of Christian belief and tradition such as Christianity once supposedly had at its Jewish birthplace Jerusalem, but that had been lost since the tender youth of the new belief everywhere in the world as a result of the pernicious influence of Greek culture. The sources for study of the origin and history of Christianity in Syriac-speaking northern Mesopotamia are scanty and one-sided. Their historical value and religious concepts are not always clear; they are consequently much-debated, and they are therefore sufficient ground for busy scholarly activity and written production (Drijvers 1984: I and VI).

In a small town like Edessa, Gentiles, Jews and Christians walked along the same streets, did their shopping at the common market-place, suffered from the same diseases, epidemics and wars, and therefore shared a lot of ideas and concepts about which they talked with each other. They were buried in the same cemeteries, caves around the city, and got the same education if they could afford it. They lived on each others' doorsteps, shared common experiences and usually spoke the same language. Our literary sources do not cover this important middle-ground, but stress the differences, so that Gentiles, Jews and Christians appear as almost totally different groups in society. To detect that common middle-ground, we have to look at magical texts, mainly of later date, which display a mixture of religious ideas, Gentile, Jewish and

Christian, and share a certain terminology. The entire population of a town like Edessa celebrated a pagan religious feast at the end of the fifth century, and must have done so in earlier times too. All people want to be healed from their illnesses and sorrows, and therefore go to the magician, whether he be a Gentile sorcerer, a Jewish rabbi, or a Christian monk (Drijvers 1982: 35–43). Religious texts stress ideological differences; religious practice is often a shared experience of a basically social character.

All the existing sources for the study of Edessene Christianity stem from the second half of the second century AD or from later times and tell us nothing about the historical origins of the local Church except legendary tales which have their own intrinsic value, but only emphasize our lack of solid evidence.

LEADING INFLUENCES IN SYRIAN CHRISTIANITY

The first figure we can lay our hands on is Tatian the Assyrian, who was a pupil of Justin Martyr in Rome and went back to his homeland about AD 177. Tatian is known for his *Oratio ad Graecos*, a philosophically tainted theological treatise. The divine *logos*, God's eternal Word, holds a central position in Tatian's theology. The *logos* functions as creator and as saviour and is the unifying principle that unites God and man. The only way to reach salvation and regain man's original immortality is by practising an austere sexual asceticism, *enkrateia*. Basically Tatian's doctrine is – at least from a theoretical viewpoint – rather simple. The first man, Adam, was created by the divine *logos* as an immortal being composed of body, soul and mind. The soul is man's life-giving principle; the mind (*nous*) is a divine entity and embodies Adam's immortality. When the first man, however, made the wrong use of his God-given free will, he lost the divine mind, also called his light robe, and consequently became a mortal and therefore a sexual being. Salvation from this state of unhappiness and sin is brought about only by sexual asceticism, by keeping body and soul pure so that the *logos* – that is, Jesus as the divine mind – can dwell in man's soul and in this way bring him back to his original state of immortality. *Enkrateia* is the only way of undoing the Fall; acquiring the indwelling of God's mind through asceticism is a spiritual process of regaining paradise lost. This on the face of it simple scheme dominates the mainstream of Syrian Christianity. It lies at the root of its concept of the saint, the

129

representation of immortal life among mortals, and it exercised an enormous influence on Manichaeism as it developed during the third century. Such a theory of creation and salvation is fundamentally a philosophical one, based on the anthropological concepts of contemporary Middle Platonism, and the process involved is therefore timeless. Incarnation and crucifixion are absent in Tatian's theology and all the emphasis is laid on knowing the truth about God and man, on moral and theoretical instruction about the possibility of man's free will to tame his passions and to undo what went wrong *ab origine* (Elze: 1960; Whittaker: 1982).

Tatian is also known as the author of the so-called *Diatessaron*, a gospel harmony based on the four canonical gospels which were made into one running story. It consists of deliberately chosen passages from the four gospels and opens with the prologue of John's gospel which contains central notions of Tatian's philosophical theology, especially the *logos*. The *Oratio ad Graecos* and the *Diatessaron* mutually elucidate each other. The basic scheme of Tatian's theology was the guiding principle in composing the *Diatessaron* and selecting the relevant passages, whereas the *Diatessaron* itself can be read as a scriptual commentary on the *Oratio* (Drijvers and Reinink 1988: 91–110). Tatian probably wrote the *Diatessaron* in Syriac, but a Greek version was available too, to which the fragment found at Dura-Europos testifies. Tatian's gospel harmony became the canonical New Testament text for the Syriac-speaking Church. Towards the end of the fourth century AD Ephrem Syrus, who died in AD 373, still wrote an extensive commentary on it. The *Diatessaron* text also exercised decisive influence on the Syriac translations of the four separate gospels, which were mainly based on Antiochene versions of the New Testament.

One may wonder why Tatian composed his *Diatessaron*, since a whole range of different gospel versions were already known. Like his teacher Justin Martyr, Tatian was a strong opponent of the Marcionites, who formed the majority of the Christians in large areas in Syria. Marcion was the first Christian theologian who during the first half of the second century AD interpreted the gospel message in the framework and with the terminology of Middle Platonism. Starting from St Paul's antitheses of law and grace, Old Testament and New Testament, Judaism and the Gospel for the Gentiles, Marcion formulated the doctrine of two gods. The God of the New Testament is the unknown hidden

God of grace, a stranger, and father of Jesus Christ. The God of the Old Testament is the creator, characterized by envy, evil justice and an iron law of retaliation. Marcion consequently abolished the Jewish Holy Book and retained from the gospels and letters only a heavily censored Gospel of Luke and some Pauline letters, of which Galatians is the most important. Marcion considered large parts of the later New Testament as falsified, forgeries brought about by the followers of the evil creator. He moreover discovered substantial contradictions between those parts of the gospel that describe Jesus as the Son of the Jewish Creator, and other passages that picture him as the Son of the unknown God of grace. In other words, Marcion's interpretation and purification of the Christian Gospel were a consequent attempt to emancipate the Christian sect from its Jewish origins. Marcion made use of the Platonic distinction between a highest god and a demiurge to differentiate the gracious stranger God from his Jewish evil antagonist (Harnack 1960; Drijvers 1987–8). The composition of the *Diatessaron* was an endeavour on Tatian's side to smooth out all the real and supposed contradictions in the four gospels through making them into one continuous story. Like Marcion, Tatian's theological views directed this process of selecting gospel passages and making them into a whole. Indeed, the canonical New Testament itself is the final result of theological controversies and the product of a winning party.

The impact of Marcionism on Syrian Christianity can also be inferred from the works and doctrine of Bardesanes (Bardaisan), the philosopher at the court of King Abgar the Great of Edessa. From his school we possess a dialogue on free will, the so-called *Book of the Laws of Countries*, which is identical with his dialogue with Antoninus *Concerning Fate*. The title is due to a large collection of laws of foreign peoples (*nomima barbarika*) at the end of this treatise, brought together in order to defend free will against fate and laws of nature. All these laws are of the type that says: 'All Persians marry their mothers and sisters, although not all of them are born under the planet constellation that predicts and commands such horrible behaviour. Free will is therefore stronger than fate.' The dialogue opens with a startling question:

> If God is One, as you say He is, and He has created mankind intending you to do what you are charged to, why did He not create mankind in such wise that they could not sin, but

131

always did what is right? Thereby His desire would have been fulfilled. Bardaisan said to him: 'Tell me, my son Awida, what do you think: The God of the Universe is not One, or He is One and does not desire man's conduct to be good and just?' (Drijvers 1965: 5; Drijvers 1966: 60–95)

This conversation contains precisely Marcion's starting-point, from which he concluded that the creator is an evil deity, because he created mankind in the wrong way. Bardaisan tries to demonstrate that there is one God, creator as well as saviour, who made man a being with a free will. God is therefore not to be blamed for all wrong and evil in the world. Although Bardaisan, unlike the Marcionites and Tatian, was not an advocate of asceticism, he developed a cosmology and soteriology which are rather similar to Tatian's ideas. The divine *logos* was the main actor in the creation of the cosmos, when he imposed order on the material elements (*stoicheia*) that had got into chaotic confusion just by an unlucky accident, and made the entire world out of them. But the *logos*, identified with Jesus, also is the divine teacher who instructs man about what is right and wrong, and how he should use his free will in order to ban evil from the world. Again incarnation and crucifixion do not occur in Bardaisan's religious philosophy, in which the divine *logos* as an eternal intellectual principle plays the main role (Drijvers 1966).

Asceticism of Tatianic origin is the dominant element in the apocryphal Acts of the apostle Judas Thomas. These Acts were written in Syriac in the beginning of the third century and probably found their origin at Edessa (Drijvers 1989: 289–303). Judas Thomas's main activity is breaking up marriages of upper-class people by persuading the women to abstain from sexual intercourse with their husbands. Thomas also preached this gospel of sexual abstinence to young recently married couples, who then spent their first night together silently sitting opposite each other without even touching! Thomas takes the prototype of this spiritual marriage to be the situation before the Fall, when man and woman were naked and not ashamed of each other (Genesis 2: 25). At that time they were the true 'sons of God', 'which were born, not of blood, nor of the will of the flesh, nor of the will of man, but of God' (John 1: 12–13). Sexual abstinence, *enkrateia*, brings man back to this situation of paradisiac immortality. Judas Thomas himself is the prototype and paradigm of such a spiritual rebirth. He is a totally unhistorical fictional personage, a combination of Thomas Didymus, that is, Thomas the Twin – the Syriac name Thomas (*tauma*) means twin – and Judas; the latter is not Iskariot, but was identified with Judas the brother of James, the brother of the Lord, and consequently seen as a brother of Jesus too. Judas Thomas is therefore Jesus' twin brother and in a sense identical with the Lord himself (Klijn 1970: 88–96; Drijvers 1984: I, 15–17). Sexual abstinence makes man into a true son of God, a twin of Jesus the only Son of God, who is his heavenly double and dwells as divine spirit in him. In this way man is brought back to his original immortality when he had not yet lost the divine spirit. There is one simple message: abstain from sex and you will be like Adam and Eve in paradise. The same theme can be detected in the other writings under the name of Judas Thomas: the *Gospel of Thomas* preserved in a Coptic version in the gnostic library of Nag Hammadi, and the *Book of Thomas the Contender* found at Nag Hammadi too. These works also betray a Syrian origin, have much in common with the *Acts of Thomas*, and display Tatianic theological concepts. The often remarkable or bizarre Gospel quotations in the *Gospel of Thomas* are related to the text of Tatian's *Diatessaron* and are another sign of Tatian's considerable influence (Baarda 1983: 165).

Marcionites, followers of Bardaisan, enkratite Christians, and perhaps other groups too, seem to have dominated the Christian scene at the beginning of the third century in Syria and Edessa, when in 216 Mani was born. Mani proclaimed himself the apostle of Jesus Christ as did Paul, and developed the various elements of Christianity in the Syrian area into a radically dualistic system. Marcion and Bardaisan provided him with essential elements for the construction of his cosmological and soteriological myth, which is dominated by two opposing principles, light and darkness. These have fought a permanent fight from the time before the creation of our visible world. Then darkness discovered the world of light and attacked it. According to the Manichaean myth the god of the world of light sent his son, the first man, to the evil darkness in order to repel it to its own domain. But the first man was conquered and held captive by the darkness. The result of it was that light particles, represented by the first man, have been imprisoned in evil and dark matter, out of which this world and man's body were created. Passing over all the complicated details of this cosmological and anthropological myth, the essence of it is that light particles are incarcerated in the world and in man and ought to be freed so that they can return to their origin, the world of light. Manichaeans were therefore austere ascetics with a special diet, in order not to damage the light particles that are to be found everywhere. They had a negative view of our world, but a rather optimistic view of man, who is able to save himself and his divine essence through rigid asceticism. Besides Marcion and Bardaisan, Tatian and the Syrian enkratites contributed to their complicated system. Tatian's *Diatessaron* was the Bible of the Manichaeans, and the various apocryphal Acts, in particular the *Acts of Thomas*, were their favourite reading (Lieu 1985: 1–59; Nagel 1973: 171–82).

Manichaeism was a missionary religion and Manichaean missionaries travelled all over the eastern part of the Roman Empire to preach their saving message and to heal people from their deadly illnesses. At this time healing was a physical as well as a spiritual activity; Mani was known and announced himself as a doctor from Babylon. One of the best-known Manichaean missionaries was Adda or Addai, who was active in the Syrian and Mesopotamian region during the second half of the third century AD. Manichaeism spread quickly and everywhere in the Syrian area Manichaean communities came into existence, among other places, at Edessa. Like St Paul, Mani wrote letters to his various congregations and quotations from his letter to the Edessenes have been preserved in the so-called Cologne Mani Codex, a miniature Greek codex discovered in Egypt. It contains a history of Mani's life and of the Manichaean Church and is a first-class source for our knowledge of Manichaeism. The work most likely was originally written in Syriac, which was also in fact the main language of the Manichaeans in which Mani wrote all his works (Cameron and Dewey 1979; Koenen and Römer 1988).

So far we have seen that Christianity in the Syrian area was a highly variegated phenomenon consisting of different groups: Marcionites, Bardaisanites, enkratite Christians of Tatianic character to whom we owe the *Acts of Thomas* and other Thomas literature, and Manichaeans (Drijvers 1984: I and VI). All these groups show philosophical characteristics in accordance with the mainstream of contemporary philosophy of the first centuries AD, and in particular Marcionites and Manichaeans embody anti-Jewish ideas.

The success of Manichaeism in particular gave the impetus to a counter-movement on the part of other Christians which would develop into a fourth-century orthodoxy having close links with Antioch. Their propaganda tract is the so-called *Doctrina Addai*, in which the famous apocryphal correspondence between the Edessene king Abgar V Ukkama ('the black') and Jesus forms the kernel of the legend of the king's conversion to the new belief (Drijvers 1991a: 492–500). The legend came to the knowledge of Eusebius, who incorporated the correspondence into the first book of his *Church History* (I 13). Eusebius tells us that he translated the correspondence from Syriac into Greek from a Syriac original from the royal archives at Edessa. This story sounds trustworthy. In any case the church historian had a copy of the Abgar legend that allegedly came from the Edessene archives. The name Addai, however, was so unfamiliar to Eusebius, because no apostle or disciple with this name was known in the early history of the Jerusalem community, that he changed it into Thaddaeus, one of the seventy.

The Abgar legend opens by telling us that the Edessene king sent an embassy to the Roman governor of Syria with letters regarding state affairs. The embassy, of which Hanan the royal secretary was a member, met large crowds on their way to Jerusalem to see Jesus. The Edessene ambassadors joined them, saw Jesus' healings and other miracles in Jerusalem, noticed the hate of the Jews who wanted to kill Jesus, and went home as eye-witnesses of Jesus' public life. They brought detailed word to King Abgar, who thereupon sent a letter to Jesus. The king invited Jesus to Edessa, a town large enough for the two of them, so that he could be safe from the Jews and moreover could heal King Abgar from a chronic illness. The embassy went back to Jerusalem, where they found Jesus in the house of the Jewish high priest. Abgar's letter was read out to him and Hanan returned with a reply to Edessa. The letters are worth quoting verbatim:

> Abgar Ukkama, to Jesus, the Good Physician, who has appeared in the country of Jerusalem. My Lord: Peace. I have heard of Thee and of Thy healing, that it is not by medicines and roots Thou healest, but by Thy word Thou openest the eyes of the blind, Thou makest the lame to walk, cleansest the lepers, and makest the deaf to hear. And unclean spirits and lunatics, and those tormented, them Thou healest by Thy word; Thou also raisest the dead. And when

I heard of these great wonders which Thou dost, I decided in my mind that either Thou art God, who has come down from heaven and dost these things, or Thou are the Son of God, who dost all these things. Therefore, I have written to request of Thee to come to me who adore Thee, and to heal the disease which I have, as I believe in Thee. This also I have heard, that the Jews murmur against Thee and persecute Thee, and even seek to crucify Thee, and contemplate treating Thee cruelly. I possess one small and beautiful city, and it is sufficient for both to dwell in it in quietness.

Jesus' reply to Abgar's letter is as follows:

Blessed art thou, who, although thou hast not seen Me, believest in Me, for it is written of Me, Those who see Me will not believe in Me, and those who see Me not, will believe in Me. But as to that which thou hast written to Me, that I should come to thee, that for which I was sent here is now finished, and I am going up to my Father, who sent me, and when I have gone up to Him, I will send to thee one of my disciples, who will cure the disease which thou hast, and restore thee to health; and all who are with thee he will convert to everlasting life. Thy city shall be blessed, and no enemy shall again become master of it for ever. (Phillips 1876: 4–5)

As a result of Jesus' promise to Abgar the apostle Addai arrived at Edessa, sent there by Judas Thomas. Addai stayed with Tobias son of Tobias, a Jew from Palestine, until King Abgar learnt about his coming and invited him to court. There Addai healed the king and some of his nobles, preached the gospel and got the opportunity to speak to the entire population of Edessa, which assembled at royal orders in a large square. Everybody, even some Jews and pagan priests, converted to the new belief (Drijvers 1985: 88–96). The original Abgar legend with the correspondence was in the course of time extended with various additions, all with a propagandistic aim, until it reached its final form some time during the first half of the fifth century AD. The original legend, however, has nothing to do with a supposed early or even later conversion of the Edessene dynasty, but has a clear anti-Manichaean propagandist aim. Addai, one of the best-known Manichaean missionaries in the Syrian area, was transformed into a Christian apostle.

Just as Mani wrote to Edessa, Jesus also sent a letter in which he promises to convey an apostle. The text of this passage in Jesus' letter is very similar to the pericope in John's Gospel where Jesus promises to send the Paraclete, John 16: 7–8:

> Nevertheless I tell you the truth; It is expedient for you that I go away; for if I go not away, the Comforter will not come unto you; but if I depart, I will send him unto you. And when he is come, he will reprove the world of sin, and of righteousness, and of judgement.

In Jesus' letter to Abgar he promises to send an apostle, who, so to say, takes the place of the Paraclete, the Comforter, in the passage in John's Gospel. It is noteworthy that Mani considered himself the promised Paraclete. The text from John's Gospel in the wording of the *Diatessaron* was his main apostolic legitimation and link with the Christian tradition. In Manichaeism Addai is an apostle of Mani, the promised Paraclete. In the Abgar correspondence Jesus promises an apostle, who turns out to be Addai. There are more elements in the Abgar legend that indicate its anti-Manichaean aim, but the most important thing is that the legend proclaims a *prestige de l'origine*. Christianity is much older and therefore much more prestigious than Manichaeism and its local appearance in the time of King Abgar Ukkama and Jesus, when the apostle Addai came to Edessa, is linked with the centre of Christianity itself. That is the reason why the legend tells us that Addai stayed with Tobias son of Tobias, a Jew from Palestine, and that even some Jews converted to the new belief. The royal house of Edessa and in particular King Abgar Ukkama plays an important role in this ingenuous and sophisticated story, because Mani had special connections with the Sassanian court and possibly other royalties, perhaps even Queen Zenobia of Palmyra. Most of the stories about Mani's miraculous healings are set in a royal court and centre around princely personages (Drijvers 1983: 171–85). The propaganda of the Abgar legend and correspondence is stimulated by the Manichaean mission in and around Edessa and by the historical context of Mani's public performances.

THE JEWS OF EDESSA AND THE ORIGINS OF SYRIAC-SPEAKING CHRISTIANITY

After this rough sketch of Syrian Christianity, Judaism and in particular the Jews at Edessa ask for attention. Edessa had a Jewish community that perhaps comprised about 12 per cent of the population. This percentage is based on the number of the known tomb inscriptions, of which four out of fifty are Jewish; three are written in Hebrew and one in Greek (Segal 1965: 40; Segal 1970: 41–3). A similar percentage of Antioch's population was possibly Jewish too, but there is a lot of guesswork here. Some members of the Jewish congregation were merchants in silk, since Edessa was a main station on the silk road to China. They were therefore men of a certain wealth and position in society. But a considerable number of the Jews must have belonged to the rank and file of the Edessene population. There was at least one synagogue, which was made into a church of St Stephen in the first half of the fifth century when Rabbula, the tyrant of Edessa, held the bishop's see. Edessa's Jews had therefore a certain weight and influence, which also becomes clear from the fact that the city is mentioned in the Targum on Genesis 10: 10 and is identified with biblical Erekh (Segal 1970: 1–3). But the main argument for the importance and distinction of Edessa's Jews is usually taken from the supposedly rapid growth of Christianity and the role attributed to the Jews in this process of conversion. The idea, however, of a substantial role of the Jews in the Christianization of Edessa is ill-founded, since it is based only on a particular interpretation of the *Doctrina Addai*.

Some scholars construct a link between the Abgar legend and the famous conversion of the royal house of Adiabene to Judaism as told by Flavius Josephus (*Antiquities* XX 2, 3; Segal 1980: 171–91; Oppenheimer 1983: 14–17). Just as Queen Helena and King Izates of Adiabene converted to Judaism, so King Abgar of Edessa embraced the Christian belief. Others believe that an elsewhere unknown Christian apostle Addai brought the gospel directly from Jerusalem to Edessa, so that original and pure elements of the early Christian message were preserved in this North Mesopotamian kingdom. In the Thomas gospel consequently, unknown words of Jesus himself that were completely forgotten in the rest of the world, would have been saved (e.g. Robinson and Koester 1971: 114–58). The use of Syriac, an

Aramaic dialect not unlike that which Jesus himself spoke, has also exercised a certain attraction. Imagine, Jesus' own words and early traditions safeguarded in a kind of sacred language; the original gospel untainted by Hellenism. Such a view of Syriac-speaking Christianity breathes a nostalgic longing for original purity, as if Edessa were a kind of sacred enclave in a corner of the evil world that was chosen and protected by the Lord himself. Edessa, however, was as Hellenized as the rest of Syria and the Roman Empire in general, and Christianity in this Syriac-speaking region was not an isolated phenomenon different from Antioch and other main centres. On the contrary, there was a continuous exchange of writings and ideas between Antioch and Edessa along the road that connected the two cities.

If we examine the entire early Christian literature from the Syrian region and from Edessa in particular, Jews are seldom mentioned and usually completely ignored. They do not occur in Tatian's writings, or in the *Acts of Thomas* and in the remaining Thomas literature. They are not found in Manichaean texts, or in Bardaisan's treatises, apart from a note on the Jewish Law. The *Doctrina Addai* is the only writing that mentions the Jews, and then in a twofold way. They are the crucifiers, but on the other hand the object of Christian propaganda. A typical propaganda element in the Abgar legend is that Hanan and the Edessene ambassadors met Jesus in the house of the high priest. If the high priest at Jerusalem invited Jesus to his house and gave him the opportunity of receiving foreign embassies, Christianity could not possibly be a wrong belief for Jews! According to the *Doctrina Addai* some Jews converted to Christianity upon the preaching of Addai and confessed that the Messiah was the Son of the Living God. Two pagan priests also converted (Drijvers 1980: 33–5). The same opponents, Jews and Gentiles, occur in Addai's farewell sermon before he dies (Phillips 1876: 41; Howard 1981: 87). The apostle warns his flock:

Do not be a stumbling block to the blind, but make the path and road smooth in a rough place, between the crucify-ing Jews and the erring pagans. With these two parties alone you have a warfare that you might demonstrate the truth of the faith which you hold. Those fighters for the truth are, however, not very militant or warlike. When you are silent, your modest and honourable appearance joins the battle for you with those who hate truth and love falsehood.

Such phrases are typical of a minority group without real power to convert people of different belief. It even seems that Christians instead of converting Jews were friends with them and may have gone so far as to visit the synagogue (Howard 1981: 87; Drijvers 1985: 94–5).

> Beware, therefore, of the crucifiers and do not be friends with them, lest thou be responsible with those whose hands are full of the blood of the Messiah. Know and bear witness that everything which we say and teach in regard to the Messiah is written in the books of the Prophets and is laid up with them.

Christians who, unlike Marcionites, Manichaeans and some other gnostic groups, wanted to keep the Jewish Holy Book, the Old Testament, as part of their Bible, because creation and salvation were parts of the only God's provident plan for the world, were obliged to reinterpret the Law and Prophets in such a way that Old Testament and New Testament formed a real unity. The doctrine of the divine *logos* active in creation and salvation is one way of solving this problem. In other words, these Christians had to come to terms with the whole Jewish tradition and heritage through fitting it into a Christian context. If Syrian Christianity consequently preserved a great many Jewish traditions in its literature, even some that are not to be found elsewhere, this is not a proof of a substantial Jewish part in the formation of the Church in Syria, but only of a Christian urge to adapt and assimilate Old Testament and other Jewish traditions to its own ideological concepts (Brock 1979: 212–32). The struggle of an orthodox Christian minority with, in particular, Marcionites compelled the Church to deal with Jewish material without identifying itself with Judaism.

It is precisely for this reason that the Syriac-speaking Christians produced their own Syriac translation of the Old Testament, the Peshitta. It was in their interests to possess a version that was different from the Hebrew text and the Aramaic targumim which were in use among the Jews. Even if the extant Peshitta version shows signs of an influence from certain targumim, this again is not a decisive indication of the Jewish origin of the Peshitta (*contra*

Vööbus 1958b; Brock 1979: 212–23; Weitzman 1982: 277–98). Moreover, nowhere in the Jewish sources is a special Syriac translation of the Old Testament, unlike existing Greek translations, recorded. The Edessene and other Syrian Jews did not need a Syriac translation, whereas the Christians wanted it to define themselves as different from the Jews. It is of special interest that some passages in the Syriac Peshitta show a certain Christian colouring, whereas more philosophically tainted books like the Wisdom of Solomon were translated in a highly tendentious manner to make them into Christian books in accordance with the mainstream of Syrian Christianity (Drijvers 1986: 15–30).[2] The same phenomenon can be observed in the writings of Theophilus of Antioch at the end of the second century AD. Theophilus' strong emphasis on the continuity of the revelation to the Jews with that to the Christians does not imply a positive relationship with the Jews. On the contrary, it is meant to demonstrate that all the rest were in error and only the Christians have held the truth (Theophilus, *To Autolycus* 2, 33).

All the available evidence points in the direction that Syriac-speaking Christianity in northern Mesopotamia and in the East Syrian region was mainly of Gentile origin and that some of these Christians were more attracted by Judaism than the Jews were drawn to Christianity. 'Do not be friends with the Jews' was Addai's warning in his farewell discourse to his flock. And these words only apply to that group which wanted to keep the Jewish Bible as part of the Christian revelation.

As in Antioch, we do not know much about the situation in Edessa in the fourth century. Some information can be gathered from the works of Ephrem Syrus, who after the fall of Nisibis in 363 spent the remaining ten years of his life as the champion of orthodoxy at Edessa (Murray 1982a: 755–62; Griffith 1986: 22–52). Ephrem Syrus does not address himself to the Jews as a separate community at Edessa, but deals with members of the Christian Church who were attracted to Jewish customs and feasts and frequented the synagogue. From Ephrem's viewpoint, Jews were on a par with Marcionites, Bardaisanites, Manichaeans, and even pagans, in so far as Christians still clung to pagan practices. Ephrem therefore comments on the Jews in his anti-heretical writings which are meant only for his own threatened flock. Ephrem has a revealing remark: 'he who prays with the Jews prays with Barabbas the robber' (Drijvers 1985: 97–8). Jewish religious customs were apparently so appealing to the Christians that Ephrem's community was robbed, or Ephrem felt it like that. When the same Ephrem attacks the Arians in his third homily, *On Faith*, he speaks within this context at great length about Jewish practice that was common among Christians. In particular, circumcision, the observance of the sabbath, and the great feasts had an enormous attraction. Ephrem's sermon is intended only for internal Christian use. The situation at Edessa in Ephrem's time can be compared to religious relations at Antioch where John Chrysostom (*c.* 349–407), who in his *Homilies against the Jews* attacked Jewish customs that were practised in the Antiochene Christian community (Wilken 1983). Fixing the boundaries of the Christian Church and Christian self-definition have always implied polemic against the Jews. This situation did not of necessity give rise to actual hostility between groups and individuals in the towns of the eastern part of the Roman Empire. All the evidence shows that Judaism appealed to pagans and Christians alike and that the Christians used and took over large parts of Jewish writings for their own use, which implies regular contacts on all levels. This in particular holds true when Christianity was still a small minority in comparison with Jews and Gentiles, who represented traditional, well-established religions.

The situation changed, however, during the fourth century. Particularly after Julian the Apostate's plan to rebuild the temple at Jerusalem in 363, Christian anti-Jewish feelings became much stronger. At that time the legend of Helena, Constantine's mother, who was said to have discovered the True Cross at Jerusalem, emerged. The story claims Jerusalem as a Christian place *par excellence*, where the True Cross was found notwithstanding severe Jewish opposition (Drijvers 1991b). A version of the Helena legend found its way to the *Doctrina Addai* and was adapted to the fictitious chronology of the Abgar legend. The *Doctrina* tells the story of Protonice, the wife of the Emperor Claudius (AD 41–54), who came as a pilgrim to Jerusalem, visited Christ's tomb and discovered the True Cross, which she gave to James, Christ's brother, who was at that time the leader of the Christian community at Jerusalem. The name Protonice is fictional, but bears a symbolic meaning. It signifies 'first victory' and stands for the first victory of the True Cross over the Jews.

At the beginning of the fifth century Christians felt free to attack the Jews in a tone of complete religious fanaticism, and to destroy synagogues in order to get rid of a threatening rival. This happened at Edessa in the time of Bishop Rabbula (Drijvers 1985: 102).

Summarizing, it can be stated that Edessa and the Syriac-speaking region in northern Mesopotamia had close links with Antioch and that the religious situation in both cities is comparable. As in Antioch, Christianity at Edessa is mainly of Gentile origin and does not show substantial influence from Judaism, let alone an original Judaeo-Christianity coming directly from Jerusalem. However, Edessene Christians were attracted to Jewish religious practice and were obliged to take over and to reinterpret Jewish holy writ in their struggle against the influential Marcionites and other gnostics. The final victory of Christian orthodoxy in about AD 400 meant both a final break with and open hatred against the Jews. In the foregoing period we may assume a pattern of social relations between Gentiles, Jews and Christians, which the official leaders of the Church did not like at all. In this pattern Judaism was a traditional well-established belief system, whereas the Christians were revolutionary newcomers who recruited their followers mainly among the Gentiles. On the other hand, they had to deal with Jewish writings and practices, and it was this paradox which caused them such severe problems.

NOTES

1 The *Manichaean Psalm-Book*, preserved in a Coptic version (ed. Allberry 1938) goes back to a Syriac original. See also Baumstark 1941: 117–26; Säve-Söderbergh 1949. For magic bowls with Syriac texts, Hamilton 1971; Naveh and Shaked 1985.

2 A different view of Peshitta authorship is explored by M. Weitzman in chapter 7, pp. 147–173 of this volume (eds).

BIBLIOGRAPHY

Allberry, C. R. C. (1938) *A Manichaean Psalm-Book*, Part II, Stuttgart.

Baarda, Tj. (1983) *Early Transmission of Words of Jesus: Thomas, Tatian and the Text of the New Testament*, Amsterdam.

Baumstark, A. (1941) Review of C. R. C. Allberry, 'A Manichaean Psalm-Book Part II', *Oriens Christianus* 36: 117–26.

Bellinger, A. R. and Welles, C. B. (1935) 'A Third-Century Contract of Sale from Edessa in Osrhoene', *Yale Classical Studies* 5: 95–154.

Brock, S. (1979) 'Jewish Traditions in Syriac Sources', *Journal of Jewish Studies* 30: 212–32.

Cameron, Averil (1986) 'Redrawing the Map: Early Christian Territory after Foucault', *Journal of Roman Studies* 76: 266–71.

Cameron, R. and Dewey, A. J. (1979) *The Cologne Mani Codex Concerning the Origin of his Body*, Missoula, Mont.

Dihle, A. (1982) *The Theory of Will in Classical Antiquity*, Berkeley, Calif.

Dillemann, L. (1982) *Haute Mésopotamie orientale et pays adjacents*, Paris.

Downey, G. (1961) *A History of Antioch in Syria from Seleucus to the Arab Conquest*, Princeton, NJ.

Drijvers, H. J. W. (1965) *The Book of the Laws of Countries. Dialogue on Fate of Bardaisan of Edessa*, Assen.

Drijvers, H. J. W. (1966) *Bardaisan of Edessa* (Studia Semitica Neerlandica 6), Assen.

Drijvers, H. J. W. (1972) *Old-Syriac (Edessean) Inscriptions*, Leiden.

Drijvers, H. J. W. (1977) 'Hatra, Palmyra und Edessa. Die Städte der syrisch-mesopotamischen Wüste in politischer, kulturgeschichtlicher und religionsgeschichtlicher Beleuchtung', *Aufstieg und Niedergang der römischen Welt* 11 8, Berlin and New York.

Drijvers, H. J. W. (1980) *Cults and Beliefs at Edessa* (EPRO 82), Leiden.

Drijvers, H. J. W. (1982) 'The Persistence of Pagan Cults and Practices in Christian Syria', in N. G. Garsoïan, Th. F. Mathews and R. W. Thomson (eds) *East of Byzantium: Syria and Armenia in the Formative Period*, Washington DC, 35–43.

Drijvers, H. J. W. (1983) 'Addai and Mani. Christentum and Manichäismus im dritten Jahrhundert in Syrien', *IIIe Symposium Syriacum 1980, Orientalia Christiana Analecta* 221: 171–85.

Drijvers, H. J. W. (1984) *East of Antioch. Studies in Early Syriac Christianity*, London.

Drijvers, H. J. W. (1985) 'Jews and Christians at Edessa', *Journal of Jewish Studies* 36: 88–102.

Drijvers, H. J. W. (1986) 'The Peshitta of *Sapientia Salomonis*' in *Scripta Sigma Vocis: Studies presented to J. H. Hospers*, Groningen, 15–30.

Drijvers, H. J. W. (1987–8) 'Marcionism in Syria: Principles, Problems, Polemics', *The Second Century* 6: 153–72.

Drijvers, H. J. W. and Reinink, G. (1988) 'Taufe und Licht. Tatian, Ebionäerevangelium und Thomasakten', *Text and Testimony. Essays in honour of A. F. J. Klijn*, Kampen: 91–110.

Drijvers, H. J. W. (1991a) 'The Abgar Legend', in W. Schneemelcher (ed.) *New Testament Apocrypha*, Vol. 1, trans. R. McL. Wilson, Cambridge, Louisville, 492–500.

Drijvers, J. W. (1991b) *Helena Augusta. The Mother of Constantine the Great and the Legend of Her Finding of the True Cross*, Leiden.

Elze, M. (1960) *Tatian und seine Theologie*, Göttingen.

Goodenough, E. R. (1964) *Jewish Symbols in the Greco-Roman Period*, Vols 9, 10 and 11, *Symbolism in the Dura Synagogue*, New York.

Griffith, S. H. (1986) 'Ephraem, the Deacon of Edessa, and the Church of the Empire', in Th. Halton, and J. P. Williman (eds) *Diakonia: Studies in Honor of Robert T. Meyer*, Washington, DC, 22–52.

Gutmann, J. (ed.) (1973) *The Dura-Europos Synagogue: A Re-Evaluation* (*1932–1972*), Missoula, Mont.

Hamilton, V. P. (1971) 'Syriac Incantation Bowls', unpublished PhD thesis, Brandeis University.

Harnack, A von (1960) *Marcion. Das Evangelium vom fremden Gott*, reprint, Darmstadt.

Howard, G. (1981) *The Teaching of Addai*, Chico, Calif.

Klijn, A. F. J. (1970) 'John XIV, 22 and the Name Judas Thomas', *Studies in John presented to J. N. Sevenster*, Leiden, 86–96.

Koenen, L. and Römer, C. (1988) *Der Kölner Mani-Kodex: Über das Werden seines Leibes* (Papyrologica Coloniensia, XIV), Opladen.

Kraeling, C. H. (1935) *A Greek Fragment of Tatian's Diatessaron from Dura* (Studies and Documents III), London.

Kraeling, C. H. (1956) *The Excavations at Dura-Europos, Final Report VIII, 1, The Synagogue*, New Haven, Conn.

Kraeling, C. H. (1967) *The Excavations at Dura-Europos, Final Report VIII, 2, The Christian Building*, New Haven, Conn.

Lieu, S. N. C. (1985) *Manichaeism in the Later Roman Empire and Medieval China: A Historical Survey*, Manchester.

Meeks, W. A. and Wilken, R. L. (1978) *Jews and Christians in Antioch in the First Four Centuries of the Common Era* (SBL Sources for Biblical Study 13), Missoula, Mont.

Millar, F. (1971) 'Paul of Samosata, Zenobia and Aurelian: the Church, Local Culture and Political Allegiance in Third-Century Syria', *Journal of Roman Studies*: 1–17.

Murray, R. (1975) *Symbols of Church and Kingdom: A Study in Early Syriac Tradition*, Cambridge.

Murray, R. (1982a) 'The Characteristics of the Earliest Syriac Christianity', in N. G. Garsoïan, Th. F. Mathews and R. W. Thomson (eds) *East of Byzantium: Syria and Armenia in the Formative Period*. Washington, DC, 3–16.

Murray, R. (1982b) 'Ephraem Syrus', *Theologische Realenzyklopädie IX*, Berlin and New York: 755–62.

Nagel, P. (1973) 'Die apokryphen Apostelakten des 2 und 3. Jahrhunderts in der manichäischen Literatur', *Gnosis und Neues Testament*, Berlin: 149–82.

Naveh, J. and Shaked, S. (1985) *Amulets and Magic Bowls: Aramaic Incantations of Late Antiquity*, Jerusalem.

Oates, D. (1968) *Studies in the Ancient History of Northern Iraq*, London.

Oden, R. A. (1977) *Studies in Lucian's 'De Syria Dea'* (Harvard Semitic Monographs 15), Missoula, Mont.

Oppenheimer, A. (1983) *Babylonia Judaica in the Talmudic Period*, Beihefte zum Tübinger Atlas des Vorderen Orients, Reihe B, Geisteswissenschaften XLVII, Wiesbaden.

Phillips, G. (1876) *The Doctrine of Addai, the Apostle*, London.

Robinson, J. M. and Koester, H. (1971) *Trajectories Through Early Christianity*, Philadelphia, Pa.

Säve-Söderbergh, T. (1949) *Studies in the Coptic Manichaean Psalm-Book: Prosody and Mandaean Parallels*, Uppsala.

Schmitt, R. (1980) 'Die Ostgrenze von Armenien über Mesopotamien, Syrien bis Arabien', *Die Sprachen im römischen Reich der Kaiserzeit*, Beihefte der Bonner Jahrbücher 40: 187–214.

Segal, J. B. (1965) 'The Jews of North Mesopotamia before the Rise of Islam', *Sepher Segal*, Jerusalem: 32–63.

Segal, J. B. (1970) *Edessa: 'the Blessed City'*, Oxford.

Segal, J. B. (1980) 'When did Christianity come to Edessa?' in B. C. Bloomfield (ed.) *Middle East Studies and Libraries: a Felicitation Volume for Professor J. D. Pearson*, London, 179–91.

Teixidor, J. (1989) 'Les derniers rois d'Edesse d'après deux nouveaux documents syriaques', *Zeitschrift für Papyrologie und Epigraphik* 76: 219–22.

Vööbus, A. (1958a) *A History of Asceticism in the Syrian Orient* Vol. I (Corpus Scriptorum Christianorum Orientalium, Subsidia 14), Louvain.

Vööbus. A. (1958b) *Peschitta und Targumim des Pentateuchs*, Stockholm.

Weitzman, M. P. (1982) 'The Origin of the Peshitta Psalter', in J. A. Emerton and S. C. Reif (eds) *Interpreting the Hebrew Bible: Essays in honour of E. I. J. Rosenthal*, Cambridge, 277–98.

Whittaker, M. (1982) *Tatian: Oratio ad Graecos and Fragments*, Oxford.

Wilken, R. L. (1983) *John Chrysostom and the Jews: Rhetoric and Reality in the Late 4th Century*, Berkeley, Calif.

7

FROM JUDAISM TO CHRISTIANITY: THE SYRIAC VERSION OF THE HEBREW BIBLE

Michael Weitzman

INTRODUCTION

The state of the question

There has long been debate about the religious context in which the Syriac version of the Hebrew Bible (the 'Peshitta' – here called P) would have been first produced. The date of the translation is usually put somewhere between the first and third centuries AD, but the context might be either Jewish or Christian. On the one hand, the translation was made from the Hebrew and shows the influence of Jewish exegesis. Again, it exhibits parallels with targums – that is, with Jewish biblical versions written in dialects that belong under the heading of Aramaic, as does the Syriac of the Peshitta itself. On the other hand, the translation has been preserved by the Church, and only by the Church. There is no evidence of its use in the synagogue, though the translator of the targum on Proverbs (Nöldeke 1872), the biblical commentator Nachmanides and the compiler of a midrash attested in a fifteenth-century manuscript (Neubauer 1878: 39–42) showed academic interest in it.

These general considerations do not determine the religious background of P and opinion today remains divided between the hypotheses of Jewish and Christian authorship. It is therefore necessary to work through P's version of the books of the Hebrew Bible, in search of changes of substance, or at least of emphasis, which might reflect the theology of the translator(s). Such clues are rare, because for the most part P translates literally – though not at the expense of intelligibility. Theologically significant passages are, however, more numerous than previous discussions have allowed. The present chapter sets out to reconstruct the religious beliefs of the translators on the basis of that internal evidence. It also suggests that the roots of those beliefs lie in the Hebrew Bible, and then follows them forwards into the Syriac-speaking Church in which P was preserved.

Arguments for a Jewish context

P was translated from a consonantal Hebrew text which coincided largely with the Massoretic Text (MT), i.e. the text handed down among the Jews to the present day. This is clear from occasional misreadings in P (e.g. at Numbers 6: 25 *w-yḥnk* 'may He be gracious to thee' was read *w-yḥyk* 'may He preserve thee'). But, of course, use of the Hebrew does not demonstrate Jewish authorship of the translation, as the example of Jerome would be enough to prove.

Again, there are many examples of Jewish exegesis in P (e.g. at Exodus 40: 17, the idea that the Tabernacle was set up on a Sunday, found also in bShabbath 80b), as J. Perles's pioneering work showed. Although the evidence was exaggerated somewhat by Perles, and more so by Heller, hundreds of striking parallels with rabbinic sources remain (Maori 1975). Yet Jewish exegesis is no conclusive proof of Jewish origin either. It might in theory stem from a Christian community with Jewish roots or with Jewish contacts. For example, the Old (Curetonian) Syriac version of Matthew 23:5 translates *phylakteria* by the authentic Jewish term, viz '(the straps of) their Tephillin' (*teplayhon*). Again Jerome (*PL* 25, 843) in his commentary on Hosea 3:2 has a homiletic explanation – the 15 shekels symbolize the date of Passover on the 15th of Nisan – which reappears in bḤullin 92a.

Another common argument for the Jewish origin of the translation invokes its many verbal parallels with the targums. Scholars have frequently exaggerated the parallels, forgetting how much similarity is inevitable between translations of the same text into dialects of the same language, even if the actual translations are independently made. Some have even supposed that P (at least in the Pentateuch) is not a direct translation from the Hebrew at all.

On this theory, P is based on a targum partially revised in conformity with MT and transcribed into Syriac characters.

Some striking parallels indeed exist, e.g. the rendering of Hebrew *taḥaš* (NEB: 'porpoise') by *sasgonā*, 'many-coloured' in both P and the targums. Such parallels are particularly striking in the Pentateuch and the Minor Prophets (Gelston 1987: 178–190). The parallels are, however, too few to show that P depends regularly on any targum. Indeed, P's treatment of the Hebrew text very often differs from that of any known targum. Furthermore, P often deals with obscure passages by simply omitting them; and unlike the targums it tolerates some bold anthropomorphisms. The parallels rather indicate a 'common exegetical tradition' (Maori 1975: xvii) that dictated the proper Aramaic equivalent of certain Hebrew words and phrases. This is no sure proof of Jewish authorship, since the targum tradition might have lived on in a Christian community of Jewish descent.

Supporters of the theory of Jewish translators have also appealed to biblical citations in Syriac patristic authors and translation literature, and in works of Arabic authors whose biblical text is based on P. Many of these citations represent looser translations than the text of the biblical manuscripts of P. As the known targums are inclined (in varying degrees) to paraphrase, these loose citations are claimed to preserve an otherwise lost 'targumic' stage in the development of P. However, this argument neglects other possible causes of the looseness – faulty memory on the part of a patristic writer, metrical constraints on authors of Syriac verse, freedom in the translation *from* Syriac in the case of Arabic works. The Jews had no monopoly on loose translation.

Arguments for a Christian context

No more conclusive, however, are the arguments often proposed in favour of a Christian context for the translation, familiar from B. J. Robert's influential book (1951: 222; but see also Bloch 1918–19: 219). Some renderings, as we shall see, could be read as references to Christ, or appear to echo the New Testament. Values which (at least at first sight) fit the Church rather than the Synagogue have also been detected, notably an 'air of negligence apparent in the translation of the Levitical law, particularly in the sections concerning clean and unclean animals' (Davidson 1839: 60). We shall return to such passages, which are certainly of of theological interest. For the moment, however, one must note that they do not by themselves prove Christian origin outright. First, some of the arguments are factually wrong. In particular, as regards dietary laws, Emerton (1962) has shown that P in fact identifies in accordance with Jewish tradition all the creatures involved, apart from a few forbidden birds. The gaps in P's ornithological expertise do not in themselves prove that he was not a practising Jew. Second, in individual passages a seemingly Christian feature may be due to quite different factors, e.g. the influence of the standard Greek translation – the Septuagint (LXX). Third, ideas that some have assumed to be exclusive to Christianity may have existed also in certain currents of Judaism.

Summary

Previous generations, then, could not agree on the question of Jewish versus Christian context. For them, Judaism was represented by the rabbinic texts – Mishnah, Midrash, Talmud – and so the alternatives were sharp: the context had to be either rabbinic Judaism or Christianity. The problem was that much of the evidence, as we shall see, fits neither alternative well. The explanation lies in the diversity which the last few decades have revealed within both religions. In particular, not all Judaism was rabbinic. It follows that, rather than devise a litmus test between two possibilities called 'Judaism' and 'Christianity', we have to build up a theological profile of the translation, and only then compare it with the different tendencies, Jewish and Christian, known to us.

THE PESHITTA OF CHRONICLES

Jewish or Christian?

Chronicles may seem an odd point to begin, especially as its canonicity was questioned in the Syriac Church. It was thus excluded from the Nestorian canon, and also from the Syriac scholarly tradition that stretched from the 'Massoretic' manuscripts of the Bible to the scholia of Bar Hebraeus (Brovender 1976: 70; Beckwith 1985: 307–9). It demands our attention, however, because in Chronicles P diverges far more than in any other book from the Massoretic Hebrew text. In other books,

P translates straightforwardly as a rule, with very little explicit theological (or other) comment. In Chronicles, however, the translator was not able to hide behind the text, because – as argued in detail elsewhere (Weitzman 1993) – his Hebrew exemplar seems to have suffered damage. This forced him to guess and consequently to reveal his own assumptions and attitudes.

In some of these guesses, the translator shares the grief and shame of Israel in exile, e.g. 1 Chronicles 29: 16, part of David's prayer (1 Chronicles 29: 10–19), which in P has partly been freely composed by the translator, presumably faced with a largely illegible Hebrew text:

> and thee do we praise, O Lord our God, that thou mayest save us from all the nations that harm and revile us, saying: Where is your God that ye worship?

Similarly at 2 Chronicles 15: 5–7:

> and in those former times, when we feared not our God, there was no peace ... for great evil came upon all the inhabitants of the earth, and we were scattered in every nation and among different cities and lands, for we had forsaken the Lord our God and refused to hearken to his servants the prophets; and he too has requited us for our deeds.

Yet another reference to the exile is introduced at 1 Chronicles 16: 20: 'and ye were led captive'.

We must remember that exile meant not only political helplessness, but also disgrace and sin (Daniel 9: 7–8). Indeed at Daniel 9: 16, the cry that 'thy people has become a reproach' is rendered by P: 'thy people has been scattered to every place'. Ezekiel's message (39: 23) that Israel were exiled for their sins is echoed in a Jewish prayer recited at every festival: 'because of our sins we were exiled from our land' (Baer 1868: 352).

It might be suggested that P of Chronicles is the work not of a Jew sharing this grief, but of a Christian who was gloating over the exile of the Jews as proof of their rejection, as do, for example, Tertullian (*Against Marcion* 3, 23 (4)) and Aphraates (*Demonstrations* 19).[1] However, a hostile propagandist could hardly have simulated the heartfelt ring of the prayers above, or placed in God's mouth the promise that 'the sons of wickedness shall not exile him again' (1 Chronicles 17: 9). Even a Jewish Christian is

unlikely to have felt such sorrow at the plight of the Jews as is
expressed in P on 2 Chronicles 15: 5–7. Jewish Christianity is
characterized by retention of Jewish laws – something hardly
typical of P in Chronicles, as we shall see – rather than by Jewish
national identification.

The participation in Jewish suffering identifies the translator as
a Jew. A positive reference to the historical Israel at 2 Chronicles
6: 18 confirms this:

MT: can indeed God dwell with man on earth?
P: in faith the Lord caused his presence to dwell upon
      his people Israel.

Hebrew *'umnām* 'indeed' was interpreted as *'ĕmūnāh* 'faith'.
Compare the statement (discussed on p. 156) introduced by P at
2 Chronicles 31: 18, that 'all Israel were sanctified in faith'.

The translator again links himself with past generations of Jews
at 1 Chronicles 29:15:

MT: we are before thee sojourners like all our forefathers;
      our days on earth are like a shadow and there is no
      hope
P: and we are sojourners before thee, insignificant
      [z'orin] in the world; and thou didst rule over our
      fathers formerly and command them by which way
      they should go, that they might live

For the most part, the 'midrashic' reputation of P on Chronicles
is due to its divergence from MT. That divergence, however,
reflects not the translator's method but, it may be argued, the
poor physical quality of the Hebrew text before him. In such
passages, one would better speak not of a midrash, but of a loose
rendering made up by the translator, confronted with an often
illegible Hebrew text. The hypothesis of a damaged *copy* explains
many puzzling features of this translation: (a) the omission of
portions of the text, ranging from a few words to several verses,
(b) the replacement of other portions of the text of Chronicles by
parallel passages of the Bible, and (c) curious guesses in passages
(e.g. 2 Chronicles 20: 22) where the Hebrew text would have
been straightforward had the translator only been able to read it.
The hypothesis was originally advanced by S. Fraenkel, who did
not, however, appreciate its power to explain category (c) and so
classified many such renderings as 'targumic'.

Attitude to Jewish law

If the translator identified with the Jewish people, he nevertheless departs on occasion from rabbinic and even Pentateuchal norms, as follows.

The calendar

The Hebrew text of Chronicles tells of Solomon's seven-day feast which marked the dedication of the Temple. It was immediately followed by the seven-day feast of Tabernacles, with a closing festival (Heb. *'ăṣeret*) on the eighth day. Solomon then dismissed the people 'on the twenty-third day of the seventh month' (2 Chronicles 7: 10). P agrees that Solomon feasted for two weeks, though in v.9 he seems to invert their order ('seven days of the festival and seven days of the dedication of the house') and makes no reference to a closing festival. The surprise in P comes in v.10: 'on the day of the full moon [i.e. on the fifteenth day – compare P on 1 Kings 12: 32] of Tishri the king dismissed the people'. The fifteenth day of Tishri is in fact the first day of Tabernacles; but the translator seems to be under the impression that Tabernacles ended a day (or eight days) before that date.

Again, the Hebrew at 2 Chronicles 8: 13 tells us that Solomon offered sacrifice on the feasts of Unleavened Bread, Pentecost and Tabernacles. For Pentecost (Heb. *ḥag ha-šābūʿōt*), however, P writes: 'the feast of the fast' (*ʿēdā d-ṣawmā*). Fasting on Pentecost is forbidden in rabbinic Judaism; according to bPesaḥim 68a, it was one of the three days in the year when even the ascetic Mar son of Rabina did not fast. Fraenkel suggested that the translator confused this feast with the Day of Atonement; he did not try, however, to account for this elementary mistake. Finally, the vague translation of 'Passover' as 'festival' (*ʿēdā*) in 2 Chronicles 30 and 35 reinforces the impression of indifference to halakhah (Jewish law).

Hours of prayer

The Hebrew text of 1 Chronicles 15: 21 lists the Levites designated 'to play with harps upon the *šeminit*'. The last Hebrew word, literally 'eighth', is a musical term of uncertain meaning. Now P substitutes numbers of its own: 'These uttered praise on the harp every day at the third, sixth and ninth hours.' These hours of prayer are alien to rabbinic Judaism, which specifies not points but intervals of time (e.g. mBerakoth 4: 1 – 'The morning prayer may be said until noon'). In the Church, however, these canonical hours of prayer – terce, sext and none – were established at a very early date. Clement of Alexandria noted that 'some fix hours for prayer, such as the third, sixth and ninth' (*Miscellanies* 7: 7). Tertullian commends these hours, because of their importance in the New Testament and because their number recalls the Trinity (*On the Prayer* 25). These hours indeed appear as designated for prayer from the earliest days of the Church. Peter prayed at the sixth hour, i.e. at noon (Acts 10: 9). The ninth hour is called the 'hour of prayer' (Acts 3: 1). This was the hour when Cornelius prayed even as a 'God-fearer' attached to the Jewish community, i.e. before his conversion to Christianity. It was also the hour of Jesus' final prayer (Matthew 27: 46, Mark 15: 34, Luke 23: 44–6). Their observance by Cornelius, and their occurrence in P, suggest that these hours of prayer originated in some form of Judaism, though not in rabbinic Judaism – before being adopted by the Church.

Priests and Temple

Here too we find surprising departures from rabbinic and even biblical norms. At 2 Chronicles 13:11, P says that the candelabrum was lit up by a 'boy lamplighter'; the Mishnah, however, imposed this task on the priests themselves (mTamid 3: 9). At 2 Chronicles 31: 3 P identifies the animals for the 'continual' sacrifice (the Tamid) as bulls, instead of the lambs prescribed at Numbers 28: 3. Both renderings in P arise from misreading of the Hebrew – *lĕ-na'ar* instead of *lĕ-bā'ēr* at 2 Chronicles 13: 11, *bāqār* instead of *bōqer* at 2 Chronicles 31: 3. Most surprising is P's rendering of the last word of 2 Chronicles 31: 18, together with v.19:

> for holy were the sons of Aaron the priest; holy was their flesh; and they drew not nigh unto women.

This is not a gloss (*pace* Brock 1979: 217) but a mistranslation. The Hebrew speaks of the priests *bi-śĕdē migraš 'ārehem* 'in the fields of the common-land of [i.e. around] their cities'. The translator, however, mistook the consonants *bśdy* 'in the fields' for *bśr* 'flesh'. Hebrew *migraš* ('common-land' for grazing animals) comes from the root *grš* 'drive out', which can also mean 'divorce'; the translator may have thought of the latter, whence 'celibacy'. The reference is not confined to the priests' hours of service in the Temple, for entry there was forbidden not only to women but to all non-priests (Numbers 18: 4, Nehemiah 6: 11). P is asserting rather that the priests led a celibate life. This is alien to rabbinic Judaism, but is reminiscent of the Essenes, who considered themselves priests, and, according to Josephus (*Jewish War* II 8, 2 (120)), were celibate.

These renderings which conflict with rabbinic Judaism belong to two distinct categories. Some embody a rule (halakhah) which we know (or can presume) to have actually been practised in non-rabbinic circles. For example, in view of the external parallels, the rendering at 1 Chronicles 15: 21 must reflect a real practice of praying at the third, sixth and ninth hours. Of course many other examples exist of divergence from rabbinic halakhah – e.g. in the Dead Sea Scrolls, or the apocryphal book of Susannah (which in a capital case demands death for witnesses whose testimony is broken down under examination, in contrast to mMakkoth 1:4). Similarly Josephus (e.g. *Antiquities* IV 280) and Philo (e.g. *On the Special Laws* III 182 (195)) do not interpret 'eye for an eye' invariably, like the rabbis (bBaba Qamma 84a), to mean monetary compensation. Hence divergences in P from rabbinic halakhah need cause no surprise.

By contrast, it would be dangerous to suppose that the translator was actually familiar with a practice of fasting on Pentecost or leaving a boy to light the Temple lamp. It seems rather that the many guesses which the difficult text forced upon the translator happened to include some which bore on halachic matters. The content of the translator's guesses may be noteworthy, but the central point is his ignorance of rabbinic norms. These are not rules of Jewish life (halakhot), but inventions (pseudo-halakhot).

Prayer, charity and faith

Yet with regard to certain other commandments, the translator is well informed, even assiduous. He often introduces the idea of prayer. For example, at 1 Chronicles 16: 29 the sense of the Hebrew ('and come before him') is expanded in the Syriac: 'with the prayer of your mouths'. References to 'cymbals' and other musical instruments in the Hebrew are replaced in P by 'praise', 'voice' and 'mouth' (1 Chronicles 15: 28, 2 Chronicles 29: 25–7, 30: 21). At 1 Chronicles 16: 42, P departs from the Hebrew to stress that 'righteous men offered praise not with instruments [five are listed] but with goodly mouth and pure and perfect prayer and righteousness and integrity'. Those people who, according to the Hebrew, 'sought' (*drš* or *bqš*) or 'returned to' (*šwb*) the Lord are said instead to have 'prayed before him' (1 Chronicles 22: 19, 2 Chronicles 15: 4, 15, etc.). In the Hebrew of 2 Chronicles 14: 3, King Asa, having suppressed heathen worship, calls upon the Jews 'to seek the Lord the God of their fathers and to perform the Torah and the commandments'. P renders the first half of Asa's call by 'Come let us pray before the Lord God of our fathers'; the second half, on performing the Torah, is omitted. Finding his text of David's prayer in 1 Chronicles 29 largely illegible, the translator composed a prayer of his own, concluding with the earliest known text of the Jewish Kaddish prayer (v.19):

> *d-netqadaš šmāk rabā w-neštabaḥ b-'ālmā da-brayt*
> that thy great name be sanctified and praised in the world
> that thou hast created.

Another commandment evidently important to the translator was charity, for at 1 Chronicles 23:5 he writes, apparently once more guessing at a text he could not read:

> and David set over the poor and needy, providers and over-seers who might feed and provide for the poor – one [provider] over ten [needy people] – and they lacked nothing.

Faith is another virtue introduced in this translation. At 1 Chronicles 29: 17, P twice substitutes inward faith for the 'rectitude' (i.e. upright action) of the Hebrew, so that David now says:

> And I know, O God, that thou searchest the heart, and delightest in faith [*haymānutā*]; and I by the faith of my heart have uttered all this praise.

To the reference already noted at 2 Chronicles 6: 18 to Israel's faith, we may add 2 Chronicles 31: 18. MT speaks of the whole company (*qāhāl*) of priests, who hallowed themselves in their *'ĕmūnāh* – i.e. conscientiously, or because of their permanent standing. P instead declares that 'all Israel were sanctified in faith'. The rabbinic sources, by contrast, generally prefer to stress observance.

Place and time

The place-names which the translator sometimes substitutes for the names in the Hebrew text hint at his location. Thus Heb. Ṣōbā' (1 Chronicles 18: 3, etc.) becomes Nisibis, 'Ăram Ma'ăkāh (1 Chronicles 19: 6) becomes Haran, and Carchemish (2 Chronicles 35: 20) becomes Mabog, some 40 km to the south. The rendering of the Hebrew 'ăšērāh by nemrā 'leopard' (2 Chronicles 31: 1, etc.) suggests that the translator knew of a leopard-cult, such as is reported in the sixth century by Jacob of Serug (ed. Martin, 1.64) in Haran. All these point to the area stretching eastwards from Edessa, which was also the centre for the Syriac dialect.

The frequency of Greek loan-words for central religious concepts – nāmosā 'law' and diatīkī 'covenant' – indicates Hellenistic influence. Compare P's verdict (2 Chronicles 24: 16) that Jehoiada 'ran many races' for God's temple – an idiom drawn from the Greek games (cf. 1 Corinthians 9: 24–7).

The painful awareness of exile suggests a date no earlier than AD 70. Indeed a date no earlier than AD 100 is suggested by the presence of the Latin loan-word carruca, not attested in Latin itself until Pliny (Natural History XXXIII 140). This loan-word is also found in P in Joshua (11: 6, 9; 24: 6), 1 Kings (10: 25, 20: 33) and Isaiah (66: 20).

A further indication of time is that the myriad (talents) of bronze donated towards Solomon's temple (1 Chronicles 29: 7) become, in P, 'Corinthian bronze'. Pliny (Natural History XXXIV 1) places the Corinthian first in his list of bronzes, valuing it 'before silver and almost before gold'. He calls it an alloy of gold, silver and copper (XXXIV 3; XXXVII 12). The explanation of Bar Bahlul (ed. Duval, 1888–96: 1238) in Arabic broadly agrees ('part silver, part gold and part copper'). Corinthian bronze is first mentioned by Cicero, as having aroused the greed of Verres and others (Verrines II 2 34, etc., 'In defence of Roscius of Ameria' 46). Most of the literary references, however, belong to the opening centuries AD, and include Josephus' record (Jewish War V 201) that the most precious gate to the sanctuary in Jerusalem was of Corinthian bronze. Two other Peshitta references to 'Corinthian bronze', both in relation to Temple vessels, are at 1 Kings 7: 45 (Heb: neḥošet memoraṭ [burnished]) and at Ezra 8:27 (Heb: neḥošet muṣhab [yellowed]). (See further Jacobson and Weitzman,

1992.) P's reference in Chronicles to Corinthian bronze can hardly be earlier than the first century BC. This is of course consistent with (though less precise than) the *terminus post quem* indicated by the loan-word *carruca*, namely the first century AD.

A *terminus ante quem* is given by the quotations from the P version of all these books, including Chronicles, by the Syriac Church father Aphraates in AD 344. Within these limits, a more precise date could tentatively be based on the phrase *be-'ālmā di brā* '(May his name be hallowed) in the world that he created' in the Kaddish, which is quoted in the Peshitta of Chronicles. As argued elsewhere (Weitzman, 1993) that phrase may have originated in the Jewish anti-gnostic campaign which rabbinic writings first attest in the second century AD (e.g. R. Isaac in Genesis Rabba 1: 7). If so, we may tentatively assign P, which quotes the Kaddish, to the third century.

To summarize, the translator of P identifies with the Jewish people, but sets little store by the ritual demands of the halakhah (apart from prayer). This combination of Jewish identification with neglect of ritual is also attested by Philo (*On the Migration of Abraham* 89–93), who complains that some Jews believed that they had penetrated to the inner meaning of the commandments and therefore 'casually neglected' (*rāthumōs oligōrēsan*) their observance. No doubt other Jews were lax in observance even without such a philosophical system. One could indeed cite the book of Esther, whose heroine's acts give no hint of Jewish observance.

Altogether, the translator seems to have been working alone, with limited background knowledge and a poor Hebrew exemplar. One has the impression of an enclave in a pagan city, rather like the Jews of Dura-Europos. Judah son of Bathyra II had founded a rabbinic academy as near as Nisibis, but the translator was too isolated even to replace his crumbling copy of the Hebrew text.

OTHER CANONICAL BOOKS

Here the evidence can be surveyed only very briefly; it awaits a fuller examination.

Jewish law

Many theological features found in Chronicles recur (albeit less frequently) elsewhere. An example of non-rabbinic halakhah occurs at Exodus 13: 13, where P (with Philo and Josephus) extends the law of redemption of asses to all unclean animals, against mBekhoroth 1: 2. Again, the time when Ezra (9: 5) prayed, i.e. the hour of the evening sacrifice, becomes in P the 'ninth hour'. This was half an hour too early for the sacrifice, according to the rabbis (mPesaḥim 5: 1). Rather, it agrees with the non-rabbinic hours of prayer found at 1 Chronicles 15: 21.

One area where the translators were especially vague was sacrifice. The trespass-offering (*'āšām*) is simply rendered 'offering' throughout P. The three specific types of offering at Joshua 22: 23 become 'sacrifices and other worship'. P renders Jeremiah 7: 5: 'You are the Temple of the Lord (if only you pursue justice)'. Compare the 'temple of men' at Qumran (4QForilegium 6), though Paul (1 Corinthians 3: 16) provides the closest parallel. At Psalm 48: 14, P's hostility extends to Jerusalem: 'destroy her citadels' (Weitzman 1982: 290–3).

In two passages, P has a rendering that the rabbis actually forbade. At Ruth 2: 4 (Heb: 'the Lord be with you'), P changes 'the Lord' in Boaz's greeting to 'peace'. Such substitution is condemned as sectarian in mBerakoth 9: 5. At Leviticus 18: 21, P's rendering of the prohibition ('to impregnate a foreign woman') is forbidden in mMegillah 4: 9, even though it had been upheld by R. Ishmael (jMegillah 4: 10).

Two more features of the translation, apart from the content, point to non-rabbinic Judaism. First, the translators themselves seem often to have consulted the Greek of the Septuagint. Thus at Ruth 4: 6, where MT has 'my duty as kinsman', P renders 'for my lack of faith', a mistake which could only arise from misreading the Greek (ΑΓΧΙΣΤΕΙΑΝ as ΑΠΙΣΤΙΑΝ. Again, P incorporates some passages found in LXX but not MT, e.g. the Prayer of Azariah and the Song of the Three after Daniel 3: 23, and many couplets in Proverbs (after 9: 12, 18; 11: 16a; 13: 13; 14: 22; 18: 22; 25: 20; 27: 21). Second, the very fact that P includes the Writings[2] suggests non-rabbinic origin. Targums on the Writings were forbidden by Gamliel I (mMegillah 1: 8). It was at the table of Johannan (son of) the excommunicate that his grandson Gamliel II found – and destroyed – a targum on Job (bShabbath 115a).

Today's rabbinic Judaism does possess targums on the Writings, but no earlier reference can be found than Hai Gaon (AD 939–1038; see Ginzberg 1929: 85–7). A century later, Rashi could still declare (on bMegillah 21b): 'There is no targum on the Writings.' If P had been a rabbinic product, Rashi would have been quite wrong and his ignorance hard to explain.

Israel and the nations

The attitude of P in Chronicles, namely identification with the sufferings (and guilt) of Israel, is paralleled also in Ezra 9: 14–15: 'we have transgressed . . . and cleaved to unclean nations. . . . Leave for us a remnant.'

Elsewhere, however, P is less sympathetic to the Jewish people. At Jeremiah 31: 32, P makes God say: 'I rejected them [Israel]', apparently reading *bāḥaltī* rather than MT *bā'altī*. (Further instances are discussed in the *Journal of Theological Studies* 38 (1987), p. 466 and 41 (1990), p. 226.) In Psalms, P often introduces the 'elect' (for Hebrew *ḥāsīd* 'pious') – a term eschewed in rabbinic Judaism because of its use by sectarians, witness the Dead Sea Scrolls and the New Testament (see further Weitzman 1993). At Malachi 3: 17, P (unlike LXX and rabbinic tradition) promises that at the end-time God will make a new congregation (Heb. *sĕgullāh*).

The Gentiles, on the other hand, are viewed positively. P renders Deuteronomy 33: 3 as 'he [God] loves the peoples' (while LXX and the rabbinic targums restrict the object to Israel), continuing: 'all his saints he has blessed'. This esteem for the nations may explain P's characterization of the proselyte (Heb. *gēr*) as 'he that turns unto Me'. This seems to be an interpretation of the Greek *prosēlytos*, whose original meaning is 'one who has gone to'.

The hereafter

At Job 7: 7, P reverses the original sense and makes Job affirm the immortality of the soul: 'the spirit lives and my eye shall again see good'. P introduces the same doctrine at 30: 23 and 42: 6 ('I shall be resurrected upon dust and ashes' – compare the added verse 17a in LXX). In Proverbs, P introduces 'hope' at 2: 7, 8: 21 ('that all who love me may inherit hope'), 10: 24, 11: 3

and 13: 12; similarly the valorous wife 'will rejoice on the last day' (31: 25). Such expectation bred disdain for material wealth. P thus transforms Proverbs 22: 7 ('the poor will rule the rich') and Ecclesiastes 10: 19 ('money humbles and misleads').

Many of the features just noted are accentuated in P's version of the Apocrypha. In Ecclesiasticus (notably ch. 32), P removes all favourable references to sacrifice (Winter 1977: 239–42). In the original of Wisdom (3: 8), the nations *serve* the righteous; in P they *are* the righteous (Drijvers 1986: 18). In both books, Winter and Drijvers observe that P seems hostile to Jewish law as such, and also commends poverty.

POSSIBLE CHRISTIAN ELEMENTS

The clearest possible evidence of a Christian translator would be the finding of specific references to Christ in his translation. Certain passages have been thought to support that interpretation, so it is essential to consider the strength of this case. (The passages are listed (i-xvi) and discussed in the appendix; see pp. 169–71.)

In all the passages in question the original was difficult to interpret and P adheres closely to the Hebrew or in (i) (Isaiah 7: 14) and (xi) (Hosea 13: 14), to the Greek. Even in (x) (Daniel 9: 26) 'slay' is a reasonable interpretation of 'cut off'. It may be that a Jewish translator, unable to fathom the sense of the original, conveyed what he could of the form. Perhaps he never consciously considered the implication of the resulting translation.

In some passages, it is in any case clear that a purely Jewish context will provide a perfectly adequate explanation: thus in two cases the usage is already in the Septuagint text (see i; xi); references to the Messiah may as well be Jewish as Christian (see, for example, ii); and again, references to the Redeemer can be to God not to Christ (as, for example, iii); others could be simple confusion (as iv, vii, viii). Taking the whole case together, these passages, even if all reference to Christ cannot be formally disproved, fall well short of demonstrating Christian origin.

UNITY AND DIVERSITY IN THE PESHITTA

The evidence in the sections above has been drawn from many different biblical books. To what extent can we legitimately combine this evidence into a single picture of the translation? Is it possible to decide whether we are faced by a range of different translators at different times? Or is there at least enough coherence to speak of a tendency or school which lies behind the whole work?

Lexical considerations

The Peshitta of the different biblical books is not homogeneous. Lexical usage throws up some striking differences; for example, the Hebrew words for 'city', *'ir* and *qiryah*, are rendered in some books by Syr. *qritā*, in others by Syr. *medi(n)tā*. Nor is translation technique uniform; for example, an especially literal approach is found in Song of Songs and Qohelet. Such differences virtually exclude the possibility that one translator is responsible for P on the whole Hebrew Bible.

Arguments for diversity examined: treatment of anthropomorphisms

Barnes (1901) went further, denying that any single school could have produced the P version of the whole Hebrew Bible. His first argument was that P in the Prophets and Psalms bears far more influence from LXX than in the Pentateuch. Perhaps, however, the translator had greater need to consult LXX in the Prophets and Psalms simply because they are far more difficult than the Pentateuch.

Secondly, Barnes claimed to find in Psalms 'a dread of anthropomorphisms, of which the translators of the Pentateuch were free'. Certainly P in the Pentateuch preserves references to God's hand and voice; God hears and even smells (Genesis 8: 21), and men see him and the pavement beneath his feet (Exodus 24: 10). In the Psalms, by contrast, as Barnes notes, 'shield' regularly becomes 'helper'; in particular, 'sun and shield' (84: 12 [11]) become 'nourisher and helper'. 'Rock' too becomes 'helper' or simply 'God' or 'trust', though its commonest rendering is 'might(y)' or 'strengthener'.

Yet the contrast between the Pentateuch and the Psalter is less clear on closer scrutiny. It is in Psalms that P expresses the desire to 'see the face of God' (42: 3 – MT as traditionally vocalized signifies merely 'appearing before' him). Conversely, those particular anthropomorphisms which P avoids in Psalms are equally

162

avoided in the Pentateuch (and elsewhere). Thus 'shield' likewise becomes 'help(er)' at Genesis 15: 1, Deuteronomy 33: 29, 2 Samuel 22: 31, Proverbs 2: 7, 30: 5. Similarly 'rock' becomes 'mighty' at Deuteronomy 32: 4, 1 Samuel 2: 2, Isaiah 17: 10 and many other passages. Again, as Loewe (1952: 271) has shown, cases where God is said to 'repent' (Hebrew *nḥm*) are invariably changed (albeit into a variety of expressions) throughout P. It seems, *pace* Barnes, that there were certain anthropomorphic expressions which all the P translators were equally anxious to avoid. It just so happens that these expressions are especially frequent in the Psalter.

Arguments for a single school

There are further common features to indicate that the different books were translated by a single school. First of all, there is a common philosophy of translation. The version keeps close to the original Hebrew, but strives above all to be intelligible. To that end, P will often change grammatical elements. Whole words or phrases not intelligible to the translator are often simply omitted. P differs from the targums authorized by rabbinic Judaism, which are fed by an all-embracing exegetical tradition. Few if any difficulties in the Hebrew text left those targums at a loss for a rendering. By contrast, P was often forced to make sheer guesses based on limited knowledge.

The impression of a single school is reinforced by some specific peculiarities running through the translation, such as the use of the Greek loan-word *nāmosā* to render Heb. Torah. Another such feature is the distortion of 'Aram' to 'Edom', apparently because 'Aramean' had come to mean 'pagan'. Furthermore, P in one biblical book sometimes quotes another. For example, the woman described in the Hebrew (Proverbs 7: 11) as 'flighty and rebellious' (*hōmiyyāh wĕ-sōrāret*) becomes in P 'rebellious and gluttonous', with the same adjectives (*mārod, 'āsoṭ*) as P on Deuteronomy 21: 20. Altogether, one may reasonably at least attempt a synthesis of our findings in the P version of the whole Hebrew Bible. The most obvious obstacle is the inconsistent attitude to the Jewish people – now contrite self-identification, now the hostility of an outsider.

THE BELIEFS OF THE TRANSLATORS

In the light of the evidence assembled above, it is now possible to attempt a reassessment of the two alternative hypotheses from which we began.

Christian context

The hypothesis of a translation made in a Christian context could hardly apply to Ezra and Chronicles, in which books the translator identifies himself with the Jews. One might, however, posit a Christian context for the remaining books. It could be urged that Ezra (with Nehemiah) and Chronicles should be treated separately, since they share some peculiarities (e.g. the rendering of 'singers' as 'servants') and are usually grouped together in (or omitted together from) Syriac biblical manuscripts or canonical lists. On this view, perhaps the Christians translated the biblical books in roughly the traditional Jewish sequence (Beckwith 1985: 309) and stopped short of Ezra-Chronicles. Later, having forgotten Hebrew, they commissioned Jews to complete the translation. Alternatively, perhaps P on Ezra-Chronicles is all that survives of an old Jewish translation of the whole Bible into Syriac. The Christians made a new translation of every book except Ezra-Chronicles, which were of lesser interest or authority.

There are difficulties, however, in viewing P on Ezra-Chronicles either as an afterthought or as the sole relic of a Jewish translation of the whole Hebrew Bible. The former theory requires Jews and Christians to have worked together in a surprisingly harmonious fashion, given the unkind remarks which *ex hypothesi* the Christian translators had already made elsewhere. On the other hand, the latter theory fails to explain the remarkable homogeneity of the manuscript tradition of P. Had an earlier Jewish version existed, one would have expected many passages where two substantially different alternative renderings survive, each independently derived from the Hebrew, representing the old version and the new. In fact, however, such passages are few indeed.

The hypothesis of Christian origin is also open to a more general objection. Given the status of the Septuagint as the Bible of the church, it calls for explanation that Christians should instead have translated from the Hebrew and so produced a translation frequently at odds with the Septuagint version. At Edessa, it would not have been difficult to translate from Greek, which had of course been a familiar language there ever since Seleucid times.

Jewish context

If P is a Jewish translation, it certainly differs from rabbinic Judaism. We need only recall its three fixed hours of daily prayer, its depreciation of sacrifice, and its emphasis on faith and hope rather than observance. Some non-rabbinic form of Judaism, however, could well have had these features.

One problem in the theory of non-rabbinic as of any other Jewish origin is the inconsistent attitude towards Israel. One might answer that the translation represents two stages in the history of the community of Edessa. In the first, they are an enclave. Despite commercial contacts with Nisibis (Segal 1970: 41), they are estranged on a religious level from the main Jewish centres in the Holy Land and Babylon. Their religion revolves about the individual and the local community, rather than Jewry at large or rabbinic halakhah. By the second stage, represented by Ezra-Chronicles, some catastrophe (perhaps the massacre under Trajan) has strengthened their solidarity with the Jewish people.

All in all, the likeliest explanation is that P on the whole Hebrew Bible is of non-rabbinic Jewish origin. An implication of this view is that the institution of targum extended well beyond rabbinic Judaism; this would account for the appearance, in the Syriac Church, of targumic elements not paralleled in P. On Genesis 49:23, for example where the Hebrew has *ba'ălē ḥiṣṣīm*, Ephrem[3] quotes not only P (*māray godē* = 'chiefs of bands') but also a rendering agreeing with Onkelos, namely *ba'lay palgutā* 'masters of dissidence'. Further targumic elements that crop up in the Syriac fathers but not in P – notably the 'second death' of sinners – are noted by Brock (1979: 218–23).

One problem remains: if P on the whole Hebrew Bible is of Jewish origin, how did it become the Bible of the Syriac Church? This question of the relationship between the Jews who produced the translation and the Christians who preserved it must now be considered.

A HISTORICAL RECONSTRUCTION

Where did P's non-rabbinic Judaism originate? From a traditional Jewish viewpoint, P's Judaism represents a mere falling away from a pre-existing rabbinic standard. It is, however, worth considering an alternative possibility: the origins of the translators' religion may lie in a popular anti-cultic movement that goes back to biblical times.

Practices of worship suggest a possible reconstruction. In the Pentateuch sacrifice is prescribed twice daily, and prayer is not prescribed at all. It may be that practice in the Temple before the exile followed this model, while the Levites in the provinces developed an independent regular prayer-cult 'evening and morning and noon-day' (Psalm 55:18 [17]). The latter alone survived into the Babylonian exile, where Daniel is represented as turning in prayer to Jerusalem thrice daily (Daniel 6:11). The second Temple restored the sacrificial ritual of the priests but combined it with the prayer-cult, led as ever by the Levites. Chronicles justifies the latter by tracing psalmody and the Levitical choirs back to David, at the origin of the Temple.

Prayer, then, was offered in the second Temple, but as an accompaniment to sacrifice. This primacy of sacrifice is continued in a tradition which aligns the times of prayer with those of sacrifice. Thus at Qumran, prayer was offered twice daily (*pace* Jungmann 1953), at daybreak and nightfall (1QS 9:5, 1QH 12:4–7, 1QM 13–14), the points when sacrifice had been offered (Jubilees 6:14). For the rabbis too, prayer replaced sacrifice, so that the additional sacrifice of feast days was represented by an additional service. However, they extended the times, so that, for example, the morning prayer could be said until midday. It is worth noting that R. Judah b. Ilai is less lenient and so, for example, extends the morning prayer to the fourth hour only.

All this time the simple prayer-cult – without sacrifice – had survived, especially in the Diaspora. To P it is central. It appealed to God-fearers, and doubtless to full converts, among the Gentiles. Despite the victory of the rabbinic system among the Jews, the prayer-cult survived in the Church.

The prayer-cult was not merely characterized by thrice daily hours of prayer. Having grown up away from the central sanctuary, it may have tended to depreciate sacrifice and outward ritual, and instead to emphasize inward faith. Such an attitude can already be detected in Proverbs. That book, like P, refers favourably to prayer (15:8, 29), while sacrifice is presented negatively throughout. The wicked man's sacrifice is an abomination (15:8, 21:27). Sacrifice is inferior to just behaviour (21:3), and may even be a prelude to immorality (7:14). It is true that Proverbs 3:9,10 commends payment of first-fruits, but this seems a social rather than cultic obligation. Again like P, Proverbs prefers to emphasize faith (3:6, 16:20, 28:25, 29:25). It is not suggested here that P was especially influenced by Proverbs. Rather, both independently reflect the values of the prayer-cult. Other well-known attacks on the sacrificial cult by biblical writers (Isaiah 1:11, Jeremiah 7:22, Amos 5:21–2, Psalm 40:7 [6], 50:9–14) may be influenced by the same movement. Rabbinic Judaism, by contrast, strove to preserve whatever it could of the central sacrificial cult.

Jews whose practice was confined to the prayer-cult could well have come to adopt Christianity. Christianity would have preserved their dearest religious values – prayer, charity and faith – and yet given them a rationale for continuing not to observe the rituals. This may be the case for the community represented by P.

This movement from prayer-cult to Christianity can perhaps be paralleled in the epistle to the Hebrews, written to prevent the relapse of newly converted Christians. The intended recipients of the letter must have been of Jewish origin, in view of the traditional title of the epistle and the assumption throughout that its recipients will in any case accept the authority of the Hebrew Bible. Yet the author expresses no concern that they might revert to Jewish ritual observance. The hypothesis that their background had been a non-rabbinic Judaism like that of P would explain this combination. It would also explain other elements – apart of course from the belief in Christ – which the author expects his readers to share: faith (6: 12, and ch. 11), hope (6: 11, 19; 7: 19), the elevation of prayer and charity as true sacrifice (13: 15–16), and the view of scriptural laws as mere symbols (9:9) or shadows (10:1). It is altogether fitting that Hebrews (10: 5–7) should quote Psalm 40: 7–9 to argue that God does not desire sacrifice. A line can be traced from the Israelite prayer-cult that inspired those verses, through the non-rabbinic Judaism with which the audience of Hebrews had grown up, to the Christian faith of the author of the letter.

The community addressed in Hebrews is usually located in the west (cf. 13: 24), but this process of conversion from non-rabbinic Judaism to Christianity may have repeated itself all over the Diaspora. In Mesopotamia it may have been precipitated by the massacres of the Jews at the end of Trajan's reign (Eusebius, *Church History* IV 2; Eusebius, *Chronological Tables* 2). No longer was there any hope that this exile (like the first) would end speedily. Exile was felt as a badge of shame and sin (cf. already Daniel 9: 7–8). Some Jews finally accepted the argument, still purveyed by Aphraates centuries later, that there was no future prospect of the fulfilment of the biblical prophecies of ingathering; and they accepted the inference that the Messiah had already come and that the historical Israel had been rejected.

Others became convinced that their survival as Jews now depended on observance of the Torah and adherence to the rabbinic commandments. These are the Jews of whom Aphraates speaks in the fourth century. They observe the dietary laws prescribed by the rabbis, who forbade all Gentile cooking and Gentile wine (Aphraates, *Demonstrations* I 733; cf. mAbodah Zarah 2: 4, 6). It is difficult to accept Neusner's view (1971: 147) that the Jews known to Aphraates practised a Judaism based on the Hebrew Bible alone. Aphraates' references to dietary laws show rather that the Jews who by the fourth century had not joined the Church were precisely those who accepted rabbinic halakhah.

This historical reconstruction is offered with reserve. In conclusion let us recall the main facts that it seeks to explain. The translator sometimes identifies himself with the Jewish people. The translation is frequently at odds with rabbinic norms. Some features (e.g. the hours of prayer, explicit emphasis on faith) are familiar to us from the Church rather than the Synagogue. Until we reach P on the Apocrypha, however, there are no *undeniably* Christian statements. Finally, P was preserved by the Church alone. To account for all these features, we must posit a line that ran from some non-rabbinic form of Judaism into Christianity. The P translations of the different books of the Hebrew Bible lie somewhere near the beginning of that line. In these translations we may hope to glimpse that Judaism out of which the Syriac-speaking Church grew.

APPENDIX OF ALLEGED REFERENCES TO CHRIST IN THE PESHITTA

(i) Isaiah 7: 14: 'Behold a virgin [*btultā*] shall conceive.'
See Bloch (1918–19: 218). This rendering coincides, however, with LXX (parthenos), and may merely reflect the influence of that version.
(ii) Isaiah 16: 1 '(and to the rest of the earth) send the son (Heb. *kar*, Syr. *bar*) of the ruler of the earth'.
Messianic interpretation of this passage was widespread, as attested both by Targum ('they shall bring tribute to the King Messiah') and by the Vulgate (*emitte [domine] agnum dominatorem terrae*).
(iii) Isaiah 25: 6 'the feast of our heavenly and mighty redeemer.'
For Heb. *šěmānīm měmuḥāyīm* 'fattened dainties', the translator wrote two Syriac words of similar sound: *mahyānan šmayānā* 'our heavenly redeemer'. The redeemer is taken by van der Kooij (1981: 274) to be Christ. Note, however, that elsewhere this title may indicate God (Isaiah 60: 16 [9a1], Wisdom 16: 7).
(iv) Isaiah 25: 7 'the sacrifice (*nekstā*; Heb. *massēkāh*) slaughtered for all the peoples shall be swallowed.'
Hebrew *massēkāh něsūkāh* 'web woven' is interpreted through the similar-sounding Syriac root *nks* 'slaughter, sacrifice'. This passage too is considered Christian by van der Kooij (p. 276). One might further take the 'swallowing' of this sacrifice to refer to the Eucharist.
(v) Isaiah 53:8 '[some] of the wicked ones of my people touched him.'
P read the Hebrew as: *mip-pōšěʿē ʿammī nāgěʿū lō*. MT, however, has *mip-pešaʿ ʿammī negaʿ lāmō*, meaning literally: 'through the sin of my people, a stroke to them.'
(vi) Zechariah 12: 10 'and they shall look to me through him that they pierced.'
This passage is mentioned by Bloch, p. 219. MT has: 'and they shall look to me, the one that they pierced'. The verse is applied at John 19: 37 to Jesus' death: 'they shall look upon the one that they pierced'. P introduces a different (though arguably equally Christian) nuance, that man will look to God ('me') *through* a pierced one. Yet Christian reference is not certain. The translator may simply have changed the preposition (from Heb. *ʾēt* to Syr. *b-*), as often elsewhere, simply in the effort to make sense of the puzzling Hebrew text. We may note that the rabbis applied this

verse to the Messiah 'son of Joseph' who would be slain (bSukkah 52a).

(vii) Psalm 2: 12 :'kiss the son' (Heb: *naššĕqū bar*).

(viii) Psalm 110: 3 'thee O child (Syr. *ṭalyā*; Heb. *ṭal* 'dew') I have begotten.'

On these two passages from Psalms see Weitzman (1982: 294). Although both read like references to Christ, this is not the only possibility. Both may instead simply be literal translations forced on the translator in difficult passages and not necessarily reflecting his conscious beliefs.

(ix) Daniel 9: 24 'and for the Messiah, holy of holies.'

The word traditionally vocalized *li-mšōăḥ* 'to anoint' was instead taken as *lam-māšīăḥ*. As Wyngaarden (1923: 30) observes, the holiness of the Messiah seems a Christian idea. The cause may simply, however, be assimilation to Heb. *māšīăḥ* in v. 26.

(x) Daniel 9: 26 'the Messiah shall be slain (*netqṭel*).'

The Hebrew less specifically says that the anointed one (*māšīăḥ*, which, however, never means 'Messiah' in biblical Hebrew) would be cut off (*yikkārēt*). P goes on, like the Hebrew, to say that the holy city would be destroyed 'with (=by?) the king that cometh . . . its end will be in destruction . . . he will annul the sacrifices . . . it will remain in desolation'. Aphraates (p. 885) and Wyngaarden identify the slain Messiah with Christ. The whole passage could then be read as predicting the events of the first century AD, culminating in the destruction of the second Temple.

(xi) An echo of the New Testament has been detected (Bloch, p. 219) in P at Hosea 13: 14 LXX has 'Where is (Heb. *'ĕhī* read *'ayyēh*) thy cause (*dikē*), O death? Where is thy sting, O Sheol?' 1 Corinthians 15: 55 is virtually identical, except in having *nikos* 'victory' rather than *dikē*. P's rendering agrees with both. The discrepant word is rendered *zākutā(k)*, which covers both 'justification' (LXX) and 'victory' (1 Corinthians). P may well be following LXX rather than the New Testament. Indeed the range of *zākutā* may explain how an Aramaic speaker like Paul equated *dikē* with *nikos*.

(xii/xiii) Only in the Apocrypha do the arguments for Christian origin seem stronger. Thus Winter points to this hope in Ecclesiasticus 48: 10 that Elijah would 'evangelize' (*l-msbrw*, contrast Heb. *lĕ-hākīn* 'establish') the tribes of Jacob. Drijvers notes P's blessing at Wisdom 14: 7 of the wood from which the righteous appears; the original here has no mention of 'wood'. However, it is clear that the Apocrypha were translated after the canonical books,[4] and apparently not before the evangelization of the community represented by P.

(xiv) Isaiah 53: 2, where P makes the Jews confess 'we deceived him' [*dagelnāy(hy)*] can be left aside, since this is an easy corruption of *ragnāy(hy)* '(that) we desire him', which would have been a literal translation of the Hebrew.

(xv/xvi) We must also exclude straightforward renderings of two biblical passages that are especially significant for Christianity (Isaiah 9: 5; Jeremiah 31: 31 'a new covenant'). Since these renderings are perfectly literal, they need no more be Christian than the underlying Hebrew texts themselves – despite their citation by Bloch (p. 219) as Christian renderings.

NOTES

1 (1894–1907) *Aphraates' Demonstrations*, ed. D. J. Parisot, in *Patrologia Syriaca* I-II, Paris.
2 That is, the third section of the Jewish Bible, together with the Pentateuch and the Prophets.
3 (1955) *Sancti Ephraem Syri in Genesim et in Exodum Commentarii*, ed. R.-M. Tonneau, CSCO Syr. 71, Louvain.
4 In the thirteenth century, transcriptions into Hebrew characters of parts of the P version of the Apocrypha circulated among the Jews of the western Diaspora (Neubauer 1878: 39–42), who mistook these translations for Jewish works composed in Aramaic. Thus Nachmanides, whose commentary on Genesis 1: 1 cites the P version of Wisdom, believed instead that he was citing an ancient Jewish translation into 'very difficult Aramaic' (*lěšōn targūm ḥāmūr mě'ōd*) ((1963) *Kitvei Rabbenu Moshe ben Nachman*, ed. D. Chavel, Jerusalem Vol. 1, 182). The Jews, he supposed, had handed down this work of Solomon orally (in Hebrew) but wrote it down during the Babylonian exile, in their then current Aramaic. The Hebrew was not preserved, since the work was merely Solomon's wisdom and not divinely inspired. The Aramaic text, Nachmanides concludes, was later copied by Christians (*wě-ha-gōyīm he'tīqūhū*). Just as Nachmanides unwittingly adopted P on Wisdom and Judith from the Church, so too some centuries earlier a Jew had supplied a targum on Proverbs by revising P in conformity with MT. Such episodes do not prove a Jewish origin for P, still less that 'the Jews possessed it [the complete Peshitta] as late as the time of Nachmanides' (Bloch, 1918–19: 221).

BIBLIOGRAPHY

Baer, S. (1868) *Seder Avodat Yisra'el*, Rödelheim.
Barnes, W. E. (1901) 'On the Influence of the Septuagint on the Peshitta', *Journal of Theological Studies* 2: 186–97.
Beckwith, R. (1985) *The Old Testament Canon of the New Testament Church*, London.
Bloch, J. (1918–19) 'The Authorship of the Peshitta', *American Journal of Semitic Languages and Literatures* 35: 215–22.
Brock, S. P. (1979) 'Jewish Traditions in Syriac Sources', *Journal of Jewish Studies* 30: 212–32.
Brovender, C. (1976) 'The Syriac Shemahe Manuscripts: A Typological and Comparative Study', unpublished dissertation, Jerusalem.
Davidson, S. (1839) *Lectures on Biblical Criticism*, Edinburgh.
Dirksen, P. B. (1988) 'The Old Testament Peshitta', in M. J. Mulder (ed.) *Mikra. Text, Translation, Reading and Interpretation of the Hebrew Bible – Ancient Judaism and Early Christianity*, Assen/Maastricht and Philadelphia, Pa, 255–97.
Drijvers, H. J. W. (1986) 'The Peshitta of the Wisdom of Solomon', in H. L. Vanstiphout *et al.* (eds) *Scripta Signa Vocis: Festschrift J. H. Hospers*, Groningen, 15–30.
Duval, R. (ed.) (1888–96) *Lexicon Syriacum, auctore Hassano bar Bahlule*, Paris.
Emerton, J. A. (1962) 'Unclean Birds and the Origin of the Peshitta', *Journal of Semitic Studies* 7: 204–11.
Fraenkel, S. (1879) 'Die syrische Übersetzung zu den Büchern der Chronik', *Jahrbücher für protestantische Theologie* 5: 508–36, 720–59.
Gelston, A. (1987) *The Peshitta of the Twelve Prophets*, Oxford.
Ginzberg, L. (1929) *Genizah Studies*, Vol. 2 (*Texts and Studies of the Jewish Theological Seminary of America*, 8), New York.
Heller, Ch. (1911) *Untersuchungen über die Peschîttâ zur gesamten hebräischen Bibel*, Berlin.
Hirzel, L. (1825) *De Pentateuchi Versionis Syriacae Quam Peschito Vocant Indole Commentatio Critico-Exegetica*, Leipzig.
Jacobson, D. M. and Weitzman, M. P. (1992) 'What was Corinthian Bronze?', *American Journal of Archaeology* 96: 237–47.
Jungmann, J. A. (1953) 'Altchristliche Gebetsordnung im Lichte des Regelbuches von "En Fešcha" ', *Zeitschrift für Katholische Theologie* 75: 215–19.
Kooij, A. van der (1981) *Die alten Textzeugen des Jesajabuches* (*Orbis Biblicus et Orientalis*, 35), Freiburg.
Loewe, R. J. (1952) 'Jerome's Treatment of an Anthropopathism', *Vetus Testamentum* 2: 261–72.
Maori, Y. (1975) 'The Peshitta Version of the Pentateuch in its Relation to the Sources of Jewish Exegesis', unpublished dissertation (Hebrew with English summary), Jerusalem.
Martin J. P. P. (1875) 'Discours de Jacques de Saroug sur la chute des idoles', *Zeitschrift der Deutschen Morgenländischen Gesellschaft* 29: 107–47.

Neubauer, A. (1878) *The Book of Tobit: A Chaldee Text from a Unique Ms. in the Bodleian Library*, Oxford.

Neusner, J. (1971) *Aphrahat and Judaism*, Leiden.

Nöldeke, T. (1872) 'Das Targum zu den Sprüchern von der Peschita abhängig', *Archiv für Wissenschaftliche Erforschung des Alten Testaments* II, 2: 246–9.

Perles, J. (1859) *Meletemata Peschitoniana*, Breslau.

Roberts, B. J. (1951) *The Old Testament Text and Versions*, Cardiff.

Segal, J. B. (1970) *Edessa: 'The Blessed City'*, Oxford.

Tov, E. (1981) *The Text-Critical Use of the Septuagint in Biblical Research*, Jerusalem.

Weitzman, M. P. (1982) 'The Origin of the Peshitta Psalter', in J. A. Emerton and S. C. Reif (eds) *Interpreting the Hebrew Bible: Essays in Honour of E. I. J. Rosenthal*, Cambridge, 277–98.

Weitzman, M. P. (1990) 'Usage and Avoidance of the Term "Chosen People"' (Hebrew with English summary), *Language Studies* (Jerusalem) 4: xv–xvi, 101–28.

Weitzman, M. P. (1993) 'The Qaddish Prayer and the Peshitta of Chronicles', in H. Ben-Shammai (ed.) *Hebrew and Arabic Studies in honour of Joshua Blau* (Hebrew), Tel Aviv and Jerusalem, 261–90.

Winter, M. M. (1977) 'The Origins of Ben Sira in Syriac', *Vetus Testamentum* 27 237–53, 494–507.

Wyngaarden, M. J. (1923) *The Syriac Version of the Book of Daniel*, Leipzig.

8

THE DEVELOPMENT OF
RELIGIOUS PLURALISM

John North

INTRODUCTION

This book has covered a very wide range of topics: it has ranged
from the religious experience of St Paul before his conversion to
the life of Edessa in the fifth century AD. It has also used a
correspondingly wide range of approaches and techniques to discuss its topics; this is not a matter of choice but of necessity,
caused by the fragmentary and diverse character of the information
available to us about the life of the Jewish communities in the
Roman Empire, especially those of the Diaspora. Given the character of the tradition, no approach is possible except to use whatever
clues may come to hand and to use them by whatever methods
seem to advance understanding. The justification for the range of
methodology lies in the nature of the problematic of the book.

All the same, it may seem an unnecessary complication to add
still more themes in the final chapter, for its main subject is to
be the place of the pagans in the religious history of this period;
but in fact this theme is central to the book's whole conception:
the argument will be that any exploration of the character of
Diaspora Judaism or of its relationship with other groups must
take account of the religious situation in the Roman Empire as a
whole. The same logic would apply to all the other religions of
the period; if all are changing and developing in the light of their
mutual awareness, hostility and – at least potential – competition
with one another, it follows that understanding their individual
histories can never be separated from the history of their mutual
interaction. Of course the extent of their mutual intellectual

174

influence has long been one of the major themes of debate on the different religions – what did Christianity borrow from the pagans, or pagans from Christians, or either from the Jews? But these questions have generally been treated as separate issues; the question to be raised here is whether we can grasp any overall picture of the development of religious life in what was still, at least in the earlier part of this period, the pagan, Graeco-Roman world.

CONVERSION AND AFTER

It was A. D. Nock, as often in the history of ancient religions, who first grasped a profound distinction between the religious life of the Empire and that of earlier centuries. The basic contribution of his *Conversion* (1933) was the insight that in the conversions of St Paul and St Augustine we meet a new type of experience, one that on his view could not have happened in the world of pagan religions.

There can be no doubt that this insight provides a very important starting-point in the search to understand what was new in the religious life of the Roman Empire, and hence a starting-point for this chapter. But it is only a starting-point. It is of course important and interesting to show that with the conversion of St Paul we meet a new element in religious life and an unmistakable indication of the deep changes that were associated with the coming of Christianity. But the emergence of conversion cannot be treated as an isolated event in religious history; it presupposes a certain religious situation, needing itself to be placed in its context of social change. The tendency since Nock's work has been rather to pursue his interest in conversion as an individual psychological event, than to seek to explicate the context in which it would have happened, despite the tiny number of such heroic conversions known to us at all in the Roman period (though see Kee 1980: 54–73).

The character of Nock's vision has also given a very particular character to the debate: here – as elsewhere in his work – Nock saw and emphasized a profound gulf between the old religion of the pagans and the new one of the Christians, the passing world-vision and the arising one. (On the division see Fowden 1988, discussing Lane Fox 1986). It is clear that this position reflects a deeply felt conviction and one that expressed itself in a specific polemical context of its day: he was in conflict with theories that sought to find the origins of Christianity in the pre-Christian mystery cults, cults of deities who suffer, die and return to life and whose suffering and recovery in some way prefigure the salvation of their individual human adherents. The influence of such theories about Christian origins is now far less than it used to be and the case against this interpretation of the early mystery-cults has become overwhelmingly strong, particularly as regards the character of the pre-Christian mysteries themselves and the nature of the soteriology associated with them (Pettazzoni 1954; Colpe 1969; Lambrechts 1962; Duthoy 1969; Gasparro 1985).

It does not follow at all, however, that the collapse of this particular theory about the interaction of pagan and Judaeo-Christian religious developments entails accepting the total separation of the two systems. It is, of course, a theoretical possibility that religious or ethnic groups should so isolate themselves from one another that they can be treated as virtually separate societies; but in this case we know enough to be quite sure that this cannot have been the case. In fact, the surviving literature enables us to be sure that there was a great deal of mutual awareness, communication and interchange between the different religious groups in the Empire, and even outside it. The simple fact of the transfer of so many converts in the course of the centuries of the Empire from the pagan to the Judaeo-Christian side (and at least a few transfers back again) speaks for itself in this respect. Such a transfer could not have taken place at all without mutual contact, not to say conflict and resentment on all sides.

Unless the picture sketched so far is entirely to be rejected, the first requirement is simply to describe the situation of increasing complexity in religious life and in religious expectation which is the characteristic of this period. That is to say, before analysing the separate religious traditions and the separate systems of meaning that we find expressed in them, still more before starting to describe the relationships of these traditions with one another, we need an overall picture of religious change in this period.

This may seem an excessively ambitious undertaking, but in fact taking account of a long enough period of time at a broad enough level, the process of religious change in the Graeco-Roman world can, at least in some respects, be stated quite simply. It may be that the results are so general as to be unhelpful in understanding the religious situation of any particular time or any particular city.

Certainly, what follows has more resemblance to the construction of an ideal type than to a sensitive historical description of an early *polis*. On the other hand, it may be worth doing some violence to the sensibilities of those who will find this picture very crude, in order to grasp the basic direction of events. After all, one of the great weaknesses of most attempts to write the religious history of the Roman Empire is that they have lacked any overall framework of interpretation and are as a result, however sophisticated their treatment of individual religions, driven to evoking simplifying assumptions to describe their mutual effects: such are the theories that the rise of Christianity can be explained as a result of the decline of paganism (against which, Lane Fox 1986) or as a response to mass neurotic anxiety in the troubled conditions of the third century AD (cf. Dodds 1965; Brown 1972: 74–80).

The communities in the archaic Graeco-Roman world, whether they were based on city-states or on tribal systems, or were incorporated in larger imperial associations, had their own specific form of religious life. In this form, religious rituals and practices were integral to all civic, local, or family activities; and religious roles, sometimes overlapping with political ones, were ubiquitous. But there were no differentiated religious institutions or identifiable religious groups based on popular membership. There was thus no question of religion providing the individual or group with a system of power or adherence, alternative to that of the city, the tribe, or the family. This is not to say that there were no religious groups at all, but they were characteristically small elite groups of priests or priestesses, not to be joined by any act of religious commitment. On the other hand, in some sense all groups in the pagan world were religious, since they all involved some degree of cultic and ritual activity, some orientation towards the gods.

So, if we consider the situation of the Greeks and Romans who lived in city-states in these early centuries, we can say that their religious loyalty was essentially to the city's gods and goddesses, not to any religious commitment of their own choice. It is important to be clear how fundamental is this difference between the religions of ancient pagan society and those of later periods, both in terms of the religious experience of individuals and of the social significance of religion within these societies. Developed modern societies offer their members the possibility of making religious

177

choices: there may be very great pressure from family, society, even state, against the making of particular choices, or any choices at all, but at least in theory the possibility of choice exists. Again, in theory, the beliefs of the individual are supposed to determine the religion, sect, or group to which that individual belongs. In practice, of course, things may be quite different: beliefs are often inherited or unconsidered, religious commitments often habitual and unreflective. But at least the possibility is recognized and sometimes realized of losing your beliefs and, as a result, changing your religious allegiance. Beliefs are at least in this potential sense at the root of everybody's religious location.

In the world of the old civic paganism beliefs simply do not play this role; and the sequence of losing your beliefs and therefore your religious attachment was not just unusual, but virtually inconceivable. Pagans could and did experiment with foreign cults and certainly might sacrifice to foreign gods when abroad – indeed, it would always have been prudent to do so. They might also belong to, or join, a philosophical sect that held particular views about the gods and their activities. But none of this involved a fundamental decision, affecting the individual's religious loyalty and identity, as in the case of converting to or from Catholicism or Buddhism today. This is the basic insight behind Nock's contention that conversion was a new religious element in the imperial period. As we have seen already, he was thinking primarily of the psychological experience of conversion as we meet it in the case of St Paul or St Augustine; but the same observation holds true in a more social perspective, with the emphasis taken away from the drama of notable religious high-achievers, and transferred to the growth of new religious groups based on deliberate acts of religious commitment, of a type previously almost unknown.

So the basic story proposed by this chapter is one of development from religion as embedded in the city-state to religion as choice of differentiated groups offering different qualities of religious doctrine, different experiences, insights, or just different myths and stories to make sense of the absurdity of human experience (cf. Gordon 1980). One vivid way of expressing this development would be to adopt the metaphor from economic life used by Peter Berger (1969) to describe an analogous though very different religious situation in modern times – the metaphor of the market-place in religions, which he uses to analyse the process of secularization in the modern world. In these terms, the change from embedded to differentiated religion might be described as a progress (if that is what it is) from monopoly to market. The comparison with modern periods would be useful at least to this extent, that in the case of the Graeco-Roman city-state, religion and city were mutually sustaining and hence in a successful city its religious life would have a tendency to generate and maintain social solidarity. The plausibility-basis of the religion rested in the success of military, political, economic activity (cf. Gordon 1990). As the monopoly situation disappeared, there must have come a critical moment in any city's history when there was no longer a dominant group in tune with the city's own religious traditions, but a plurality of groups in tension with one another. So pluralization, here as elsewhere, would destroy the situation in which society as a whole authenticates a single shared conception of the cosmos.

The analogy, it must be admitted, becomes the less useful, the more its economic implications are pressed into service. The participants in this market were far from having anything like a shared conception of how they could legitimately dispose of their wares. The Christians, perhaps, could be said to have regarded all the rest as potential customers to whom they could offer their brand of truth; but the Jews – at least for many years – show little sign of having a similar conception; while the pagans perhaps sometimes show more interest in breaking up the market-place than in competing on terms with the other salesmen. No doubt, these are all comprehensible reactions towards a radically new situation to which they have to respond; but, given the variety of such reactions, it seems advisable to accept that the market-place image can only be partially illuminating and think instead in terms of interactions, sometimes competitive or partly competitive, between the different groups.

Whatever theory may be developed to express these dramatically changing circumstances, there can be no doubt at all that the existence of Jewish groups in the cities of the late Hellenistic period and the rise of Christian groups after the first century represent a very important part of the story. The next question to be considered is whether these particular developments might be regarded as effectively the whole of the story.

THE DIFFERENTIATION OF RELIGIOUS GROUPS

This transformation of religious life could be (and often has been) explained by means of a very straightforward hypothesis: that is, that the nature of pagan life did not (even could not) change in any serious way on its own initiative, but that it was attacked by a more evolved religious system, that is Christianity, and that the whole transformation of religious life was a simple consequence of the confrontation that resulted, essentially between pagans and Christians. It must, of course, be accepted that Christianity itself emerged from a development within Palestinian Judaism not unlike that described above for the Graeco-Roman world: Judaism as well had apparently changed from a unified religion, effectively coextensive with a people, to a set of sharply differentiated, competing groups each claiming to have a version of the truth. But it is after all the Christians who are the real initiators of the confrontation outside Palestine; and their emergence into the Gentile world could have provided the one starting-point for the differentiation of religious life.

There are, however, very good reasons for rejecting this simple view. First, it ignores the role of Judaism in interaction with pagans in Greek cities before the coming of Christianity. We know all too much about violent conflicts between Greeks and Jews in the cities of the east before the Christian era; but it also seems clear, not least from the book of Acts and the basic articulation of its plot, that Judaism was established as a visible religious presence before the time of Jesus and Paul and that there were already Gentiles, somehow associated with the life of the synagogues, to whom Paul could be thought to have made his primary appeal. Even though the stories of Acts may be far from being accurate historical accounts, it is hard to believe that the life they presuppose can be altogether fictitious. If so, then some form of interchange between identifiable religious groups was part of life in the Greek cities of the east by the first century AD.

Second, it seems very hard to separate the beginning of the religious changes under discussion from much wider social changes and movements of population in the history of the Mediterranean area. Partly, these were the result of Roman imperial expansion itself, which would have brought easterners to Rome and other cities of the west, whether as slaves or as economic migrants. In the east, however, the Roman imperialists found cities such as

Alexandria already having complex populations of diverse ethnic origins. At least some of these various migrant groups, whether in the east or west, retained the religious traditions of their original homes. The mixture of populations must be the background, not just of the Jewish presence in Hellenistic cities, but of the travelling eastern cults of the western provinces – Isis, Cybele and Attis, Mithras and so on. The Roman Empire, therefore, from its beginnings must have contained many cities with mixed religious traditions coexisting more or less peacefully.

Above all, however, the simple view assumes that there was no internally generated tendency in pagan life towards the differentiation of religious groups; but this view can hardly be maintained. The Italy of the third and second centuries BC had already seen a striking growth of autonomous religious groups evidently out of the control of the religious authorities of the time and these developments take us back to the earliest period in which Jewish sects too are known to have been already active. The evidence for what happened in Italy consists of only two basic texts (*ILS* 18; Livy XXXIX 8–19); but they provide a very convincing picture and one that can now be extended and supplemented by archaeological evidence (Gallini 1970; North 1979; Pailler 1988). It is clear that groups of worshippers of the god Bacchus were organized through large parts of central and southern Italy; this happened despite the fact that these areas were at the time far from having a united culture or even a common language; what they did share was a common political relationship with Rome and a common inheritance of contact with some aspects of Greek culture. Indeed, it is likely enough that these groups were descended from the Orphic and Pythagorean groups of the Greek colonies of South Italy, though, if so, they had radically broadened their social base as well as the nature of their religious message by the end of the third century BC.

We know this religious movement only through the eyes of its enemies, because in 187 BC the Roman Senate decided that it would destroy the cult and it seems, more or less, to have succeeded in doing so. Livy's account implies that the senators destroyed it as soon as they knew that it existed; but we need feel little doubt that this was a politically convenient pretence, and that in fact they had long known of its existence and long awaited their opportunity to destroy a cult they deeply suspected (North 1979). The violence of the persecution anticipates the action taken against the early Christians three hundred and more years later, though in fact it was methodical and thoroughgoing in a way the persecution of Christians quite failed to match, at least until the beginnings of Empire-wide persecutions in the middle of the third century AD.

We have no reason to think that the Bacchists were in open revolt against Italian city life as such or against its normal religious working. They did, however, have a cell-structure with priests and officers, and an oath which bound the initiated members together; each cell administered its own funds, presumably raised from the members. In other words, it had a structure of authority and organization and asked of its members a high degree of commitment and obedience, as well as regular worship. It was also perceived by contemporaries (again like Christianity) as a centre of dissipation and crime, whether rightly or wrongly. As in the case of the Christians the allegations of crime may simply be a convenient justification for the potentially dangerous action to be taken.

This evidence fits very badly, to say the least, with theories that emphasize strongly the continuity of the mystery-cults as social and religious phenomena. Walter Burkert (1987) has argued recently in his best polemical vein that from early Greek Eleusis to late Roman Mithraism, the mysteries hardly changed their nature: on his view, they were from beginning to end Greek in their doctrines and ideas, elitist in the character of their support, essentially elegant extras to pagan life, rather than in any sense autonomous religious groups with coherent ideas, traditions, or identities of their own. They thus never offered their adherents any alternative to the paganism of their contemporaries or any focus for radical or dissident beliefs. So Burkert, like Nock, defends a sharply defined dividing line where pagans stop and Judaeo-Christians take over.

So far as the supposed 'orientalism' of these cults is concerned, there is no doubt that Burkert has a strong case; the eastern elements had importance as authentication of this form of alien wisdom or as myths of origins, and these facts are important in themselves; but the basic structure and conception of the cults were essentially Greek, even in the case of Mithraism.

However, the question of whether the mystery-cults changed in the time of the Romans is much more difficult than the majestic sweep of Burkert's argument will allow him to accept. The evidence of the Bacchanalia is discarded without much ceremony (pp. 52–3) and even Mithraism is not allowed to have made any distinctive innovation in the tradition; indeed those characteristics that do not fit Burkert's pattern are oddly described as 'primitive' (e.g. pp. 83–4). It is of course true that the character of Bacchism in the second century, whether or not as a result of successful suppression by the Senate, does not reappear later on; and the later mystery-cults never in the same way attracted the hostility of the authorities – the most we hear of is the occasional expulsion of adherents to the Isis cult and that only in the early imperial period (Josephus, *Antiquities* XVIII 65). But that is not altogether surprising: the violent reaction to the Bacchic cult is best interpreted as an over-reaction to a completely unfamiliar phenomenon, so far as the Romans were concerned. Later cults may simply have received a more tolerant reception. Meanwhile, Burkert's position remains a difficult one, since what he is saying is that despite the quite new religious atmosphere of the imperial period, mystery-cults remain totally unaffected by events. Why should they have?

COMPETITION AND CONFLICT

It would be a great step forward towards the definition of the groups in question, and of their potential for running foul of the claims of state authority, if there were clear criteria for establishing what would count as an autonomous religious group of this new type. The only established method of attempting to classify developments is in terms of evolutionary schemes in the history of religion, the criterion of development being the soteriology of the groups in question, particularly the distinction between different forms of salvation, e.g. between this-wordly and other-worldly salvation (e.g. Kitigawa 1967). However, this approach has every possible disadvantage for the present purpose: in the first place, it privileges one particular feature of the competing religions without real justification; secondly, it picks precisely on a deeply problematic area, because although it may well be that the different mystery-cults had each their own soteriology, establishing what it was provides an insoluble problem (for discussion of the problems, Gasparro 1985). The mythical or eschatological schemes they project do not fall into such easy categories.

It would seem better to look for criteria of classification in terms of the social/religious behaviour of groups and their members rather than in the nature of the beliefs or aspirations they held. Thus possible criteria might be:

(1) existence as autonomous groups with their own organization or authority structure;
(2) the level of commitment asked of the members of the group in terms of loyalty to the cult or the rejection of other or past modes of behaviour;
(3) the existence of separate values and principles, unacceptable to other members of the society but required of members;
(4) the degree of separation from the normal life of the city, to be marked by different rituals, different calendars, different dietary rules.

On many of these criteria, and especially on the third, the degree of separation to be found in respect of Jews and Christians is clearly greater than that of the pagan mystery groups, which so far as we know accepted civic ceremonial without any hint of problems, even if they were putting their real enthusiasm in their own cult rather than in city life. The issue is often thought to be settled by the observation that pagans sometimes felt able to 'collect' initiations into different mysteries and even, in the famous case of Apuleius (*Apology* 55), to collect the symbols of various initiations into different cults:

> I have been initiated into almost all the Greek mysteries and I keep with the greatest care some symbols and tokens of my initiations, as presented to me by the priests.

The argument from such cases is not, however, compelling because the fact that some individuals combined religious experiences from various sources does not prove that others were not wholly devoted to a single one, and hence separated from other forms of religious activity – any more than the existence today of some who explore many religions proves that there are no fanatical devotees in any of them.

The most sensitive criterion available to us as to the degree of commitment asked by a cult, which is only a different way of saying the degree of power over individuals appropriated by the cultic authorities, would be the incidence of conflict with the families of members. It should not be forgotten that the Roman Empire was a place of high family authority over the individual and especially of high male authority over the family. In Rome in particular, but also wherever Roman citizens established themselves and lived by Roman laws, the legal structure of the family placed great control in the hands of the oldest living male progenitor – the *paterfamilias*. In theory, at least, so long as your father, or indeed grandfather, was still alive, you remained in his control (*potestas*): that meant that only he could own property, only he could make a contract, only with his consent could sons and daughters marry, or stay married once they were, or get divorced if they wanted to (Garnsey and Saller 1987: 126–41). In practice, no doubt, these rules must have been negotiated, elided, or evaded, so that adults could be responsible for their own affairs, as they certainly were; but the rules were not abolished or forgotten, and even in a qualified form, they must have conferred a formidable authority on fathers in conflict with their wives and children (cf. Shaw 1987).

This authority expressed itself just as much in religious practice as in any other area of activity. The *familia*, of which the *pater* was the master, included slaves and dependants as well as women and children; he was responsible for the maintaining of its sacred rites and he led it in acts of prayer and sacrifice. Sometimes these would be rites of the family's own tradition, for which the *pater* would be himself responsible, sometimes the family's correlates of rituals in the calendar of the city. It was a traditional priestly concern to see that such rituals were maintained at a family level and that those responsible for them should be clearly defined.

It is one of the most striking features of Livy's account of the Bacchanalian persecution that he opens his account with a family-based scandal. It is a story of a young man whose stepfather wishes to discredit him, in order to be able to conceal from him that he has been cheated in the administration of his rightful inheritance. The wicked stepfather persuades his wife to tell her son that she has vowed that he will become a Bacchic initiate; this dastardly plot is only foiled by the intervention of a freedwoman prostitute with a heart of gold, who protects the young man from being compromised and reveals publicly the existence of the cult. The story has often been suspected of being a fiction, derived from a New Comedy Plot, though Livy seems to have had quite good evidence that the young man and his kind-hearted friend did really exist (Livy XXXIX 19). But even if the tale is a fiction, it remains good evidence of the attitude of a writer in the very

JOHN NORTH

early imperial period; and what is most significant about it is the intersection of the power of family and of the religious group. In this particular case, the wicked stepfather is perverting the normal or expected form of that intersection: a good father and good mother would be striving to protect their children from the power of those who ran the cult and keeping them within the family's safe boundaries – or to put it another way, within their own power.

We have then a very clear indication of how conflict would arise between new cults, whether pagan or not, and the established authority of family and state; also an understanding of this pattern of behaviour in a writer too early to know anything about Christianity at all. In the pagan tradition, religion would not normally provide such an alternative focus or location of power to those established by the city or its constituent groups or families. Christianity and even Judaism might seem to provide a far more suspect location of uncontrolled power; after all, a pagan cult must have seemed preferable to a non-pagan one and we have no reason to think that pagan cults of the period – unlike those of earlier dates – rejected sacrifice or the eating of meat. Bacchists, like the initiates of most other mystery-cults, worshipped deities fully accepted by the religious authorities of their time, only in style and context did they defy authority; yet they seem to have attracted more ferocious persecution in their day than the Christians did in theirs.

The theme of opposition between family power and cult power is an important one in antiquity, as indeed it is today, as we are reminded whenever new and unrecognized cults are accused of seducing children away from parental control. It is also, of course, quite possible that early Christianity was acting as a vehicle for wider forms of social or political protest against established authority. Occasional remarks by pagan critics give colour to the suggestion and it is hard not to think that the oppressed masses of the Empire would have found in an organization so well articulated but so distant from the state, a resource for the construction of resistance whether direct or oblique. The same arguments that show the new religious forms as dissonant from family structures work at the political level as well. However, at the moment this issue is open to debate: the contention that Christianity was basically a religion of the enslaved or exploited does not stand up well to such evidence as is available (Meeks 1982; Kyrtatas 1987). That may not close the debate, but it does mean that the case for

186

a political interpretation of early Christianity will need to be re-stated in new terms.

THE IMPACT OF PLURALISM

The broad contention of this chapter is that we can illuminate the religious history of this period best by recognizing a new religious situation, in which the individual had to make his or her own choices and in which, as a result, the location of religious power became far more contentious, far more open to negotiation than it had been in the traditional Graeco-Roman world. This created a situation of competition and potential conflict between religious groups based on a voluntary commitment, which had not existed before. It is on this view one of the consequences of the competition that all the participants are affected in one way or another and to some extent forced to change to meet the new situation.

In the case of the Christians, who are on any view the intruders, their whole movement is formulated by the need to convert and to present their case to an initially unresponsive world. They take on, therefore, from the very beginning a missionary character, quite unlike the traditions of any of their competitors at the time. It is easy to forget how unusual is this enthusiasm to persuade outsiders into the fold and to slip into the assumption that some explanation must be offered for those who do not engage in the same recruiting. In many ways, this is the most radical contribution in social/religious terms that Christianity brings with it.

The pagans, on the other hand, carried the severe disadvantage that they had no such tradition of self-presentation, though here we must observe the distinction between 'paganism' as a whole and the cults within its ambit. It is perhaps misleading even to say that there was such a religion as 'paganism' at the beginning of our period, which could be offered to a potential convert from another religious tradition. It might be less confusing to say that the pagans, before their competition with Christianity, had no religion at all in the sense in which that word is normally used today. They had no tradition of discourse about ritual or religious matters (apart from philosophical debate or antiquarian treatise), no organized system of beliefs to which they were asked to commit themselves, no authority-structure peculiar to the religious area, above all no commitment to a particular group of people or set of ideas other than their family and political context. If this is the right view of pagan life, it follows that we should look on paganism quite simply as a religion invented in the course of the second to third centuries AD, in competition and interaction with Christians, Jews and others, who were seeking to convert its members to their own causes.

A different way of putting the same point would be to invent a quite separate terminology to distinguish the kind of religious life characteristic of pre-Christian paganism from what is meant by the term 'religion' today. Civic-religion (as it might be called) was concerned above all with maintaining the right relationship with the gods and goddesses and the proper rules of behaviour for dealing with birth, death, transitions and so on. In the terminology of J. Z. Smith (1978), it was 'locative' not 'utopian' to an extreme degree. Civic-religion converged on and interpenetrated with but did not contain or control morality, philosophy, eschatology and so on. But of course it is not at all true that the ancient city therefore neglected these things. They simply lay outside the area dominated or apparently dominated by priests, ritual-experts and the like.

The writers of the imperial period who have most to tell us about pagans – Arnobius, Lactantius, above all Augustine in the *City of God* – do so by their use of republican Roman writing, usually Varro's antiquarian work on Roman religion. They scour these writings of centuries before their time in order to elaborate a stereotype of Roman religion as empty, contradictory, proliferating endless gods and endless rituals without meaning, almost totally isolated from its social context. So Arnobius can present interminable lists of different types of sacrificial cuts of meat and sausages, as meaningless to his contemporaries as to us. (Arnobius, *Against the Gentiles* VII 24). What the impact of these writings was on pagan contemporaries we have no way of telling, but they have certainly influenced modern judgements very profoundly.

By the time of Julian, the pagans had evidently understood and begun to react to this weakness in their general case – a weakness we might say today of presentation rather than of substance. The notion of Hellenism, as it was used in the fourth century, was evidently intended precisely to point out that the pagan tradition did not have to be understood in the narrow terms implied by Christian polemic, but could include the whole intellectual and artistic tradition of the Graeco-Roman world (Bowersock 1990). The term provided essentially a defensive redefinition of what their cultural and religious traditions meant, at least to pagan intellectuals.

It would, however, be wrong to confuse this moment – the arrival of a self-conscious effort to defend the pagan tradition as a whole – with the origins of pagan self-awareness of themselves as a religious group among others. That self-awareness will have come at different times and places depending on local experience, about which we seldom have enough knowledge to attempt any assessment. One factor will have been the erratic incidence of local persecution, which would have had the effect of parading these eccentric malefactors and so redefining as pagan the normal and the sane. On the other hand, Pliny's letter to Trajan from Bithynia (*Letters* X 96) provides a vivid picture of how dramatically Christianity might spread, if only temporarily; he is anxious to make it clear to Trajan how successful his efforts have been in reversing its progress:

> The temples, once almost abandoned, have begun to be frequented again and the sacred rites long discontinued have been resumed; sacrificial meat, for which there had been only the very occasional purchaser, is back on the market.

Pliny is certainly not understating the situation, but, even making allowances for his own interest, it is hard not to believe that the pagans of Bithynia would have had a new sense of their religious identity from the time of this crisis onwards.

If this is a fair assessment of the impact of the new situation on the diffuse and locally embedded forms of paganism as a Mediterranean-wide religion, the next question must concern the role within the pagan world of the various forms of mystery-cults, far more narrowly defined in their membership, ritual programmes and mythical doctrines. They surely would have been in a quite different situation when it came to offering a competitive response to the seductions of Christianity or Judaism.

Mithraism seems the obvious test case for the theory, though our lack of texts originating with the devotees themselves is a severe limitation. But recent work on Mithraism has suggested two areas of great importance for this project: first, it has become increasingly clear that the monuments reflect an extremely elaborate and intellectually based eschatology, offering the soul progress towards higher states, corresponding to the higher grades of initiation in the mysteries (Beck 1988); second, aspects of the

cult have been highlighted, which suggest that its basic doctrines
may have been far more subversive of the normal assumptions of
ancient life than ever appeared likely from the cult's strong military streak (Gordon 1980). Even the central symbol of the cult –
the bull-slaying – seems to refer to, but to distance itself from or
even parody, the sacrificial ritual that lies at the root of civic
pagan practice. It seems quite reasonable to conclude that here
too we are seeing the effects of religious competition, as the search
to convince potential converts drives the Mithraists into ever more
elaborate and speculative constructions, and even into implicit
rejection of the normal pagan assumptions.

It is implicit in the argument being put forward that investigation should start from the assumption that all groups must be
affected by the new pattern of interaction sooner or later. In the
story of this interaction the place of Jewish communities was an
ambiguous but important one. They lacked the missionary clarity
of the Christians and the embedded strength of the pagans; but
they can offer a test of the hypothesis of mutual interaction that
will, at the same time, bring out the problematic nature of their
position. It has been suggested earlier that initially they must have
been in the same position as many other ethnic groups living in
the cities of the Roman Empire, that is, they would have been
perceived by their hosts as essentially foreigners, to be tolerated
as such. Like other such groups, they could therefore maintain
their own religious traditions within limits, on the grounds that
this was an inherited way of life. If the argument of this chapter
is right, so long as the Jews were indeed conceived as an ethnic
group, not as a religion, still less as a proselytizing religion, there
would be no very acute problems at least this point of
view. They would pose no threat of acquiring new members by
persuasion or seduction. Of course, there could still be other
problems – conflicts over Jewish failures, as perceived by pagans,
to assimilate successfully to the requirements of civic life; their
strange eating habits or strange deviations from the calendar could
still provide many flashpoints and sometimes did, not to mention
their tendency to open revolt.

According to the ideas of Martin Goodman (see pp. 53–78;
Goodman 1989a; 1989b), we can detect a gradual evolution away
from this position: in the first century, the Jews themselves were
not yet perceived as a religious group at all by the pagans; Goodman places the change at the time of the imposition of the *fiscus*

payable by all Jews, if they declared themselves to be Jews, in AD 70. At the same time, the Jews showed no interest (but why should they?) in any kind of mission to convert Gentiles to their cause, though there was an acceptance of those who on their own initiative sought to associate themselves to a greater or lesser degree with the Synagogue. At the same period, the Jews do not seem to have become the victims of the same type of persecution as the Christians. It would be consistent to say that they were quietist, sought no converts and were therefore left relatively alone.

Only in the course of the second and third centuries did the signs of the competition between religions begin to surface in one part of the world of Judaism: it appears in the form of an assumption among some Palestinian rabbis that an active mission to the Gentiles should after all be approved (Goodman 1989a: 179–81), but also of what may be interpreted as a ban on such conversion by the Roman authorities themselves, when they made the circumcision of non-Jews a criminal action. We know from the Aphrodisias inscription, if from nowhere else, that this ban, if that is indeed the right interpretation, was not universally respected and that an open proselyte could play what seems to be a central role in the life of a Jewish community (Reynolds and Tannenbaum 1987: 43–5). But its very existence is suggestive of a new area of conflict: the Jews (to summarize the implications of Goodman's views) have become a religion not an ethnic group; they have moved significantly towards an acceptance of mission; they have attracted official disapproval, even if inconsistently maintained.

The principal contention of this chapter has been that one aspect of the major transformation of religious life in the whole Mediterranean area in this period was the establishment of a system of interacting competing religions between which the individual could, even in a sense had to, choose. This new situation has implications not just for the individual and his or her outlook and religious behaviour, but also for whole movements which were forced to adapt to the new circumstances. The effect was a period of great religious conflict but also of creativity and adaptation. It is a basic error to start by supposing that this creativity was limited to the Christian side of the confrontation. Nor, as we have seen, is there any reason to regard the Christians as the initiators of the great changes of religious life; but their notion, shocking to much ancient opinion, of an active mission to convert

191

gained the initiative for them; others were forced to react to a situation not of their own making. Thus, in the end, the transformation affected every area of religious life.

BIBLIOGRAPHY

Beck, R. (1988) *Planetary Gods and Planetary Orders in the Mysteries of Mithras* (EPRO 109), Leiden.

Berger, Peter L. (1969) *The Social Reality of Religion*, London.

Bowersock, G. W. (1990) *Hellenism in Late Antiquity*, Cambridge, Mass.

Brown, P. R. L. (1972) *Religion and Society in the Age of St Augustine*, London.

Burkert, W. (1987) *Ancient Mystery Cults*, Cambridge, Mass.

Colpe, C. (1969) 'Zur Mythologischen Struktur der Adonis-, Attis-, und Osiris-Überlieferungen', *Festschrift W. von Soden*, Neukirchen.

Dodds, E. R. (1965) *Pagan and Christian in an Age of Anxiety*, New York and London.

Duthoy, R. (1969) *The Taurobolium: Its Evolution and Terminology*, Leiden.

Fowden, G. (1988) 'Between Pagans and Christians', *Journal of Roman Studies* 78: 173–82.

Gallini, C. (1970) *Protesta e integrazione nella Roma antica*, Bari.

Garnsey, Peter and Saller, Richard (1987) *The Roman Empire: Economy, Society and Culture*, London.

Gasparro, G. Sfameni (1985) *Soteriology and Mystic Aspects in the Cult of Cybele and Attis* (EPRO 103), Leiden.

Goodman, M. D. (1989a) 'Proselytizing in Rabbinic Judaism', *Journal of Jewish Studies* 38: 175–85.

Goodman, M. D. (1989b) 'Nerva, the *fiscus Judaicus* and Jewish Identity', *Journal of Roman Studies* 79: 40–4.

Gordon, Richard (1980) 'Reality, Evocation and Boundaries in the Mysteries of Mithras', *Journal of Mithraic Studies* 3: 19–99.

Gordon, Richard (1990) 'Religion in the Roman Empire: The Civic Compromise and its Limits', in Mary Beard and John North (eds) *Pagan Priests*, London, 235–55.

Kee, H. C. (1980) *Christian Origins in Sociological Perspective*, London, 54–73.

Kitigawa, J. M. (1967) 'Primitive Classical and Modern Religions: A Perspective on Understanding the History of Religions', in J. M. Kitigawa (ed.) *The History of Religions: Essays on the Problem of Understanding*, Chicago.

Kyrtatas, D. (1987) *The Social Structure of the Early Christian Communities*, London and New York.

Lambrechts, P. (1962) *Attis: Van Herdersknaap tot God*, Brussels.

Lane Fox, R. (1986) *Pagans and Christians*, London.

Meeks, W. (1982) *The First Urban Christians*, New Haven, Conn.

Momigliano. A. D. (1987) *On Pagans, Jews and Christians*, Middletown, Conn.

Nock, A. D. (1933) *Conversion*, Oxford.

North, J. A. (1979) 'Religious Toleration in Republican Rome', *Proceedings of the Cambridge Philological Society*: 205 (N. S. 25) 85–103.

Pailler, J.-M. (1988) *Bacchanalia* (Bibliothèque des écoles françaises d'Athènes et de Rome, 279), Rome and Paris.

Pettazzoni, R. (1954) 'Les Mystères grecs et les religions à mystères de l'antiquité. Recherches récentes et problèmes nouveaux', *Cahiers d'histoire mondiale* 2, 2: 303–12, 661–7.

Reynolds, J. and Tannenbaum, R. (1987) *Jews and Godfearers at Aphrodisias* (Cambridge Philological Society, Supplementary Volume 12), Cambridge.

Scheid, J. (1985) *Religion et piété à Rome*, Paris.

Shaw, B. D. (1987) 'The Family in Late Antiquity: the Experience of St Augustine', *Past & Present* 115: 3–51.

Smith, J. Z. (1978) *Map is not Territory*, Leiden.

INDEX

INDEX

INDEX

persecution 94, 181, 186, 189; by
Paul 34, 43–50
Peshitta 5, 7, 140–1, ch. 7 *passim*;
Apocrypha 161, 168, 170–1;
Chronicles 150–8, 164;
Pentateuch 148–9; 162–3; Psalms
162–3; 170; Writings 159; *see
also* Messiah
Pharisees 11, 37, 39–40, 60–2, 86,
114; Paul as 36–9, 43, 50, 62
Philadelphia 92–3
Philo of Alexandria 9, 10, 17, 21,
32, 54, 58–9, 63, 68–9, 72–3, 75,
118, 155
Phinehas 146, 150
phylacteries 17, 19, 86, 148
Pliny (the elder), *Natural History*
157
Pliny (the younger): on Christians
189
Porphyry, Bishop of Gaza 116
prayer 153–4, 155–6, 159, 166–7
proselytes 6, 21, ch. 3 *passim*, 160
Purim 117–18
purity 12, 13, 37

Qumran community, Qumran
writings 21, 40–1, 61, 63, 155,
159, 160, 166

rabbinic Judaism 10, 11–14, 39–40,
108, 150; and the Diaspora 5,
14–16, 18, 98, 101–2, 108, 110;
in modern scholarship 5, 83,
109; and the Peshitta 148, 153–6,
159–60, 163, 165; *see also*
Palestinian Judaism
rabbis 12–14, 39, 62, 114; in the
Diaspora 15–16, 101–2, 119; *see
also hakhamim; talmid hakham*
Rabbula, Bishop of Edessa 138, 143
revolt, first Jewish 11
Rome: Jews in 15–17, 23, 32, 37,
110, 111, 115; Jews expelled
from 59–60, 69–70
Ruether, R. 80–1

sabbath 13, 17, 67, 93; observed by
Christians 89, 90, 142

sacrifice 50, 103, 106–7, 115–16,
154, 159, 116, 188
Sardis, synagogue at 6, 81, 101–2,
110
scripture: disputes about 81, 87, 93,
115; in Greek *see* Septuagint; in
Latin 99; in Syriac *see* Peshitta;
see also Old Testament
Scythopolis 14
Sepphoris 14
Septuagint 39, 57–8, 62–3, 66, 73,
99, 150, 159, 161, 162, 164
shelikhim see apostoloi
Sibylline Oracles 57, 58, 59, 67, 73
Simon, M. 19, 79, 81, 88, 112
Stephen, Saint; death of 44–6; relics
of 119
Stern, M. 59, 69, 106
Stobi 11, 100, 102
Strabo 10, 64, 76
Strecker, G. 35, 37
synagogues: attacked by Christians
117–18, 119–20, 142–3;
Christians attending 89, 91, 94,
116, 140, 141; in Diaspora
10–11, 23–4, 58, 102, 110; as
focus of Jewish life 10–11, 22;
officials in 22–4, 100, 101–2,
110–11, 117; open to Gentiles
58, 91; in Palestine 12, 42; *see
also* Apamea; Dura Europos;
Gerasa; Julia Severa; Minorca;
Sardis, Stobi; Theodotus;
women
syncretism 4, 19, 88
Syriac *see* Peshitta; language,
Syriac

Tabernacles, feast of 18, 115, 153
Tacitus, *Histories* 5, 55, 60, 65
talmid hakham 15, 36, 39, 42, 107,
110
Talmud 4, 12, 18, 98, 109, 114
Targums 140, 147, 148–9, 159–60,
163, 165, 169
Tarsus 29–30, 33
Tatian 127, 129–31, 132, 133, 134,
137, 139
Temple, Jerusalem: Christian

criticism of 45, 50; destruction of 11, 83, 85, 106–7; in the Peshitta 154–5; rebuilding *see* Julian the Apostate

temples, pagan 102, 103–4; destroyed by Christians 116

Tertullian 84, 86–7, 95, 151, 154

Theodosius, Theodosian code 14, 17, 98, 116–17

Theodotus, son of Vettenus, synagogue of 11, 32, 42

Theophilus of Antioch 141

theosebeis see God-fearers

Thomas, Judas, Acts of Thomas 132–3, 134, 136, 138, 139; Gospel of Thomas (Coptic) 133, 138

Torah 11, 15, 37, 41, 45, 50, 168; *see also* Law; scripture

Tosefta 12

Trajan 189; Diaspora Jewish revolt under 165, 168

True cross, legend of 142

Valerius Maximus 59, 69

Van Unnik, W. 34–5, 38

Varro 188

Venosa (Venusia), Italy 23, 111

Volubilis, Mauretania 111

Wilken, R. 80, 81, 84, 89

Wisdom of Solomon 57, 66, 141, 161

women, in the synagogue 22–3

Zeno of Verona, *Tractates* 87

Zeus Hypsistos 19